KEEPING THE
Whole Child
HEALTHY AND SAFE

Reflections on
Best Practices in Learning,
Teaching, and Leadership

Edited by
Marge Scherer

Alexandria, Virginia USA

1703 N. Beauregard St. • Alexandria, VA 22311 1714 USA
Phone: 800-933-2723 or 703-578-9600 • Fax: 703-575-5400
Web site: www.ascd.org • E-mail: member@ascd.org
Author guidelines: www.ascd.org/write

Educational Leadership Editorial Staff
Margaret M. Scherer, *Editor in Chief;* Deborah Perkins-Gough, *Senior Editor;* Amy M. Azzam, *Senior Associate Editor;* Naomi Thiers, *Associate Editor;* Teresa K. Preston, *Associate Editor;* Lucy Robertson, *Assistant Editor*

© 2010 by ASCD. All rights reserved. No part of this publication may be reproduced or transmitted in any form or by any means, electronic or mechanical, including photocopy, recording, or any information storage and retrieval system, without permission from ASCD. Readers who wish to duplicate material copyrighted by ASCD may do so for a small fee by contacting the Copyright Clearance Center (CCC), 222 Rosewood Dr., Danvers, MA 01923, USA (phone: 978-750-8400; fax: 978-646-8600; Web: www.copyright.com). For requests to reprint rather than photocopy, contact ASCD's permissions office: 703-575-5749 or permissions@ascd.org. Translation inquiries: translations@ascd.org.

Cover art © 2010 by ASCD. ASCD publications present a variety of viewpoints. The views expressed or implied in this book should not be interpreted as official positions of the Association.

All Web links in this book are correct as of the publication date below but may have become inactive or otherwise modified since that time. If you notice a deactivated or changed link, please e-mail books@ascd.org with the words "Link Update" in the subject line. In your message, please specify the Web link, the book title, and the page number on which the link appears.

PDF e-book ISBN: 978-1-4166-1062-5

Paperback ISBN: 978-1-4166-2000-6

KEEPING THE
Whole Child
HEALTHY AND SAFE

Foreword vii
Molly McCloskey

Introduction: A Wish for the Good Life ix
Marge Scherer

Part 1. Back to Whole

What Does It Mean to Educate the Whole Child? by Nel Noddings 3
Why learning and health go hand in hand.

Healthy and Ready to Learn by David Satcher 12
A former surgeon general suggests ways that schools can improve the health environment.

Part 2. Promoting a Healthy Life

Finding Our Way Back to Healthy Eating: A Conversation
  with David A. Kessler by Amy M. Azzam 25
Are "designer foods" making our kids unfit? And what can schools do about it?

A Supersize Problem by Eric K. Gill 31
Why cafeteria food, vending machine policy, P.E. programs, and even cooking classes merit scrutiny.

Sleep: The E-ZZZ Intervention by Christi A. Bergin and David A. Bergin . . 37
Healthy sleep habits can boost students' memory, self-control, and speed of thinking.

A Place for Healthy Risk-Taking by Laura Warner 44
Challenge and choice are hallmarks of the new physical education.

Keeping Teachers Healthy by Rick Allen............................ 54
As role-models and for themselves, educators, too, need to take care of themselves.

Part 3. Protecting Students, Working with Bullies

Bullying—Not Just a Kid Thing by Doug Cooper and Jennie L. Snell 59
Bullying affects just about every person in a school.

Civility Speaks Up by Steve Wessler 67
Students and teachers can learn how to interrupt the language of hate.

Words Can Hurt Forever by James Gabarino and Ellen deLara 78
Emotional bullying and harassment exact a high price on the atmosphere of a school.

Fights Like a Girl by Laura Varlas 87
Educators have the chance to redefine power for girls.

How We Treat One Another in School by Donna M. San Antonio
  and Elizabeth A. Salzfass 92
What schools can do to help both the bullied and the bullies.

R U Safe? by Johanna Mustacchi 108
Eighth graders share with younger kids their top 10 Internet safety tips.

Part 4. Helping Students Cope with Life Challenges

Success with Less Stress by Jerusha Conner, Denise Pope,
  and Mollie Galloway 121
How to lower students' anxiety when it comes to schoolwork.

Helping Self-Harming Students by Matthew D. Selekman 130
Guidelines on responding to students who cut or hurt themselves.

Reaching the Fragile Student by Sue Zapf 143
Helping kids who face tough odds on the home front.

Peers Helping Peers by Margo A. Mastropieri, Thomas E. Scruggs,
  and Sheri L. Berkeley 150
Students with special needs benefit from peer support.

Silence is Golden by Judith Gaston Fisher 160
Elementary students find mindfulness calms their emotions.

When a Student Dies by Michael Jellinek, Jeff Q. Bostic, and Steven C.
  Schlozman 167
How to help students and staff grieve for the loss of a classmate.

Part 5. Teaching Values, Building Character

Democracy at Risk by Deborah Meier..........................179
School is the place where kids can learn how to practice democracy.

"Hobo" Is not a Respectful Word by Sarah Hershey
   and Veronica Reilly..186
A service learning unit opens kids' eyes to poverty in their community.

No More Haves and Have–Nots by Joyce Huguelet................195
A school finds a way to keep its students from feeling left out.

Waging Peace by Robert Blair..................................201
If armed conflict is ever to end, the young must learn the skills of peace-making.

Part 6. Creating Healthy and Safe Schools

Centers of Hope by Joy G. Dryfoos.............................213
Community schools bring together an array of helping hands.

A Full-Service School Fulfills Its Promise by Eileen Santiago,
   JoAnne Ferrara, and Marty Blank............................222
A school and community offer families direct access to resources that improve their lives.

A Coordinated School Health Plan by Pat Cooper................230
How to create a systemwide program that helps families transcend poverty.

Coordinated School Health: Getting It All Together by Joyce V. Fetro,
   Connie Givens, and Kellie Carroll..........................242
How one state coordinates and manages new and existing health-related programs.

Part 7. Rounding Out the Curriculum

Teaching Strategies for Naturalist Intelligence by Thomas Armstrong...255
Bringing the natural world into classroom learning.

Teaching Strategies for Intrapersonal Intelligence
   by Thomas Armstrong..260
When students need quiet time and a change of pace.

Teaching Strategies for Bodily-Kinesthetic Intelligence
   by Thomas Armstrong..264
How to make physical learning a part of everyday learning.

Appendix

Learning, Teaching, and Leading in ASCD's
  Healthy School Communities................................ 271
ASCD's recommendations for integrating health and learning.

Study Guide

Study Guide for Keeping the Whole Child Healthy and Safe
  by Naomi Thiers and Teresa Preston 281
Questions to think about and ways to act on the ideas presented in this book.

Foreword

The 21st century demands a highly skilled, educated work force and citizenry unlike any we have seen before. The global marketplace and economy are a reality. Change and innovation have become the new status quo while too many of our schools, communities, and systems use models designed to prepare young people for life in the middle of the last century. We live in a time that requires our students to be prepared to think both critically and creatively, to evaluate massive amounts of information, solve complex problems, and communicate well, yet our education systems remain committed to time structures, coursework, instructional methods, and assessments designed more than a century ago. A strong foundation in reading, writing, math, and other core subjects is as important as ever, yet insufficient for lifelong success.

These 21st century demands require a new and better way of approaching education policy and practice—a whole child approach to learning, teaching, and community engagement. What if decisions about education policy were made by first asking, "What works best for children?" What if the education, health, housing, public safety, recreation, and business systems within our communities aligned human and capital resources to provide coordinated service to kids and families? What if policymakers at all levels worked with educators, families, and community members to ensure that we as a society meet our social compact to prepare children for their future rather than our past?

The answers push us to redefine what a successful learner is and how we measure success. It is time to put students first, align resources to students' multiple needs, and advocate for a more balanced approach. A child who enters school in good health, feels safe, and is connected to her school is ready to learn. A student who has at least one adult in school who understands his social and emotional development is more likely to stay in school. All students who have access to challenging academic programs are better prepared for further education, work, and civic life.

ASCD proposes a definition of achievement and accountability that promotes the development of children who are healthy, safe, engaged, supported, and challenged.

ASCD's Whole Child Tenets

- Each student enters school **healthy** and learns about and practices a healthy lifestyle.
- Each student learns in an intellectually challenging environment that is physically and emotionally **safe** for students and adults.
- Each student is actively **engaged** in learning and is connected to the school and broader community.
- Each student has access to personalized learning and is **supported** by qualified, caring adults.
- Each graduate is **challenged** academically and prepared for success in college or further study and for employment in a global environment.

ASCD is helping schools, districts, and communities move from rhetoric about educating the whole child to reality. No single person, institution, or system can work in isolation to achieve such results so we have launched a Web site for educators, families, community members, and policymakers to share their stories, access resources, assess their progress, and advocate for children. Join us at www.wholechildeducation.org. Our children deserve it. Our future demands it.

—Molly McCloskey
Host of the Whole Child Podcast

Introduction

A Wish for the Good Life

Marge Scherer

Reading the *Wall Street Journal* in my dentist's office right before the past Christmas holiday, I saw a piece about what kids wanted from Santa this year. The Santas at the local malls reported that along with all the requests for Elmos and iPods were quite a few wishes for eyeglasses, school shoes, and a job for mom or dad.

It reminded me of a book I read as a child, whose title I can't recall, about a Depression-era family of four kids who each decides to make a wish. When the daughter in the book can't make up her mind what to wish for, she asks her father for advice, and he tells her that he would wish for good health. The child in the novel is surprised, and I--growing up a healthy child in a family of four kids--remember feeling skeptical, too. Why would anyone waste a perfectly good wish on "good health"? Later in the book, the reasoning becomes clear when the dad gets sick. Although he eventually gets better, the family learns a number of lessons in the meantime about what is truly valuable in life.

Certainly if we adults had our wishes, health—and safety, too—would be gifts that all kids could take for granted. Unfortunately, though, these basic ingredients of the good life increasingly belong to fewer children. The recent report *America's Children: Key National Indicators of Well-Being* (2009) concludes that hard economic times threaten to roll back gains made since 1975 in health, safety, and education for children. The percentage of children in poverty is predicted to rise in 2010 to 21 percent. The obesity epidemic is expected to grow as parents turn to cheap fast food to feed families. Children are likely to experience both a decline in safety due to higher rates of violent crime and a setback in social connectedness as the housing crisis affects their families. In addition, the report predicts that fewer children will be participating in early childhood education programs, known to boost their success in school.

With all this bleak news, and no chance of turning back the clock to what seemed to be gentler times for children, what can schools and educators do to grant the wish of health and safety to children? That is the question that authors explore in this fourth in a four-book series of e-books on educating the whole child. Knowing that what we teach kids today will shape their future well-being, the authors look at the issues from many angles, addressing both physical and mental health and safety.

The book is divided into seven sections. In the first part, "Back to Whole," author Nel Noddings explains why schools should be involved in teaching the whole child and why health and safety aren't just extras to add to the curriculum. Noddings describes the seven aims of education, noting that schools too often concentrate on one: imparting basic academic skills. She makes the case for integrating the other aims: health, vocation, citizenship, worthy family membership, worthy use of leisure, and ethical character. Also in Part 1, Dr. David Satcher, former U.S. surgeon general, weighs in on the issues of good nutrition and physical activity and describes how they influence children's readiness to learn.

In Part 2, "Promoting the Healthy Life," our authors continue to connect health with learning as they explore the dangers of, and remedies for, our nonnutritious snacking habits, our supersize problem, our sleep-deprived children, our inactivity, and more. A piece on keeping teachers healthy reminds us that our children need the adults in their lives to take care of themselves, too.

The third section, "Protecting Students, Working with Bullies," looks closely at a safety problem that mimics society's one-upmanship and often manifests itself in school. Our authors talk about the roles adults and students can play in interrupting the language of hate, combating bullying, and creating an environment where kids and adults feel safe to live and learn.

Part 4 circles back to "Helping Students Cope with Life Challenges." Among the challenges authors describe are anxiety, stress, and even the death of a fellow classmate. Our authors tell how we can guide children toward choosing healthy responses to the realities from which adults cannot always protect them.

Part 5 takes a proactive stance toward "Teaching Values, Building Character." What better guarantee that schools are safe and healthy than assurance that students within our schools respect others' rights, value social justice, and can practice self-control? As Deborah Meier notes, schools are the ideal laboratory for students to learn the skills needed to live in a democracy. Articles in this section talk about effective ways to help children understand and practice civic participation, tolerance, equity, and peace-keeping.

The sixth part of our book, "Creating Healthy and Safe Schools," gives educators the larger picture of school/community cooperation. The exemplary partnerships illustrate the ways coordinated programs link students and their families to vital resources, providing the social connectedness our children crave. In the Appendix, ASCD describes the role of the principal in "Learning, Teaching, and Leading in Healthy School Communities."

We end our book with Part 7, "Rounding Out the Curriculum." Although health and safety are not just curriculum topics, they definitely should be formal parts of learning, according to Thomas Armstrong. He spells out strategies that help students learn from nature, enlarge knowledge of self, and develop physical skills.

We hope you enjoy this e-book compiled from *Educational Leadership* and other ASCD publications. Our hope is that all four "whole child books" will help you keep students engaged, challenged, supported, healthy, and safe. May they also reinforce your abiding faith in children, who despite their phenomenal resilience rely on their teachers so very much.

—Marge Scherer
Editor in Chief, *Educational Leadership*

Part 1

Back to Whole

What Does It Mean to Educate the Whole Child?

Nel Noddings

In a democratic society, schools must go beyond teaching fundamental skills.

Public schools in the United States today are under enormous pressure to show—through improved test scores—that they are providing every student with a thorough and efficient education. The stated intention of No Child Left Behind (NCLB) is to accomplish this goal and reverse years of failure to educate many of our inner-city and minority children. But even if we accept that the motives behind NCLB are benign, the law seems fatally flawed.

Some critics have declared NCLB an unfunded mandate because it makes costly demands without providing the resources to meet them. Others point to its bureaucratic complexity; its unattainable main goal (100 percent of students proficient in reading and math by 2014); its motivationally undesirable methods (threats, punishments, and pernicious comparisons); its overdependence on standardized tests; its demoralizing effects; and its corrupting influences on administrators, teachers, and students.

All these criticisms are important, but NCLB has a more fundamental problem: its failure to address, or even ask, the basic questions raised in this issue of *Educational Leadership*: What are the proper aims of education? How do public schools serve a democratic society? What does it mean to educate the whole child?

The Aims of Education

Every flourishing society has debated the aims of education. This debate cannot produce final answers, good for all times and all places, because the aims of education are tied to the nature and ideals of a particular society. But the aims promoted by NCLB are clearly far too narrow. Surely, we should demand more from our schools than to educate people to be proficient in reading and mathematics. Too many highly proficient people commit fraud, pursue paths to success marked by greed, and care little about how their actions affect the lives of others.

Some people argue that schools are best organized to accomplish academic goals and that we should charge other institutions with the task of pursuing the physical, moral, social, emotional, spiritual, and aesthetic aims that we associate with the whole child. The schools would do a better job, these people maintain, if they were freed to focus on the job for which they were established.

Those who make this argument have not considered the history of education. Public schools in the United States—as well as schools across different societies and historical eras—were established as much for moral and social reasons as for academic instruction. In his 1818 *Report of the Commissioners for the University of Virginia*, for example, Thomas Jefferson included in the "objects of primary education" such qualities as morals, understanding of duties to neighbors and country, knowledge of rights, and intelligence and faithfulness in social relations.

Periodically since then, education thinkers have described and analyzed the multiple aims of education. For example, the National Education Association listed seven aims in its 1918 report, *Cardinal Principles of Secondary Education*: (1) health; (2) command of the fundamental processes; (3) worthy home membership; (4) vocation; (5) citizenship; (6) worthy use of leisure; and (7) ethical character (Kliebard, 1995, p. 98). Later in the century, educators trying to revive the progressive tradition advocated open education, which aimed to encourage creativity, invention, cooperation, and democratic participation in the classroom and in lifelong learning (Silberman, 1973).

Recently, I have suggested another aim: happiness (Noddings, 2003). Great thinkers have associated happiness with such qualities as a rich intellectual life, rewarding human relationships, love of home and place, sound character, good parenting, spirituality, and a job that one loves. We incorporate this aim into education not only by helping our students understand the components of happiness but also by making classrooms genuinely happy places.

Few of these aims can be pursued directly, the way we attack behavioral objectives. Indeed, I dread the day when I will enter a classroom and find *Happiness* posted as an instructional objective. Although I may be able to state exactly what students should be able to do when it comes to adding fractions, I cannot make such specific statements about happiness, worthy home membership, use of leisure, or ethical character. These great aims are meant to guide our instructional decisions. They are meant to broaden our thinking—to remind us to ask *why* we have chosen certain curriculums, pedagogical methods, classroom arrangements, and learning objectives. They remind us, too, that students are whole persons—not mere collections of attributes, some to be addressed in one place and others to be addressed elsewhere.

In insisting that schools and other social institutions share responsibility for nurturing the whole child, I recognize that different institutions will have different emphases. Obviously, schools will take greater responsibility for teaching reading and arithmetic; medical clinics for health checkups and vaccinations; families for housing and clothing; and places of worship for spiritual instruction.

But needs cannot be rigidly compartmentalized. The massive human problems of society demand holistic treatment. For example, leading medical clinics are now working with lawyers and social workers to improve housing conditions for children and to enhance early childhood learning (Shipler, 2004). We know that healthy families do much more than feed and clothe their children. Similarly, schools must be concerned with the total development of children.

Aims of Education

> *The habits we form from childhood make no small difference, but rather they make all the difference.*
>
> —Aristotle

Democracy and Schools

A productive discussion of education's aims must acknowledge that schools are established to serve both individuals and the larger society. What does the society expect of its schools?

From the current policy debates about public education, one would think that U.S. society simply needs competent workers who will keep the nation competitive in the world market. But both history and common sense tell us that a democratic society expects much more: It wants graduates who exhibit sound character, have a social conscience, think critically, are willing to make commitments, and are aware of global problems (Soder, Goodlad, & McMannon, 2001).

In addition, a democratic society needs an education system that helps to sustain its democracy by developing thoughtful citizens who can make wise civic choices. By its very nature, as Dewey (1916) pointed out, a democratic society is continually changing—sometimes for the better, sometimes for the worse—and it requires citizens who are willing to participate and competent enough to distinguish between the better and the worse.

If we base policy debate about education on a serious consideration of society's needs, we will ask thoughtful questions: What modes of discipline will best contribute to the development of sound character? What kinds of peer interactions might help students develop a social conscience? What topics and issues will foster critical thinking? What projects and extracurricular activities might call forth social and personal commitment? Should we assign the task of developing global awareness to social studies courses, or should we spread the responsibility throughout the entire curriculum (Noddings, 2005b)?

In planning education programs for a democratic society, we must use our understanding of the aims of education to explore these questions and many more. Unfortunately, public policy in the United States today concentrates on just one of the *Cardinal Principles* proposed by NEA in 1918: "command of the fundamental processes." Although reading and math are important, we need to promote competence in these subjects while also promoting our other aims. Students can develop reading, writing, speaking, and mathematical skills as they plan and stage dramatic performances, design classroom murals, compose a school paper, and participate in establishing classroom rules.

If present reports about the effects of NCLB on the education of inner-city and minority children are supported by further evidence, we should be especially concerned about our democratic future. Wealthier students are enjoying a rich and varied curriculum and many opportunities to engage in the arts, whereas many of our less wealthy students spend their school days bent over worksheets in an effort to boost standardized test scores (Meier & Wood, 2004). Such reports call into question the notion that NCLB will improve schooling for our poorest students. Surely all students deserve rich educational experiences—experiences that will enable them to become active citizens in a democratic society.

Life in a healthy democracy requires participation, and students must begin to practice participation in our schools. Working together in small groups can furnish such practice, provided that the emphasis is consistently on working together—not on formal group processes or the final grade for a product. Similarly, students can participate in establishing the rules that will govern classroom conduct. It is not sufficient, and it may actually undermine our democracy, to concentrate on producing people who do well on standardized tests and who define success as getting a well-paid job. Democracy means more than voting and maintaining economic productivity, and life means more than making money and beating others to material goods.

The Whole Child

Most of us want to be treated as persons, not as the "sinus case in treatment room 3" or the "refund request on line 4." But we live under the legacy of bureaucratic thought—the idea that every physical and social function should be assigned to its own institution. In the pursuit of efficiency, we have remade ourselves into a collection of discrete attributes and needs. This legacy is strong in medicine, law, social work, business, and education.

Even when educators recognize that students are whole persons, the temptation arises to describe the whole in terms of collective parts and to make sure that every aspect, part, or attribute is somehow "covered" in the curriculum. Children are moral beings; therefore, we must provide character education programs. Children are artistically inclined; therefore, we must provide art classes. Children's physical fitness is declining; therefore, we must provide physical education and nutrition classes. And then we complain that the curriculum is overloaded!

We should not retreat to a curriculum advisory committee and ask, "Now where should we fit this topic into the already overloaded curriculum?" Although we cannot discard all the fragmented subjects in our present school system and start from scratch, we can and should ask all teachers to stretch their subjects to meet the needs and interests of the whole child. Working within the present subject-centered curriculum, we can ask math and science teachers as well as English and social studies teachers to address moral, social, emotional, and aesthetic questions with respect and sensitivity when they arise (Simon, 2001). In high school math classes, we can discuss Descartes' proof of God's existence (is it flawed?); the social injustices and spiritual longing in *Flatland*, Edwin Abbott's 1884 novel about geometry; the logic and illogic in *Alice's Adventures in Wonderland*; and the wonders of numbers such as φ and π.

For the most part, discussions of moral and social issues should respond to students' expressed needs, but some prior planning can be useful, too. When a math teacher recites a poem or reads a biographical piece or a science fiction story, when she points to the beauty or elegance of a particular result, when she pauses to discuss the social nature of scientific work, students may begin to see connections—to see a whole person at work (Noddings, 2005a). Teachers can also look carefully at the subjects that students are required to learn and ask, "How can I include history, literature, science, mathematics, and the arts in my own lessons?" This inclusion would in itself relieve the awful sense of fragmentation that students experience.

The benefits of a more holistic perspective can also extend beyond the academic curriculum and apply to the school climate and the issue of safety and security. Schools often tackle this problem the way they tackle most problems, piece by piece: more surveillance cameras, more security guards, better metal detectors, more locks, shorter lunch periods, more rules. It seems like a dream to remember that most schools 40 years ago had no security guards, cameras, or metal detectors. And yet schools are not safer now than they were in the 1960s and 1970s. We need to ask *why* there has been a decline in security and how we should address the problem. Do we need more prisonlike measures, or is something fundamentally wrong with the entire school arrangement?

Almost certainly, the sense of community and trust in our schools has declined. Perhaps the most effective way to make our schools safer would be to restore this sense of trust. I am not suggesting that we get rid of all our security paraphernalia overnight, but rather that we ask what social arrangements might reduce the need for such measures. Smaller schools? Multiyear assignment of teachers and students? Class and school meetings to establish rules and discuss problems? Dedication to teaching the whole child in every class? Serious attention to the integration of subject matter? Gentle but persistent invitations to all students to participate? More opportunities to engage in the arts and in social projects? More encouragement to speak out with the assurance of being heard? More opportunities to work together? Less competition? Warmer hospitality for parents? More public forums on school issues? Reduction of test-induced stress? More opportunities for informal conversation? Expanding, not reducing, course offerings? Promoting the idea of fun and humor in learning? Educating teachers more broadly? All of the above?

We will not find the solution to problems of violence, alienation, ignorance, and unhappiness in increasing our security apparatus, imposing more tests, punishing schools for their failure to produce 100 percent proficiency, or demanding that teachers be knowledgeable in "the subjects they teach." Instead, we must allow teachers and students to interact as whole persons, and we must develop policies that treat the school as a whole community. The future of both our children and our democracy depend on our moving in this direction.

References

Dewey, J. (1916). *Democracy and education*. New York: Macmillan.

Jefferson, T. (1818). *Report of the commissioners for the University of Virginia*. Available: www.libertynet.org/edcivic/jefferva.html

Kliebard, H. (1995). *The struggle for the American curriculum*. New York: Routledge.

Meier, D., & Wood, G. (Eds.). (2004). *Many children left behind*. Boston: Beacon Press.

Noddings, N. (2003). *Happiness and education*. Cambridge, MA: Cambridge University Press.

Noddings, N. (2005a). *The challenge to care in schools* (2nd ed.). New York: Teachers College Press.

Noddings, N. (Ed.). (2005b). *Educating citizens for global awareness*. New York: Teachers College Press.

Shipler, D. K. (2004). *The working poor: Invisible in America.* New York: Alfred A. Knopf.

Silberman, C. E. (1973). *The open classroom reader.* New York: Vintage Books.

Simon, K. G. (2001). *Moral questions in the classroom.* New Haven, CT: Yale University Press.

Soder, R., Goodlad, J. I., & McMannon, T. J. (Eds.). (2001). *Developing democratic character in the young.* San Francisco: Jossey-Bass.

Nel Noddings resides in Ocean Grove, New Jersey, and is Lee L. Jacks Professor of Education, Emerita, at Stanford University, Stanford, California; noddings@stanford.edu.

Originally published in the September 2005 issue of *Educational Leadership, 63*(1), pp. 8–13.

Healthy and Ready to Learn

David Satcher

Research shows that nutrition and physical activity affect student academic achievement.

Remember when children came home from school and played outside before dinner? When fast food was a novel treat, and soft drinks came in a cup small enough for a child to hold in one hand? When kids walked or rode their bikes to school and went home for lunch?

Things have changed in recent decades. Students no longer go home for lunch, restaurant serving sizes have expanded along with customers' waistlines, and many children—out of desire or necessity—stay indoors watching television or playing computer games. Only 2 percent of school-age children in the United States consume the recommended daily number of servings from all five major food groups (U.S. Department of Agriculture, 1994–1996). Schools have changed, too, selling candy, chips, and soda while offering fewer opportunities for students to be physically active.

During the last two decades, many school systems have abolished recess and cut back on physical education and extracurricular sports. According to the American Association for the Child's Right to Play, an estimated 20 percent of all elementary schools in the United States have dropped recess in favor of more classroom time (Tyre, 2004). Fewer than 25 percent of children in the United States get at least 30 minutes of *any kind* of daily physical activity (International Life Sciences Institute, 1997), and fewer than 30 percent of U.S. high school students attend physical education class every day (Centers for Disease Control and Prevention, 1999). Not surprisingly, these cultural shifts have resulted in a marked decline in children's health.

Today, 9 million children in the United States are overweight—triple the number in 1980 (Ogden, Flegal, Carroll, & Johnson, 2002). Poor nutrition and sedentary lifestyles are the root causes. The incidence of overweight in children is much higher among African American and Latino children than in other groups (Hoelscher et al., 2004; Thorpe et al., 2004).

Overweight and obesity are not just cosmetic issues—they are health issues. Childhood weight problems can lead to elevated blood pressure and cholesterol, joint problems, Type II diabetes, gallbladder disease, asthma, depression, and anxiety (U.S. Department of Health and Human Services, 2001). Severely overweight children miss four times as much school as normal-weight children and often suffer from depression, anxiety disorders, and isolation from their peers (Schwimmer, Burwinkle, & Varni, 2003). These problems often continue into adulthood, with 70–80 percent of overweight children and adolescents becoming obese adults.

A Wake-Up Call to Schools

Schools can be a powerful catalyst for change when it comes to preventing and reducing overweight and obesity. The school setting is a great equalizer, providing all students and families—regardless of ethnicity, socioeconomic status, or level of education—with the same access to good nutrition and physical activity. Because children also teach their parents, important lessons learned at school can help the entire family.

In 2004, the nonprofit organization Action for Healthy Kids released a special report identifying the link among the factors of poor nutrition, inactivity, and academic achievement (2004). It is a wake-up call to schools: Improving children's health likely improves school performance.

The relationship is based on substantial research. Well-nourished students tend to be better students, whereas poorly nourished students tend to demonstrate weaker academic performance and score lower on standardized achievement tests. The majority of U.S. children are not eating a balanced, nutrient-rich diet. Inadequate consumption of key food groups deprives children of essential vitamins, minerals, fats, and proteins necessary for optimum cognitive function (Tufts University School of Nutrition, 1995). Children who suffer from poor nutrition during the brain's most formative years score much lower on tests of vocabulary, reading comprehension, arithmetic, and general knowledge (Brown & Pollitt, 1996). In a 1989 study, 4th graders with the lowest amount of protein in their diets showed the lowest achievement test scores (School Nutrition Association). A 2001 study revealed that 6- to 11-year-old children from food-insufficient families had significantly lower arithmetic scores and were more likely to repeat a grade (Alaimo, Olson, & Frongillo). Even skipping breakfast has been shown to adversely affect student achievement on problem-solving tests (Pollitt, Leibel, & Greenfield, 1991).

That nutrition affects academic achievement comes as no revelation. After all, as children we were told to eat our breakfast before leaving for school. What may come as a surprise, however, is that physical activity also plays an important role in students' performance—even when it uses time that is normally set aside for academics.

Students who participate in daily physical education exhibit better attendance, a more positive attitude toward school, and superior academic performance (National Association for Sport and Physical Education & Council of Physical Education for Children, 2001). Two studies demonstrated that providing more time for physical activity—by reducing class time—can lead to increased test scores, particularly in the area of mathematics (Shephard, 1997; Shephard et al., 1984). Another study linked physical activity programs to stronger academic achievement; increased concentration; and improved math, reading, and writing test scores (Symons, Cinelli, James, & Groff, 1997). The President's Council on Physical Fitness and Sports states that

> Evidence suggests that time spent in physical education does not decrease learning in other subjects. Youth who spend less time in other subjects to allow for regular physical education have been shown to do equally well or better in academic classes. (1999)

The California Department of Education analyzed results of student physical fitness testing in 2001 and compared them with the same students' scores on the Stanford Achievement Test (SAT-9). The analysis showed that higher academic achievement correlated strongly with higher levels of fitness at each of the three grade levels measured (grades 5, 7, and 9). The relationship was greatest in mathematics: Girls in the higher fitness levels demonstrated higher achievement than males at similar fitness levels (2004).

Healthy Change

Educators across the United States are facilitating changes at the state, district, and school levels to improve student health. Collaborating in teams as part of the Action for Healthy Kids initiative, they are creating and distributing nutritional guidelines, educating policymakers, helping to develop school wellness policies, instituting changes in vending and other noncafeteria food sales, creating school health councils, and improving health education. The teams are successful because they are inclusive and grassroots, representing administrators, teachers, health professionals, community leaders, parents, and students.

The Arizona Action for Healthy Kids team worked in cooperation with the Arizona Department of Education and USDA Team Nutrition to create and implement a model healthy school policy in eight pilot schools (see "Arizona Healthy School Environment Model Policy"). The policy addresses food-service operation, nutrition education, food choices at school, physical education, and a healthy school environment. To facilitate implementation, each pilot school received $5,000–$10,000 as part of a USDA Team Nutrition grant. Among other improvements, participating schools replaced low- or no-nutrient foods with more healthful items, such as water, juice, low-fat milk, fruits, and vegetables.

Arizona Healthy School Environment Model Policy

Following are some guidelines for physical activity adapted from the Arizona Healthy School Environment Model Policy, modeled after the National Association of State Boards of Education (NASBE) sample policy.

Recommendations for Physical Activity
- Offer physical education courses in an environment in which students learn, practice, and are assessed on developmentally appropriate motor skills, social skills, and knowledge.
- Provide students with at least 60 minutes of physical activity on all or most days of the week.
- Discourage extended periods of inactivity (periods of two or more hours).
- Provide at least 150 minutes each week of physical education classes for elementary school students and at least 225 minutes each week for middle and high school students for the entire school year.
- Ensure that students are moderately to vigorously active in physical education classes for at least 50 percent of the time.

> ***Encouraging Lifetime Physical Activity***
> - Provide daily recess periods of at least 20 minutes for all elementary school students.
> - Provide physical activity breaks during classroom hours.
> - Encourage parents and community members to institute programs that support physical activity, such as a walk-to-school program.
>
> The complete model policy is available at www.actionforhealthykids.org. Reprinted with permission.

The pilot study found no negative impacts on vending machine or cafeteria sales once healthier options were offered. In fact, sales in some schools increased with the more healthful selections. The Healthy Food Sales and Schools Act, which has been introduced in the Arizona legislature, proposes that all schools be required to implement nutrition standards on the basis of those recommended in the initial Healthy School Environment Model Policy created by Arizona Action for Healthy Kids. A bill addressing physical education standards has also been introduced.

Several states have worked to create and disseminate nutritional standards for schools. In Idaho, the Action for Healthy Kids team developed "Idaho Recommendations for Promoting a Healthy School Nutrition Environment." The guidelines recommend that all foods and beverages available on school campuses and at school events meet USDA dietary guidelines. The state superintendent of public instruction and the state board of education endorsed the team's recommendations and distributed them to school district leaders throughout the state. Sixteen of Delaware's 19 school districts agreed to adopt health standards, beginning with the 2004–2005 school year. In Massachusetts, statewide distribution of nutritional guidelines will affect 1 million students.

Students themselves are concerned about these issues. In a 2002 poll conducted by Action for Healthy Kids, 81 percent of the 1,308 student leaders surveyed believed that schools should make eating healthy a priority, and 72 percent believed that schools should make physical activity more of a priority. In Massachusetts, the Action for Healthy Kids team is working in collaboration with the Department of Education student advisory group to educate student governments on creating nutrition and physical activity policies.

The team approach can often open doors for especially committed individuals, providing support and resources that wouldn't otherwise be available. For example, a minigrant provided by the Minnesota Action for Healthy Kids team enabled a physical education teacher to enhance her school's physical education program by weaving more activity into students' daily lives. Jo Zimmel started using pedometers at Garlough Elementary School in West St. Paul, Minnesota, to obtain a baseline measure of kids' activity levels while at school. She developed strategies to increase activity during school hours and taught kids as well as teachers how to find time for extra movement each day. At the conclusion of the program, Zimmel will evaluate the students' progress, using the pedometers to measure their post-activity levels.

Schools need not act alone to tackle the issues of good nutrition and physical activity. They can encourage community partners to sponsor an extracurricular fitness program or draw on grandparents to help start a walking club. Schools will benefit as both achievement scores and attendance improve. Students will benefit as they perform and behave better in school and experience more energy and fewer illnesses. Schools not only need to teach good eating habits and healthy levels of physical activity, but they also need to model and reinforce these habits every day throughout the building.

Aims of Education

> *Education . . . is a process of living and not a preparation for future living.*
>
> —John Dewey

What Schools Can Do

Schools can take a number of steps to promote student health.

Form a school health advisory council. Principals, superintendents, and board members do not have to change schools on their own. Instead, they need to engage a group of volunteers—including parents, students, medical professionals, business professionals, school administrators, youth group leaders, and law enforcement officials—to help conceive and implement nutrition education and physical activity programs that make sense for the local school community.

Develop a comprehensive wellness policy. With the 2004 passage of the Child Nutrition Reauthorization Act, all schools that participate in federal school meal programs will need to develop a local wellness policy. This road map needs to include guidelines for all foods and beverages sold in school as well as guidelines for teaching students how to make good decisions about what they eat. The policy must include goals for increasing students' physical activity and school strategies for promoting student wellness. Policies should include recommendations for staff training on developing nutrition education curriculums and for new approaches in physical education. In addition, policies should address program implementation, monitoring, and evaluation.

Integrate physical activity and nutrition education into the regular school day. Teachers can start classes with fun calisthenics or dancing and can incorporate nutrition information and physical activity into reading, writing, math, science, and other subjects.

Incorporate nutrition education, healthy snacks, and physical activity into after-school programs. Students who stay after school can do more than finish homework, play board games, and watch television. Time should be set aside for physical activities that engage students in fun and innovative ways. In addition, after-school programs should provide access to healthful snacks and hands-on opportunities to learn about food and nutrition. Turnkey programs, including one sponsored by Action for Healthy Kids and the National Football League, can assist schools with implementation.

Encourage staff to model healthy lifestyles. A wellness program for faculty and staff can enhance school effectiveness by strengthening morale, reducing absenteeism, and cutting insurance costs. By exercising regularly and eating healthful foods, staff can also set a powerful example for students.

By taking these fundamental steps, schools can create healthy environments and, at the same time, promote student achievement.

Resources for Improving the School Health Environment

- Model school-based approaches, a school wellness policy tool, statistics relating to childhood nutrition and physical activity, and information on joining a state team are available at www.actionforhealthykids.org.

> - For an overview of issues relating to foods and beverages in schools and for strategies to improve school health environments, read *Making It Happen: School Nutrition Success Stories*. To download a free copy, go to www.cdc.gov/healthyyouth.
> - The Centers for Disease Control and Prevention offer a tool that schools can use to identify the strengths and weaknesses of nutrition policies and programs and to develop an action plan for improvement. *School Health Index: A Self-Assessment and Planning Guide* is available at http://apps.nccd.cdc.gov/shi.

References

Action for Healthy Kids. (2004). *The learning connection: The value of improving nutrition and physical activity in our schools.* Available: www.actionforhealthykids.org/special_exclusive.php

Alaimo, K., Olson, C., & Frongillo, E., Jr. (2001). Food insufficiency and American school-aged children's cognitive, academic, and psychosocial development. *Pediatrics, 108,* 44–53.

Brown, L., & Pollitt, E. (1996). Malnutrition, poverty, and intellectual development. *Scientific American, 274,* 38–43.

California Fitnessgram correlation with SAT scores. California Department of Education. Available: www.cde.ca.gov/nr/ne/yr02/yr02rel37.asp

Centers for Disease Control and Prevention. (1999). *Youth risk behavior surveillance.* Atlanta, GA: Author.

Hoelscher, D. M., Day, R. S., Lee, E. S., Frankowski, R. F., Kelder, S. H., Ward, J. L., et al. (2004). Measuring the prevalence of overweight in Texas schoolchildren. *American Journal of Public Health, 94,* 1002–1008.

International Life Sciences Institute. (1997). *Improving children's health through physical activity: A new opportunity.*

National Association for Sport and Physical Education & Council of Physical Education for Children. (2001). *Physical education is critical to a complete education.* Available: www.aahperd.org/naspe/pdf_files/pos_papers/pe_critical.pdf

Ogden, C., Flegal, K., Carroll, M., & Johnson, C. (2002). Prevalence and trends in overweight among U.S. children and adolescents, 1999–2000. *The Journal of the American Medical Association, 288*(14), 1728–1732.

Pollitt, E., Leibel, R., & Greenfield, D. (1991). Brief fasting, stress, and cognition in children. *American Journal of Clinical Nutrition, 34,* 1526–1533.

President's Council on Physical Fitness and Sports. (1999). Physical activity promotion and school physical education. *Physical Activity and Fitness Research Digest.* Available: www.fitness.gov/digest_sep1999.htm

School Nutrition Association. (1989). Impact of hunger and malnutrition on student achievement. *School Board Food Service Research Review, 1,* 17–21.

Schwimmer, J., Burwinkle, T., & Varni, J. (2003). Health-related quality of life of severely obese children and adolescents. *Journal of the American Medical Association, 289,* 1818.

Shephard, R. (1997). Curricular physical activity and academic performance. *Pediatric Exercise Science, 9,* 113–126.

Shephard, R., Volle, M., Lavalee, M., LaBarre, R., Jequier, J., & Rajic, M. (1984). Required physical activity and academic grades: A controlled longitudinal study. In J. Limarinen & I. Valimaki (Eds.), *Children and sport* (pp. 58–63). Berlin, Germany: Springer Verlag.

Symons, C., Cinelli, B., James, T., & Groff, P. (1997). Bridging student health risks and academic achievement through comprehensive school health programs. *Journal of School Health, 67,* 220–227.

Thorpe, L. E., List, D. G., Marx, T., May, L., Helgerson, S. D., & Frieden, T. R. (2004). Childhood obesity in New York City elementary school students. *American Journal of Public Health, 94,* 1496–1500.

Tufts University School of Nutrition. (1995). *Nutrition and cognitive development in children.* Medford, MA: Author.

Tyre, P. (2004, Nov. 3). Reading, writing, recess: Is jump-rope the answer to the obesity epidemic? *Newsweek* [Online edition]. Available: www.msnbc.msn.com/id/3339666/site/newsweek

U.S. Department of Agriculture. (1994–1996). *Continuing survey of food intakes for individuals (CSFII).* Washington, DC: Author.

U.S. Department of Health and Human Services. (2001). *The surgeon general's call to action to prevent and decrease overweight and obesity.* Washington, DC: Author.

David Satcher is Director of the National Center for Primary Care at the Morehouse School of Medicine and Interim President of the Morehouse School of Medicine. He is the former Surgeon General of the United States and is Founding Chair and Board Member of Action for Healthy Kids, 4711 West Golf Rd., Ste. 806, Skokie, IL 60076; info@actionforhealthykids.org.

Originally published in the September 2005 issue of *Educational Leadership, 63*(1), pp. 26–30.

Part 2

Promoting a Healthy Life

Finding Our Way Back to Healthy Eating: A Conversation with David A. Kessler

Amy M. Azzam

Our kids eat too much—and what they're eating drives them to eat even more. In this interview with Educational Leadership, *David A. Kessler, former commissioner of the Food and Drug Administration (FDA) under Presidents George H. W. Bush and Bill Clinton, discusses why so many people overeat and what we can do to help children develop better habits.*

In his new book, The End of Overeating: Taking Control of the Insatiable American Appetite *(Rodale, 2009), Kessler describes how processed food and changing lifestyles are setting people up for a lifetime of food obsession.*

Kessler is a lifelong health advocate. Under his watch, the FDA enacted regulations requiring standardized nutrition labels on food. He's also known for his role in the FDA's attempt to regulate cigarettes. Dr. Kessler is a pediatrician and has served as the dean of the medical schools at both Yale and the University of California.

In your new book, The End of Overeating, *you paint an alarming picture of our obsession with food. What exactly is overeating?*

The journey for me started with some simple questions: Why does that chocolate chip cookie have such power over me? Once I start eating it, why can't I stop? It's the struggle with eating as much as the overeating that the book tries to explain. Why do we do what we *know* we don't want to do but end up doing anyway?

I was watching Oprah one night, and there was a well-spoken, well-educated woman on the show who said, "I eat after my husband leaves for work in the morning, I eat before he comes home at night, I eat when I'm happy, I eat when I'm sad, I eat when I'm hungry, and I eat when I'm not hungry—and I don't like myself." Obviously, this woman wasn't eating for fuel or nutrition. The question was, What was driving that woman to eat? And I could relate: I have suits in every size.

So if adults are eating like this, I would assume that children are, too.

Certainly when I grew up four or five decades ago, we used to eat at mealtimes—we didn't snack, or only occasionally. But the average child now eats almost constantly throughout the day. Rarely does that child get hungry. Some call this *grazing*.

What we've done in the United States is taken fat, sugar, and salt and put them on every corner. We've made food available 24/7, and we've made it socially acceptable to eat anytime. We've made food into entertainment. These cultural effects lead to constant eating. The definition of overeating is eating more calories than you expend—more calories in than out. So you have a net weight gain.

Take the average candy bar. You could eat those 300 calories in two or three minutes. But it could take an hour to work them off. The imbalance over the last 20–30 years has been on the intake side, which raises some questions: What's going on? Why do people feel compelled to eat? And why is it so hard to stop?

So why is it so hard to stop?

Take the vanilla milkshake. What is it about the vanilla milkshake that gets us to keep on drinking it? Is it the sugar, fat, or flavor? Science has shown us that sugar is the main driver. But when you add fat to that sugar, you have more consumption. And combinations of fat, sugar, and salt drive consumption—they stimulate you to come back for more.

Forty or 50 years ago, the U.S. food industry shifted from food that was locally grown to a highly interdependent food distribution network that had many advantages in terms of cost and food safety. But now that food is so highly processed, we're able to dial in the exact amount of fat, sugar, and salt that will make us come back for more.

Does this kind of "food" even meet the criteria for what food is supposed to be?

It used to be that we needed to chew the average bite of food from 20 to 30 times. Today it's a fraction of that. Food goes down in a whoosh. It's almost as though it's predigested. It's like we're eating baby food all the time. We're just constantly stimulating ourselves. We're eating for reward—not for fuel or nutrition.

What's going on today is that combinations of fat, sugar, and salt stimulate the reward circuits and get us coming back for more. The reward centers of our brain regulate such behaviors as eating, drug use, and sexual reproduction. We can now look into the brain. For people who have a hard time resisting their favorite foods, we see that fat, sugar, and salt stimulate their brains. In fact, these substances highjack the reward pathways. You can actually see this activation in their brains.

Are children more vulnerable than adults are?

There's no doubt about that. Let's go through how this works. On the basis of past learning, memories, and experience, you get *cued*. A cue could be a sight, smell, time of day, or location. For example, I walk down a street that I walked down six months earlier. I've forgotten entirely that on that previous walk, I went into a store that sold chocolate-covered pretzels. Now that I'm back on that street, I start thinking about chocolate-covered pretzels. That's a cue.

You associate these cues with the actual food itself. That cue focuses your attention. It stimulates thoughts of wanting. You get this momentary pleasure from responding to the cue—by eating the chocolate-covered pretzels. The next time you get cued, you do it again and repeat the cycle. The behavior becomes both conditioned (learned) and motivated (driven). Once you lay down those learning circuits and those motivational circuits—certainly if you do it in childhood as it's happening today—they stay with you for a lifetime.

Kids are the most vulnerable. When I was growing up, I wasn't being constantly bombarded by food. It wasn't available on every corner, in every gas station, during most of our waking hours. Now our kids are growing up, not just with food that's been highly developed to be stimulating—layered and loaded with fat, sugar, and salt, which stimulates intake—but they're also constantly bombarded with food cues.

Food has to be rewarding. It has to be pleasurable. But I certainly want food that's going to nourish me, that will make me feel full and give me fuel. I don't want food that's going to keep me coming back for more.

My colleague, Dr. Gaetano Di Chiara, one of the great pharmacologists, studies the effect of cocaine and amphetamine on the brain. He finds that cocaine and amphetamine elevate the brain's dopamine circuitry. Dopamine is the chemical that locks in your attention, that gets you focused on the drugs and drives wanting.

We always thought that food gave you a little bump in dopamine the first time, but the second and third times it did not. So I said to Gaetano, let's not use just one ingredient, let's make the food highly palatable; let's take fat and sugar, put them together, and see whether we can get rises in brain dopamine. And we got exactly that—not only the first time, but repeatedly.

What are the repercussions for childhood obesity in the United States?

Let me give you an example. An average 2-year-old knows how to compensate for his or her eating. If the child eats more calories at lunch, he or she will typically eat fewer calories later on in the day. But by 4 or 5 years old, children lose the ability to compensate because they've been exposed to diets that are high in fat, sugar, and salt. They're now eating for reward—and not for fuel.

The greatest gift you can give someone is to lay down healthy eating patterns from the beginning, to find foods that are rewarding as well as healthy. If you continually expose children to fat, sugar, and salt, they will find these foods to be their friends. They will use them to feel good. If that's the case, it's hard to break the habit. Yes, you can retrain the brain, but you do it by laying down new neural circuitry, new learning on top of old.

How can schools help with laying down this new learning?

Once we understand that the constant availability of fat, sugar, and salt conditions and drives our behavior as well as the behavior of our kids, it has profound implications—for school lunch programs, for vending machines, for when we eat, for how we use food, and for how we educate. The best thing that schools can do is to teach kids about nutrition and help them understand that fat, sugar, and salt— although they taste good for the moment—will only stimulate them to come back for more. That if they use food as a reward or for purposes other than for nutrition and fuel, they're contributing to laying down that neural circuitry. That if they use food to regulate mood, then they're going to be stuck in that cycle for the rest of their lives.

Kids look at that huge plate of food now and say, "That's what I want." That's a hard cycle to break. And it's having a profound effect on their health. In the past, adults would get type 2 diabetes in their 40s or 50s, then live for two or three decades with the disease, developing eye disease, kidney disease, cardiovascular disease, and other complications. But kids are now getting type 2 diabetes—at 10 years old! What's going to be the effect of living, not for two or three decades with the disease, but for four, five, and six decades? That concerns me as a pediatrician.

Limiting where we eat, when we eat, and what we eat is vitally important with kids. But we can't just deprive our kids or give them rules. If kids feel deprived, it's not going to work. You've got to give them the tools so they can understand what good nutrition is so they will want to eat foods that will sustain, satisfy, and nourish them.

There are going to be problems if our kids eat foods layered with fat, sugar, and salt for lunch at school, if they use vending machines there, and if stores around the school also sell products layered with fat, sugar, and salt.

We all got into this jam together. We created this problem in the last four or five decades—and it's going to take all of us to undo it. You can't just do it at home, you can't just do it in the schools—you have to do it together.

David A. Kessler, M.D., is former Commissioner of the Food and Drug Administration. He is a pediatrician, lawyer, and author. **Amy M. Azzam** is Senior Associate Editor, *Educational Leadership*, aazzam@ascd.org.

Originally published in the December 2009/January 2010 issue of *Educational Leadership*, 67(4), pp. 6–10.

A Supersize Problem

Eric K. Gill

School wellness policies tackle overweight students, declining physical activities, and everpopular vending machines.

An estimated 17 percent of U.S. children are overweight, and policymakers are turning to schools to help students trim down and shape up. The Centers for Disease Control (CDC) and Prevention reports the number of overweight children ages 6–11 has doubled in the past 20 years; for adolescents 12–19 years old, the overweight figure has tripled. The CDC found that 80 percent of all high school students fail to eat the recommended daily allowance of fruits and vegetables, while more than 60 percent of U.S. children consume too much saturated fat (U.S. Department of Health and Human Services, 2006).

These statistics arrive 40 years after President Lyndon B. Johnson signed the Child Nutrition Act. At the time, many children in poor urban and rural communities came to school hungry and went home unfed. The law acknowledged the relationship between "nutrition and the capacity of children to develop and learn," and the government pledged to assist states "through grants-in-aid and other means, to meet more effectively the nutritional needs of our children" (Child Nutrition Act of 1966, Section 2).

Today's overweight epidemic is also occurring predominantly within the nation's poorest urban and rural areas. The CDC reports childhood overweight numbers are highest among Mexican American boys, non-Hispanic black girls, American Indian youth, and non-Hispanic white students from low-income families. In its well-meaning effort to feed the nation's poorest children, it seems the United States has succeeded at feeding them poorly.

Generation Extra Large

Among the many causes of today's overweight problem are fast-food chains, snack-food companies, and beverage manufacturers, which target young people and encourage consumption through promotional tie-ins, two-for-one deals, and free beverage refills. Apparently, these marketing strategies work. The CDC claims the average daily consumption of soft drinks among young girls doubled from 1978 to 1998, while consumption of carbonated sodas nearly tripled among boys during the same 20-year span.

As Coca-Cola boasts, "More than 1.3 billion times a day someone enjoys one of our beverages" (The Coca-Cola Company, n.d., para. 2).

Meanwhile, magazine covers tout sugar-free, low-carb, high-fiber, polyunsaturated foods for kids. Last fall, Mickey Mouse even scurried into the act when Disney announced it would revamp the children's menus at its theme parks with healthier foods.

The renewed focus on adolescent eating habits arrives as districts participating in federally funded school-meals programs are required to develop local wellness policies. The Child Nutrition and WIC (Women, Infants, and Children) Reauthorization Act of 2004 requires districts partaking in subsidized school breakfast and lunch programs to establish nutrition guidelines and physical activity goals by the end of the 2006–07 school year.

"The U.S. wellness policy requirement reinforces the actions many schools and districts had already begun in order to support the needs of the whole child," said Theresa Lewallen, ASCD's director of Healthy School Communities. "Successful, sustained implementation will only come about, however, if schools and communities work together to ensure that students learn in environments that help them develop lifelong healthy habits."

Mirroring ASCD's whole child approach, the CDC is promoting a Healthy Youth! initiative with its Coordinated School Health Program. The underlying theme is cooperation. "Schools by themselves cannot, and should not be expected to, address the nation's most serious health and social problems," the CDC declares on its Web site. "Families, health care workers, the media, religious [and] community organizations that serve youth, and young people themselves also must be systematically involved" (CDC, 2005, para. 1).

Imogene Clarke, director of Student Nutrition Services for Richland One School District in Columbia, S.C., is optimistic parents will participate in improving children's health. Richland One has more than 24,000 K–12 students enrolled in 47 schools. It implemented a Healthy and Nutritious Environment policy in compliance with the Reauthorization Act of 2004, and one goal is to curtail consumption of sodas.

"We don't have a say-so over what students bring for lunch from home, but we asked parents for their cooperation in not sending carbonated beverages to school, and you'd be surprised how many have complied," said Clarke, who supports schools taking an assertive role in child nutrition. "I think because we have students for such a long time during the day, it's an excellent opportunity for us to safeguard their health."

Penny McConnell, director of Food and Nutrition for Fairfax County Schools in Virginia, agrees: "We need to provide an environment, a wellness policy, and partnership where students are ready to learn. I stress the term 'partnership' because I think it's important that we work with parents, teachers, nurses, and students."

In South Carolina, Clarke pointed out, culture plays a huge role in what children learn to eat. "I'm African American, and I don't prepare food the way my mother did, but with lower-income families, you buy and eat what you can afford."

Despite the data showing a preponderance of overweight problems among poor American students, experts agree that nutrition education is important for everyone, regardless of economic levels.

"Parents also need to be educated, and they need to take an active role in planning family exercise programs," said McConnell of Fairfax, which is ranked 11th in highest per capita income among U.S. counties. "Nutrition education impacts what students eat—before and after school. Parents need to work with us and become role models."

The Fairfax County school district, which has about 164,000 K–12 students enrolled in 239 schools, implemented a progressive "competitive foods" policy in 1986. Although Fairfax schools allow vending machines, McConnell explained they incorporate electronic timers designed to prevent sales of sodas during school hours.

Soul Foods and Whole Children

Fabiola Gaines, a nutritionist who codeveloped the Soul Food Pyramid, echoed ASCD's whole child approach. "We need to explain proper eating habits to children, and I think through nutrition education in schools, children will influence their families," she said.

Gaines said it's critical to relate to children on a socioeconomic level. "You have to understand the culture of the community you're trying to work with," said Gaines, a partner with Hebni Nutrition Consultants in Orlando, Fla., and coauthor of cookbooks for diabetics. "With the cookbooks, we're trying to give healthier alternatives for traditional soul foods. Our forefathers needed those foods because you can't work in the fields all day and eat salads. The problem is we're still eating those traditional foods, but we're driving to the mailbox."

Gaines, who runs an after-school program for kids, reports that half of the participants are overweight. To curtail this, she started a cooking class that encompasses nutrition education and exercise. However, she remains realistic about teaching students to eat healthy.

"We're not trying to get them to lose weight at first. We're just trying to get them to stop *gaining* weight—to exercise and burn more calories."

Fairfax County offers a similar program. "We have a wonderful 4th grade cooking class, and the kids are taking the recipes home," McConnell said, noting that the district's Web site offers a nutrition calculator for parents, students, and teachers that encourages them to tally calories and vitamins on food and beverage labels. Fairfax also implemented a food-tasting program in which each school principal selects a focus group of lunch buyers and nonbuyers. Vendors bring in new foods for evaluation, and students rate their favorites.

"Choices are important for children," McConnell said. "It's my job to make sure they are healthy choices."

The Weight of History

After decades of neglecting the overweight problem, everyone seems to have something to say about childhood obesity, a term some psychologists find offensive. Although a lot of children are overweight, they argue it's insensitive and counterproductive to label them as obese.

No matter how students are labeled, Gaines is primarily concerned with changing their behaviors. "We have to get the physical activities back in schools if we want to address the child obesity issue," she insisted. "When I see a 10-year-old diabetic come into my office with type-2 [adult onset] diabetes, I think, 'Wait a minute. This can't be happening to American children.'"

The consequences of ignoring adolescent overweight problems could be dire if recent studies are accurate predictors: The University of California–Berkeley reported that "26–41 percent of overweight preschool children will become overweight adults" (2000, para. 2). *Family Economics and Nutrition Review* estimated "more than $68 billion" is spent annually on "direct" overweight-related U.S. health care costs (Facts About Childhood Obesity and Overweightness, 1999).

Although the economic costs to society are burdensome, the physical and emotional costs to individuals could be devastating. ASCD's Lewallen believes society has a responsibility to help students develop healthy eating habits and daily physical activities. In fact, she said it's critical if we hope to nurture whole children.

"Each child must have the opportunity to learn and to be physically and emotionally healthy," Lewallen said. "It is the mutual responsibility of schools, families, communities, and governments to make this happen. Our children deserve nothing less."

References

Facts about childhood obesity and overweightness. (1999, January). *Family Economics and Nutrition Review, 12*(1).

Centers for Disease Control (CDC). (2005). Healthy youth! Coordinated school health program. Retrieved November 13, 2006, from www.cdc.gov/healthyyouth/cshp

Child Nutrition Act, 42 U.S.C. § 1771 (1966). Retrieved November 13, 2006, from www.fns.usda.gov/cnd/Governance/Legislation/Historical/CNA-Oct-4-2005.pdf

The Coca-Cola Company. (n.d.). Corporate responsibility. Retrieved November 13, 2006, from www2.coca-cola.com/citizenship

University of California–Berkeley Department of Nutritional Sciences. (2000, January). Childhood overweight: A fact sheet for professionals. Retrieved November 13, 2006, from nature.berkeley.edu/cwh/PDFs/bw_health_prof.pdf

U.S. Department of Health and Human Services. (2006, May). Nutrition and the health of young people. Retrieved November 13, 2006, from www.cdc.gov/healthyyouth/nutrition/pdf/facts.pdf

---

Eric K. Gill is a former staff writer for ASCD's Newsletters and Special Publications.

Originally published in the January 2007 issue of *Education Update, 49*(1).

Sleep: The E-ZZZ Intervention

Christi A. Bergin and David A. Bergin

The answer to low achievement and misbehavior might just be a good night's sleep.

Nikki is supposed to be working on a lab experiment in her chemistry class. Instead, she is slumped in her seat, twirling a piece of hair, and staring at nothing in particular as she yawns loudly and says, "I'm sooooo tired!" Take a stroll through an average school and you will see students in many classes yawning, "spacing out," or dozing with their heads on their desks. Some students fall asleep before the morning announcements are over. Such sleepy students can be found in any elementary, middle, or high school.

Do some of your students appear sleepy, spacey, or groggy? Do they misbehave or have lower-than-expected achievement? It is common knowledge among parents that when toddlers are irritable, unreasonable, hyper, and unfocused, it must be nap time. Although K–12 students may have outgrown nap time, their achievement and behavior are affected by lack of sleep.

To see how this works, consider the story of one student, as told by Dahl and Lewin (2002). Jay, a 10th grader, routinely stayed up until 3 a.m. and woke up at noon during the summer. When the school year began, he tried to go to bed at 10 p.m. but couldn't fall asleep until 3 a.m. He got up at 6 a.m. for school the first week but was exhausted. When the weekend came, he stayed up late and slept most of the day on Saturday to "catch up." He continued this pattern for several weeks.

Sometimes he would oversleep and miss class, or he would fall asleep during class. His teachers and parents became angry, and Jay became irritable, had difficulty paying attention, and began failing his classes. This increased his anxiety, which made it harder for him to sleep. Eventually Jay was diagnosed with attention deficit/hyperactivity disorder and depression.

Many students, like Jay, are sleep deprived, and their sleep deprivation has significant implications for the classroom.

What Are the Results of Sleep Deprivation?

Sleep-deprived students tend to be more restless, irritable, and impulsive than other students (Bates, Viken, Alexander, Beyers, & Stockton, 2002). They also may be more depressed and have lower self-esteem than their classmates who sleep more (Fredriksen, Rhodes, Reddy, & Way, 2004). The effect can go in both directions—sleep deprivation may cause emotional disorders such as depression or anxiety, and emotional disorders may cause poor-quality sleep.

Another consequence of sleep deprivation is lower academic achievement. Poor sleepers are more likely to fail a grade than other students are, even when they do similar amounts of homework (Kahn et al., 1989). Third graders who have good sleep habits have higher grades in 5th grade than other students, after controlling statistically for earlier test scores (Buckhalt, El-Sheikh, Keller, & Kelly, 2009). Sleep deprivation decreases motivation, concentration, attention, and coherent reasoning. It decreases memory, self-control, and speed of thinking and increases the frequency of mistakes.

Note that students do not have to feel sleepy to experience these negative effects. People who are sleep deprived adapt; they may not report feeling sleepy even though their functioning has diminished (Beatty, 2001; Horowitz, Cade, Wolfe, & Czeisler, 2003).

Most of these studies are correlational, so you might wonder whether the positive outcomes linked to more sleep are really due to something else, such as healthy family routines. To test whether sleep causes these outcomes, researchers asked parents of students in grades 4 and 6 to put their children to bed earlier or later than usual for three nights in a row (Sadeh, Gruber, & Raviv, 2003). They found that students who went to bed an average of 30–40 minutes earlier improved in memory, motor speed, attention, and other abilities associated with math and reading test scores. Thus, even modest, temporary increases in sleep can have substantial effects on students' classroom functioning.

How Much Sleep Do Students Need?

As students grow, their need for sleep gradually diminishes. A good rule of thumb is "10 for 10"—10 hours of sleep for 10-year-olds. Younger children need more, and older children need less—except during puberty, when they typically need 9–10 hours. Adolescents who are growing rapidly or participating in sports may need even more sleep time.

Many U.S. students of all ages do not get enough sleep, but adolescents tend to be more sleep deprived than younger children. In fact, about 85 percent of adolescents are reported to be mildly sleep deprived, and 10–40 percent may be significantly sleep deprived (Dahl & Lewin, 2002).

Several changes in adolescence contribute to sleep deprivation. First, adolescents wake up more easily during the night than younger children (Carskadon & Dement, 2000). Second, adolescents stay up late for sports, homework, and jobs. Third, adolescents easily shift to a "night-owl" pattern. From ages 3 to 17, children tend to get up at the same time, about 7 a.m., but adolescents stay up about two and one-half hours later than younger children (Snell, Adam, & Duncan, 2007).

Adolescents often get less sleep on school nights and then sleep excessively on weekends (Ohayon, Carskadon, Guilleminault, & Vitiello, 2004). When they go to bed later on weekends than on school nights, they experience a "jet-lag" effect each week, and their school achievement may suffer. Research has shown that high school students who earn *A*s or *B*s tend to have a small discrepancy between school-night and weekend bedtimes. In contrast, students with a discrepancy of two hours or more are more likely to earn lower grades (Wolfson & Carskadon, 1998).

Given the evidence above, improving students' sleep should be of great concern to educators. Indeed, it may be among the lowest-cost approaches to improving student learning.

What Can Schools Do?

The first thing schools can do is communicate with parents about the importance of sleep, including a consistent bedtime, even on weekends. When teachers notice signs that a student might be sleep deprived they should contact the student's parents. Parents can then stay in tune with their children's sleep needs by observing how easily they wake up in the morning. They can prevent sleep problems by eliminating conditions that disturb sleep—such as noise, stress, light, lack of exposure to daylight, and some medicines—and ensuring that children avoid large meals, exercise, TV viewing, computer use and caffeine consumption in the hour before bedtime (Roehrs & Roth, 2008). And they can enforce a consistent bedtime, with no more than two hours difference on weekends.

Although parents play a key role, schools also can help prevent sleep deprivation. Here are a few ideas:

- Given the start time for most U.S. high schools, ensure that school activities such as basketball games or play practices end by 9 p.m. When traveling overnight with students for sporting events, science fairs, band competitions, or other school-sponsored activities, make sure students have a healthy bedtime. Some educators want to appear "cool" by encouraging late-night activities during such trips, but these activities undermine student achievement.

- Do not assign homework that requires staying up late. Give plenty of lead time for large projects. Convey to students that you would rather that they turn in homework late than pull an "all nighter." Be flexible about due dates so that students can juggle multiple commitments while getting adequate sleep.
- Advocate for a later start time for high schools. In one study, adolescents who transitioned from middle schools whose start time was 8:25 a.m. to a high school whose start time was 7:20 a.m. did not go to bed earlier (Carskadon, Wolfson, Acebo, Tzischinsky, & Seifer, 1998). As a result, they slept an hour less each night. In contrast, seven high schools in Minneapolis changed their start time from 7:15 a.m. to 8:40 a.m. Most students did not go to bed later, as some had feared, so they got 5 more hours of sleep per week (Wahlstrom, Davison, Choi, & Ross, 2001).

Changing the Cycle

Students with delayed sleep cycles, like Jay, can be gradually introduced to a healthier schedule by going to bed earlier in increments of 15–30 minutes over several weeks (Ollendick & Schroeder, 2003). Radical changes in sleep habits, as Jay attempted, are not as successful. For students with serious sleep problems, physicians or therapists might be enlisted to help with underlying medical, social, or emotional problems.

Parents and schools need to join forces to help students develop healthy sleep habits. If they do so, students' socioemotional well-being and academic achievement should improve, and educators' jobs should become easier.

References

Bates, J., Viken, R., Alexander, D., Beyers, J., & Stockton, L. (2002). Sleep and adjustment in preschool children: Sleep diary reports by mothers related to behavior reports by teachers. *Child Development, 73*(1), 62–74.

Beatty, J. (2001). *The human brain: Essentials of behavioral neuroscience.* Thousand Oaks, CA: Sage.

Buckhalt, J. A., El-Sheikh, M., Keller, P., & Kelly, R. J. (2009). Concurrent and longitudinal relations between children's sleep and cognitive functioning: The moderating role of parent education. *Child Development, 80*(3), 875–892.

Carskadon, M., & Dement, W. (2000). Normal human sleep. In M. Kryger, T. Roth, & W. Dement (Eds.), *Principles and practice of sleep medicine* (3rd ed., pp. 15–25). Philadelphia: W. B. Saunders.

Carskadon, M., Wolfson, A., Acebo, C., Tzischinsky, O., & Seifer, R. (1998). Adolescent sleep patterns, circadian timing, and sleepiness at transition to early school days. *Sleep, 21*(8), 871–881.

Dahl, R., & Lewin, D. (2002). Pathways to adolescent health: Sleep regulation and behavior. *Journal of Adolescent Health, 31*(6), 175–184.

Fredriksen, K., Rhodes, J., Reddy, R., & Way, N. (2004). Sleepless in Chicago: Tracking the effects of adolescent sleep loss during the middle school years. *Child Development, 75*(1), 84–95.

Horowitz, T., Cade, B., Wolfe, J., & Czeisler, C. (2003). Searching night and day: A dissociation of effects of circadian phase and time awake on visual selective attention and vigilance. *Psychological Science, 14*(6), 549–557.

Kahn, A., Van de Merckt, C., Rebauffat, E., Mozin, M., Sottiaux, M., Blum, D., et al. (1989). Sleep problems in healthy pre-adolescents. *Pediatrics, 84*(3), 542–546.

Ohayon, M., Carskadon, M. A., Guilleminault, C., & Vitiello, M. V. (2004). Meta-analysis of quantitative sleep parameters from childhood to old age in healthy individuals: Developing normative sleep values across the human lifespan. *Sleep Medicine Reviews, 27*(2), 1255–1273.

Ollendick, T., & Schroeder, C. (2003). *Encyclopedia of clinical child and pediatric psychology.* New York: Kluwer Academic.

Roehrs, T., & Roth, T. (2008). Caffeine: Sleep and daytime sleepiness. *Sleep Medicine Reviews, 12,* 153–162.

Sadeh, A., Gruber, R., & Raviv, A. (2003). The effects of sleep restriction and extension on school-age children: What a difference an hour makes. *Child Development, 74*(2), 444–455.

Snell, E. K., Adam, E. K., & Duncan, G. (2007). Sleep and the body mass index and overweight status of children and adolescents. *Child Development, 78*(1), 309–323.

Wahlstrom, K., Davison, M., Choi, J., & Ross, J. (2001). *Minneapolis Public Schools start time study.* University of Minnesota, Center for Applied Research and Educational Improvement. Available: www.cehd.umn.edu/carei/Reports/docs/SST-2001ES.pdf

Wolfson, A., & Carskadon, M. (1998). Sleep schedules and daytime functioning in adolescents. *Child Development, 69*(4), 875–887.

Christi A. Bergin (berginc@missouri.edu) is Associate Research Professor and

David A. Bergin (bergind@missouri.edu) is Associate Professor and Codirector of the Educational Psychology Program at the University of Missouri, Columbia.

Originally published in the December 2009/January 2010 issue of *Educational Leadership*, 67(4), pp. 44–47.

A Place for Healthy Risk-Taking

Laura Warner

At Francis W. Parker Charter Essential School, Wellness classes combine challenge and choice to help adolescent students grow.

Eating sushi. Talking with your parents about drugs or alcohol. Playing basketball. After each of these prompts, the students in my Wellness class rearrange themselves in a series of concentric circles that indicate their comfort level with the action described. I use this activity, called challenge circles, in the first week of school to set the stage for the coming year.

First, I create three concentric circles using ropes or cones on the floor. The inner circle is *comfort*, the middle is *stretch or risk*, and the outer circle is *panic*. Then I ask students to stand in the circle that represents their comfort level when asked to do a range of activities. We start off with relatively innocuous activities (*eating pizza*) and then ramp it up (*talking with your parents about sex; telling a close friend you disagree with him or her*). Finally, I connect it back to Wellness class and to physical activity using such prompts as *running the mile for fitness testing* or *getting sweaty in class*.

At the end of this activity, students have seen the wide range of comfort levels within our class. One student might feel completely at ease taking free throws but be sent right into the panic zone by something like swimming in the ocean. Playing soccer, with those hard balls flying through the air, is scary for many students, but it can be a place of true comfort for an athlete. Challenge circles are a great reminder for middle school students that what is true for them may not be true for their classmates.

Early adolescents are often described as developmentally egocentric, meaning that they struggle to differentiate between their own thoughts and the perspectives of others and often feel as though they are on stage, being constantly watched and judged by their peers. So seeing this visual demonstration of the differences in how their classmates perceive risk and comfort can be especially powerful. To debrief the circles activity, I ask questions like, Were we ever all standing in the same circle at the same time? What were some of the similarities or differences in our group? In which circle do you think the most learning occurs?

At Their Own Pace

Risk and challenge are an integral part of Wellness classes at the Francis W. Parker Charter Essential School in Devens, Massachusetts, where all 7th–10th graders attend these classes four days a week. We ask students to push themselves—to try new things that challenge their sense of comfort, but without the threat of actual harm. Our Wellness program includes an integrated curriculum combining aspects of health classes with physical education, games, and fitness. We offer a mixture of conventional games such as floor hockey and soccer and more unusual activities such as rock climbing, yoga, walks, and large-group tag.

The three full-time Wellness teachers frame activities so that students understand their range of options for participation and entry. When teaching middle school students to play football, for instance, I often remind them that they don't have to be able to throw a perfect spiral to be successful. I encourage them to see the fun and strategy in making up new plays or working with their team to trick the offense or defense.

For sports like this, I often split my classes in half, letting one group of kids play competitively while taking a smaller group of students aside to provide more explicit instruction and a less threatening introduction to the game. This helps students enter into the curriculum at their own place. When they are comfortable and exhibit some mastery, we can push them to go just a little further.

You don't need a ropes course to explore risk-taking or challenge. Any physical activity can involve risk—from trying yoga, to using an exercise ball for the first time, to pushing yourself to play all-out in a game of Frisbee even when you're worried about looking stupid in front of your friends. Our students complete "the dreaded mile run" twice a year to assess their cardiovascular fitness, and this event comes at a time in their lives when they are acutely aware of their own bodies and sensitive to how others perceive them. For teenagers (and some adults), running when they think that others might be watching can be a trying proposition, and we need to acknowledge the social and emotional chances our students are taking.

As a public charter school, we enroll approximately 75 new students each year through a lottery system. As these students enter Parker from more than 40 different schools and towns, I've heard them say things like, "I'm not good at gym," or "I'm just not athletic." I've always felt that my mission was to dispel those assumptions. For me, physical activity classes have become less a place for students to learn to throw a softball well, and more a place for them to learn to throw aside some assumptions about themselves and practice taking risks.

Challenge by Choice

At Parker, we use the *Adventure Curriculum for Physical Education* series developed by Project Adventure (www.pa.org) as the foundation of much of our program (Panicucci, 2007; Panicucci, Constable, Hunt, Kohut, & Rheingold, 2002–2003). That organization's Challenge by Choice philosophy recognizes that any activity or goal poses a different level of challenge for each person and that authentic personal change comes from within. Challenge by Choice creates an environment where participants are asked to search for opportunities to stretch and grow during the experience. [Students learn] how to set goals that are in neither the comfort nor the panic zone, but in that slightly uncomfortable stretch zone where the greatest opportunities for growth and learning lie. (Project Adventure, n.d.)

Incorporating this viewpoint into our physical education classroom offers a new way of thinking about how to assess students' needs and how to work in what psychologist Lev Vygotsky called *the zone of proximal development*—the place where optimal learning can occur (Nakkula & Toshalis, 2006).

For example, we play volleyball in groups of mixed gender, age, and ability. A student with solid ball-handling skills might be ready to try working with others to get the ball over the net using strategy instead of just slamming it back toward the other team; another student might be struggling to serve underhand, so I might let him or her throw the ball over the net instead of serving. Although I dread the phrase "I can't," I've learned to work with it. "You can't play volleyball?" I respond. "That's a big statement. Can you throw the ball? Can you help with the rotation? Have you tried learning to serve? To bump? To set?" We start from the beginning, and although not every student will become Olympian Misty May-Treanor, they often find out they are actually pretty good at something they would never have guessed they would be.

Teens Need to Play

In our Wellness program, we have taken the idea of Challenge by Choice one step further by working to adopt this mind-set throughout the year. We believe that learning to take healthy risks is particularly appropriate for teenagers.

In the Western world, the term *adolescence* is often viewed as synonymous with *bad decisions*—early sexual encounters, reckless driving, parties without parental supervision, and other impulsive deeds done without regard for consequences. We know that the teenage years are tumultuous, that middle schoolers teeter between childlike and adultlike behavior, and that high schoolers often push the limits of the rules.

In *The Romance of Risk*, Lynn Ponton (1997) states that "risk-taking is the major tool that adolescents use to shape their identities" (p. 275). She emphasizes that parents (and, we can safely assume, teachers) need to "promote opportunities for their adolescents to undertake positive challenges, not simply as an alternative to more dangerous risks but also because of their intrinsic value in contributing to the development of healthy, confident adults" (p. 280).

Cynthia Lightfoot (1997) suggests in *The Culture of Adolescent Risk-Taking* that sharing risks offers a way for adolescents to show a new side of themselves to others and to recreate themselves in relationship with their peers. Lightfoot considers adolescent risk behaviors a developmentally natural form of play, just as normal as imaginative or fantasy play in elementary school children.

Generally, as students move up in grade level, the amount of play that schools provide or encourage significantly decreases. Yet teens are in desperate need of creative play. Their transition between childhood and adulthood—wavering back and forth from dependence to independence—means that they still need to be able to relax, be silly, and act like kids. If adolescents naturally play by searching for novel and exciting experiences that make them feel alive and that bring them closer to their peers, doesn't it make sense to try to channel this developmental need into positive activities at school?

Many of the social aspects of our physical activity classes can replicate some features of traditional play, as students negotiate rules and develop ways to act toward one another. By offering activities like capture the flag or other games that allow for spontaneity, flexible thinking, and imagination, we can begin to integrate opportunities for risk-taking and play into our classes.

Bringing Risk-Taking into P.E.

Although fitness and sports should be an important part of a comprehensive physical education program, we can go beyond the traditional P.E. class—not only by changing the activities we offer, but also by changing our own mind-set, attitude, and expectations. We can't do this well, however, in schools where students take physical education for only one term a year, or where teachers are expected to get to know 200–500 students. Although class ratios in many schools may be capped at 25–30 students per teacher, many physical education teachers see individual students only briefly as they rotate through "specials" for one quarter of their year.

As a member of the Coalition of Essential Schools founded by Theodore R. Sizer (www.essentialschools.org), Parker is guided by the belief that teachers should know students well. Our abilities to assess the needs of each student, to have honest and timely conversations, and to build trust are directly related to our small student loads.

An emphasis on differentiated instruction also helps. Instead of requiring that all students approach physical games in exactly the same way, we should acknowledge that students have different learning styles and proficiency levels. Why not offer students a tee to hit the softball, or operate on the principle that there are no strike-outs and that the score doesn't matter?

During a game of kickball, 7th grader Katie said to me, "I'm not kicking. Jackie will do it for me; I just want to run." Such a request isn't unusual, and I told her it was OK. Instead of letting her off the hook for the entire game, however, I spent a few minutes chatting with her about what exactly was keeping her from kicking—a long list that included fear that she would stub her toe, that she would miss the ball completely, and that she would look "stupid" and "everyone would laugh." Kickball puts the kicker in a visible and vulnerable place with everyone watching as he or she steps up to the plate.

After our conversation and some encouragement from her friends, Katie eventually agreed to kick. She missed the ball her first time, kicked a foul backwards over our heads the second time, and grazed the ball for a single on her third try. No one laughed. Life went on. I think she will remember moments like these, as I do, and know that she has the potential to try something that she might not immediately be good at. When we take the time to develop a strong sense of community and safety in our classes, we help make such moments possible.

Leaving a few minutes at the end of class to debrief sports activities can further strengthen the norm of exploring possibilities and encourage students to approach novel experiences with confidence instead of fear. One of the tools that I often use for such debriefing is called Captain, Crew, and Passenger. We take turns going around the circle, saying what role we most often took on during the previous activity—*captain*, meaning any kind of leadership role; *crew*, working or helping the group to succeed; or *passenger*, just listening and going along for the ride.

The message I aim to send is that there is no value judgment on these roles—we certainly couldn't be successful with 26 captains! Then, I ask the students in my classes to think about taking on different roles in future games. If they are most comfortable being a captain, I ask them to "try just listening next time. Let someone else take over. It might be hard, but it's worth trying." In the same way, I encourage habitual passengers to speak up and try out a more active role.

Finally, as educators we need to model healthy risk-taking for students. I'm relatively comfortable teaching in front of large groups, answering detailed questions about sexuality, and making a fool of myself playing games that sometimes involve clucking like a chicken or howling like a wolf. However, I also perform on the flying trapeze, and my nervousness before shows can bring me almost to tears. Having this experience of walking the line between stretching myself and full-out panic has made me more sensitive to the way students experience my class, and I make sure to share my own stories like this throughout the year.

We don't all need to fly through the air or jump out of airplanes to demonstrate our willingness to take risks—we can be silly, sing in public, laugh at ourselves, and simply let our students see us try out new lessons we aren't sure will work. Kids know when we let ourselves be vulnerable, and although it's almost guaranteed that they won't congratulate us at that moment, they will remember—and they will be more likely to let themselves be vulnerable in the future.

Providing Safe Places to Take Risks

Most of us have never mastered anything without practice. By providing spaces in school where teens can develop and nurture a sense of creativity, where they can be playful and innovative with their learning, and where we reassure them that it's OK to be less than perfect, we are offering them a chance to practice risk-taking.

Reenvisioning physical education class as a place where educators can scaffold activities to provide appropriate levels of physical, social, and emotional challenge to students may be a new approach in many schools, where the goals of physical education are more often structured around increasing student fitness, building skills in specific sports, or simply allowing students to burn off excess energy. But adolescents in the throes of emerging identity urgently need opportunities for healthy risk-taking.

Before self- and peer-assigned labels like "jock" or "geek" become entrenched in adolescents' emerging sense of identity, we should challenge their notions of what they can and cannot do. Students should be learning not only how to build their repertoire of physical skills, but also how to interact with their peers in a playful way and how to practice safe ways to fulfill their developmentally appropriate need to take risks. As physical educators, we can cultivate an atmosphere in which students push themselves to new limits, both physically and emotionally, while feeling supported by their classmates and teachers.

> ### Flying Outside Their Comfort Zone
>
> The circus art of flying trapeze is a love of mine, and I teach beginners on the weekends. For the past two years, I've brought my advisory class to the trapeze school for an end-of-year field trip.
>
> Last year Theo, an energetic and popular 8th grade boy, was looking anxious when he learned about the take-off and subsequent hanging-by-the-knees position. "It's OK," I said, "I know you can do it." He replied, "I'm really nervous." It was a real change from his usual self-assured persona.
>
> One by one, each student climbed 23 feet into the air, jumped off a platform, swung out and then hung upside-down. Most were nervous, but especially Theo, as this pushed him way outside his comfort zone into what we call "stretch" or "risk" in our classes.
>
> The most powerful part of the day was when he slowly, with encouragement, took one hand and then the other off the bar to hang by his knees. His face showed just how hard this was for him. We all learned a lot about him in those few seconds when he had to decide how much he trusted himself and the person on the safety lines and allow himself to be vulnerable in front of his peers.

> The idea of having a "shared experience" is what Lightfoot (1997) heard repeatedly when she interviewed teens about risk-taking. By telling and retelling stories about their escapades, they created narratives that became the social glue that held them together. This was true for our group; the students became closer after looking at photos from the day, laughing at their smiling and scared faces, and reveling in the accomplishment of stretching beyond their comfort zone.
> —*Laura Warner*

References

Lightfoot, C. (1997). *The culture of adolescent risk-taking.* New York: Guilford.

Nakkula, M., & Toshalis, E. (2006). *Understanding youth: Adolescent development for educators.* Cambridge: Harvard Education Press.

Panicucci, J. (2007). *Achieving fitness: An adventure activity guide, middle school to adult.* Beverly, MA: Project Adventure.

Panicucci, J., with Constable, N., Hunt, L, Kohut, A., & Rheingold, A. (2002–2003). *Adventure curricula for physical education series.* Beverly, MA: Project Adventure.

Ponton, L. (1997). *The romance of risk: Why teenagers do the things they do.* New York: Basic Books.

Project Adventure. (n.d.). *Glossary of terms.* Available: www.pa.org/about/glossary.php

---

Laura Warner is a Wellness teacher at Francis W. Parker Charter Essential School, Devens, Massachusetts; lauraw@parker.org.

Originally published in the December 2009/January 2010 issue of *Educational Leadership, 67*(4), pp. 70–74.

Keeping Teachers Healthy

Rick Allen

Staff wellness program yields results

While health education advocates are urging schools to consider the connections between student health and student achievement, some schools are targeting the health of their staff. If teachers, administrators, and other school staff are overburdened with the cares of education to the neglect of their own health, schools can count on low morale, lower productivity, increased absenteeism, and possibly higher insurance costs, say experts.

In Washoe County School District in Reno, Nev., the staff wellness program requires the district's more than 6,000 staff members and retirees to pay $40 a month—$480 annually—into a fund that runs the program.

It's a stiff price to pay, but there are ways to lighten the burden. The district's Good Health Incentive Program allows members to reduce the monthly payment by meeting certain health standards or "taking responsible actions" to meet them, says Aaron Hardy, Washoe County schools' staff wellness coordinator. Each year, employees undergo screenings for blood pressure, weight, and tobacco use. Those who merely show up to get tested pare $10 off their monthly fees.

If they meet particular criteria in the three target areas, the fee is further reduced. Indeed, a teacher could end up paying nothing, says Hardy. Joining one of the district's four weight loss programs or completing a course to quit smoking are "responsible actions" school employees can take to improve their health and reduce their payments. Participation is high: 90 percent of employees and retirees attend the screenings and try to lower their costs, Hardy says.

Responsible Actions

After Washoe officials became alarmed by rising health care costs in the 1990s, district leaders made several attempts to encourage healthy lifestyles among their employees. Although an initial wellness fair brought out 200 people its first year, the next year only 30 showed up. The district then took more drastic action by starting the current wellness program, says Hardy.

"The whole idea is very simple—the district decided to treat adults as adults. When you look at the big picture, 70 percent of health care costs are related to lifestyle behaviors," says Hardy. "The program is completely legal and was approved by the superintendent and teachers' unions. It doesn't cost the district or taxpayers anything."

The success of the program is evident, says Hardy, noting that a 20 percent reduction in staff absenteeism has saved county schools $3 million over six years.

Hardy, who has been coordinating the program for three years, has beefed up the district's Wellness Program Web site (http://www.washoe.k12.nv.us/wellness) with inspiring stories of teachers who have been successful with long-term weight loss, details of incentive programs to encourage gym workouts, and myriad four- to eight-week challenges to get school employees to exercise and eat healthy foods.

Web Is Key

"The Web site is the ticket to getting more people involved. It reminds them to do what's right for themselves," says Hardy. He has introduced a Web feature that allows employees to check their current health indicators and fee reductions online, download recipes for healthy eating, and receive health tips by e-mail.

In the last year, 54 percent of school employees participated in voluntary programs, an increase of 50 percent over the previous year, Hardy says. A voluntary program called Back to Basics, for example, describes 12 exercises to strengthen the back, has online video demonstrations, and gives incentives, such as a chance to win a reclining chair or a one-hour massage for those who commit to doing the exercises daily for a month.

The net effect of getting more school employees to take part in short- and long-term programs is "a cultural shift toward health," Hardy concludes. "We're holding adults accountable and getting them healthy, and we're helping borderline folks to stay out of the at-risk category."

School administrators are now exploring how the staff wellness model might be translated into similar health education initiatives for students, Hardy says. Because the staff program prods teachers and administrators to pursue "health and wellness from the get-go," he points out, everyone is "already on board" to find ways to mirror the program's successes for the district's 60,000 students.

Rick Allen is the project manager for ASCD Express and a staff writer for ASCD's Newsletters and Special Publications; rallen@ascd.org.

Originally published in the Winter 2004 issue of *Curriculum Update*.

Part 3

Protecting Students, Working with Bullies

Bullying—Not Just a Kid Thing

Doug Cooper and Jennie L. Snell

From "Students are just tattling" to "Boys will be boys," myths about bullying abound.

Bullying. The very word conjures up bad memories for many adults. Whether they were the target of bullying, used bullying behaviors themselves, or witnessed bullying toward others, many adults vividly recall incidents that happened 10, 20, or even 40 years ago. Perhaps because of these powerful memories, caring educators want their schools to be safe, respectful, and bully-free. They are not alone.

In the wake of school shootings and lawsuits brought against schools by victims of bullying, 11 state legislatures—California, Colorado, Georgia, Louisiana, Minnesota, Nevada, New Hampshire, Oklahoma, Oregon, Vermont, and Washington—have mandated that schools take active steps to reduce bullying. Although specific actions related to these mandates vary by state, many schools are finding that the most effective approach to bullying prevention is one that is inclusive of school staff, parents, students, and the community. Such approaches must also be comprehensive, with aligned policies and a research-based student learning component.

Since the late 1970s, Committee for Children, a nonprofit organization dedicated to helping schools address students' social and emotional development, has been conducting research and developing programs for educators, families, and communities to prevent child abuse, youth violence, and bullying (see www.cfchildren.org).

Committee for Children's researchers, program developers, and implementation specialists have learned from their work with many school districts to execute the early steps necessary for building a strong foundation to prevent bullying.

Uncovering Myths and Misconceptions

Bullying is so closely linked to childhood that it can easily be thought of as simply a child's problem. It is not. Adults play a major role depending on whether they ignore or work to prevent bullying. People who bully take advantage of an imbalance of power, such as greater physical size, higher status, or support of a peer group. Their bullying may take the form of face-to-face attacks with physical aggression, threats, teasing about perceived sexual orientation, or telling someone in a mean way that he or she can't play. Bullies often use behind-the-back behaviors, such as starting and spreading malicious rumors, writing hurtful graffiti, or encouraging others to exclude a particular child. Often, adults fail to take active steps to address the problem of bullying because they have the following misconceptions.

Everyone knows what bullying is. Bullying can often be difficult to distinguish from normal conflict and rough play. A study of the ability of lunchtime supervisors to distinguish students' play fighting, or "rough-and-tumble" play, from true aggression found that the adult supervisors were more likely to mistake aggression for play rather than the other way around (Boulton, 1996). In fact, they made errors in one out of four episodes. Adults need help recognizing bullying.

Boys will be boys. Many people perceive bullying as physical aggression—hitting, poking, or pushing—committed by boys. Bullying, however, is not limited to physical aggression or boys. Girls engage in bullying behaviors as much as boys do (Craig, Pepler, & Atlas, 2000). Some studies show that girls engage in more subtle forms of bullying, such as malicious gossip and social exclusion (Crick & Grotpeter, 1995). Other studies show that both boys and girls engage in all forms of bullying behavior.

Only a small number of children are affected. Just about every student in a school can be affected by and suffer from the long-term effects of bullying. By conservative estimates, 10 percent of school students are chronic targets of bullying, although the number may be higher (Perry, Kusel, & Perry, 1988). In addition, a school climate and culture of fear can affect more than just the students who are victims. Bullying often occurs away from adults, but students frequently witness bullying events (Hawkins, Pepler, & Craig, 2001). As bystanders, students are confused about what to do, and they fear becoming the next target.

Adults are already doing all they need to do. This misconception is one of the most challenging to overcome. First, adults might not know about bullying incidents. Many students who are targets of bullying do not tell adults. Second, students don't believe that adults will intervene even when they do report bullying. Playground observations of bullying support students' perceptions that adults rarely intervene (Craig et al., 2000). But when asked, teachers believe that they often intervene to stop bullying. Many reasons may exist for this mismatch between students' and adults' perceptions, such as adults not seeing the bullying, students not reporting it, or students not being aware of the follow-through actions that adults take after students report it. Whatever the reasons, it's clear that students believe that they need more help from adults than they are getting.

Students are just tattling. Some adults dismiss students' reports of bullying as tattling. This perpetuates students' beliefs that adults don't take reports of bullying seriously. Students and adults need to recognize and understand the difference between tattling (trying to get someone into trouble) and reporting (keeping someone safe). To counteract this misconception, adults need to be committed to listening attentively when students report bullying. Adults should gather information, take action to provide safety and assurance, and provide timely follow-up, such as checking in with the student to see whether the bullying has stopped.

Developing and Implementing Strategies

Uncovering bullying myths is an important first step. The next step is to develop and implement prevention strategies. Just as schools are familiar with installing smoke alarms, conducting fire drills, or developing earthquake and tornado preparedness procedures, schools should think through how to prevent bullying (Snell, MacKenzie, & Frey, 2002). Research shows that adults can reduce bullying among students by taking an active role in creating and implementing prevention techniques (Olweus, 1993). Even without an extensive study of the phenomenon, school staff members can ask what they can do *before* they have a bullying problem—or before it grows.

Because bullying has a hidden nature, school staff members should begin their bullying prevention efforts by examining less-structured areas of their school, such as playgrounds and hallways, to improve student behavior through supervision and established guidelines.

Make Playgrounds and Hallways Safe

Recess provides students with rich opportunities for peer interaction and social skill development; recess play may even improve some students' ability to concentrate in the classroom (Pellegrini, 1995). However, students' reports and research observations show that bullying often occurs on the playground. Bullying also occurs in school hallways, on school buses, and in the cafeteria, because students interact informally in these locations, often with little supervision (Astor, Meyer, & Pitner, 2001). With bullying prevention in mind, adults should examine and make adjustments to adult supervision, established procedures, and guidelines for student behavior on playgrounds and in other less-structured environments.

Improve supervision. Although increasing supervision typically costs money, some low- or no-cost strategies make supervision more effective. For instance, provide training in "active supervision" for playground monitors and other staff who circulate through assigned areas. Give monitors a means of communicating, such as hand-held radios, to facilitate coordination across large spaces. Maintain an adequate adult-to-student supervision ratio. Encourage all school staff members to spend some time on the playground at recess to observe student behavior in an unstructured setting, to increase their awareness of common recess problems, and to provide support for the recess supervisors' authority.

Woodway Elementary in Edmonds, Washington, for example, provided training for all of the school's stakeholders, including classroom teachers, custodians, playground supervisors, and office staff. The principal also hosted parent training in supervising play as part of the school's curriculum night. At Chautauqua Elementary in Vashon Island, Washington, bus drivers received extra training and helped develop behavioral expectations for riding on the bus.

Standing at the classroom doorway when students are changing classes provides hallway supervision and allows a teacher to greet students by name as they enter the classroom. Staff can convey tremendous caring by being present in the hallway and engaging in brief, informal conversations during transitions.

Develop specific routines. Establish clear guidelines for behavior and implement a schoolwide system for tracking, handling, and communicating about problems and disciplinary infractions. Teach rules to new students so that they learn the expectations and skills necessary for success.

To improve student behavior at recess, for example, teach and practice with students the transition routines for the beginning and end of recess. Teach common playground games to students in physical education class at the beginning of the school year and as a refresher in the spring. Provide sufficient play equipment for students in all grade levels. Assign new students "recess buddies" to help them make friends. For students who are less interested in traditional playground games, offer a range of activities, such as drawing or reading in a designated quiet area.

Incorporate social-emotional learning. Balancing structured and unstructured playtime at recess provides students with the opportunity to practice and use their prosocial skills. Teach students ways to play fairly, form friendships, join group activities, include others, show respect, and manage emotions. Define each of these skill areas by helping students understand what each is, what each isn't, and what each looks like in action on the playground. Intervene and coach students when their behavior is inappropriate.

Implement a School Discipline Policy

Another way of getting started in bullying prevention is to write an anti-bullying policy that links bullying to the school's discipline policy. An effective written policy

- Declares the school's commitment to creating a safe, caring, and respectful learning environment for all students.
- Gives a clear definition of bullying and concrete examples of specific bullying behaviors.
- States consequences of bullying in the context of a school's discipline code.

- Provides students, parents, and school personnel with a common, concrete framework for recognizing and responding to bullying.

The most effective policies include input from different groups within the school community, such as students, teachers, playground monitors, and parents. Effective policies use clear, simple language to ensure that all students, parents, and staff understand them. Place a copy in the school handbook and in the information packets provided to all students and their families, and sustain the anti-bullying message throughout the school year.

Developing a policy can be a labor-intensive process, but the result is greater personal investment in the school community by staff, students, and parents (Rigby, 1996).

Learn More About Bullying

Learning more about bullying can help adults improve their ability to recognize bullying and to take action when it occurs. A school doesn't need to complete an extensive study of bullying before beginning to make school improvements, but it can simultaneously learn about bullying while taking preventive steps.

Thinking of bullying as a kid thing is a mistake. Students would solve the problem of bullying on their own if they had the skills, knowledge, and power to do so. But they don't have the power to correct the imbalance of power that characterizes bullying. Nor do they have the power to establish a strong foundation of bullying prevention in their school. They need the help of the adults in a school community.

Be vigilant and find ways for all the adult members of the school to work together to support one another's efforts in bullying prevention. Take a whole-school approach and work proactively both behind the scenes and in view of students to build a school climate and culture in which all members—students and adults—feel safe, respected, and included.

References

Astor, R. A., Meyer, H. A., & Pitner, R. O. (2001). Elementary and middle school students' perceptions of violence-prone school subcontexts. *Elementary School Journal, 101*, 511–528.

Boulton, M. J. (1996). Lunchtime supervisors' attitudes towards playful fighting, and ability to differentiate between playful and aggressive fighting: An intervention study. *British Journal of Educational Psychology, 66*, 367–381.

Craig, W. M., Pepler, D. J., & Atlas, R. (2000). Observations of bullying in the playground and in the classroom. *School Psychology International, 21*, 22–36.

Crick, N. R., & Grotpeter, J. K. (1995). Relational aggression, gender, and social-psychological adjustment. *Child Development, 66*, 710–722.

Hawkins, D. C., Pepler, D. J., & Craig, W. M. (2001). Naturalistic observations of peer interventions in bullying. *Social Development, 10*, 512–527.

Olweus, D. (1993). *Bullying at school.* Cambridge, MA: Blackwell.

Pellegrini, A. D. (1995). *School recess and playground behavior: Educational and developmental roles.* Albany, NY: SUNY Press.

Perry, D. G., Kusel, S. J., & Perry, L. C. (1988). Victims of peer aggression. *Developmental Psychology, 24*, 807–814.

Rigby, K. (1996). *Bullying in schools and what to do about it.* London: Jessica Kingsley.

Snell, J. L., MacKenzie, E., & Frey, K. (2002). Bullying prevention in elementary schools: The importance of adult leadership, peer group support, and student social-emotional skills. In H. Walker & M. Shinn (Eds.), *Interventions for academic and behavior problems II: Preventive and remedial approaches* (pp. 351–372). Bethesda, MD: National Association of School Psychologists.

Doug Cooper (dcooper@cfchildren.org) is a program developer and **Jennie L. Snell** is a child psychologist and researcher at Committee for Children, 568 1st Ave. South, Ste. 600, Seattle, WA 98104. Both helped create *Steps to Respect: A Bullying Prevention Program.*

Originally published in the March 2003 issue of *Educational Leadership, 60*(6), pp. 22–25.

Civility Speaks Up

Stephen Wessler

*Empowered students can stop hurtful speech
and bring healing to their schools.*

Empathy and a rubber band. For one student, these are the things that made a difference.

One Friday afternoon, Rachel, a high school junior, was walking down the hallway on her way out of school. Among the hundreds of students who were talking, laughing, and gesturing as they exited the building, Rachel spotted one girl, a younger student whose name she did not know, sitting in front of a locker staring miserably across the hall as students walked by her, stepped over her, and ignored her in their rush to leave school. Rachel stopped and sat down next to the girl and asked her whether everything was OK. The girl immediately began talking, amid tears, about how every day students ridiculed her about her race and her size and spread rumors about her sexual activity.

As the girl gestured emphatically, the sleeves of her shirt rode up her arm revealing three 5-inch-long, raw cut marks. Rachel asked the girl why she was cutting herself, and she said, "the only time in my life when I don't think about how awful school is for me is when I can concentrate solely on the physical pain of cutting myself." In the past, she had put rubber bands around her wrist to remind her not to cut herself. But she was so anxious that she picked at the rubber bands until they broke.

Rachel was wearing a wide, thick rubber band around her wrist that day. She gave it to the younger girl, saying, "I'm giving this to you because I want you to remember that I care about you and because this band will not break. You won't have to cut yourself." Rachel added that she hoped the girl would talk to a counselor.

Seven months later, Rachel ran into the younger girl again. She was still wearing the broad rubber band and told Rachel that she had not cut herself since they talked.

The Power of Words

Words are the central tool of education. Whether written or spoken, words can elucidate, inform, and inspire. But they can also scare, humiliate, and disempower. Degrading slurs, jokes, and epithets are pervasive in the hallways, cafeterias, buses, locker rooms, and even classrooms of middle and high schools everywhere.

A school where degrading language, slurs, and jokes are widely used and rarely challenged is a place where violence is far more likely to occur. Some students will take the silence of bystanders as license to escalate their behavior from words to harsher words, threats, and finally violence. In every instance of violence that I have investigated in schools, first as a hate crime prosecutor and more recently when administrators asked me to help them respond to serious misconduct, I have seen this same process of escalation.

Of course, physical violence is not the only potential problem arising from hateful speech. Students who are targets of bullying and harassment may lose their health—becoming anxious or depressed, turning to alcohol and drugs, or engaging in self-harm such as cutting. Others lose their education because they are unable to put aside their feelings of humiliation, fear, or anger and concentrate on academics. Some find that their grades fall, some start skipping school, and some drop out entirely. Tragically, a few lose it all and take their own lives because of the desperation and hopelessness that a school life dominated by exclusion, intimidation, and degradation brings.

The Center for the Prevention of Hate Violence helps students find new words—words of civility and respect that can heal the wounds caused by bias and harassment. We have worked with students in the United States, the Middle East, Canada, and Northern Ireland to empower students and teachers to speak up when they hear degrading speech. Teachers can use the principles we espouse to transform the classrooms and hallways of their schools.

Empowering Students

Administrators and teachers alone cannot change school climate. A school may have the best possible written harassment policies, and administrators may consistently and fairly apply those policies. Teachers and other staff may interrupt degrading language whenever they hear it. But most incidents of bias, harassment, and disrespect occur outside the hearing and eyesight of any adult. Until we empower students to stand up and speak up, we will not change school climate.

The Center for the Prevention of Hate Violence empowers students through the Unity Project, an intensive multiyear relationship in which our staff collaborates with administrators and school faculty and staff on a variety of different interventions. Strategies include full-day workshops with student leaders, assemblies in which students work in small groups to devise strategies for reducing harassment, and intensive dialogue programs. Students learn about harassment in school, talk about bias and stereotypes, and, most important, develop strategies and skills for leadership.

Learning About Harassment

Focus groups with students help school leaders learn what degrading language and other harassment students are using and observing in school. Whenever we start working in a new school, we begin with focus groups. To encourage greater candor, we group students with similar peers: girls, boys, students of color, gaystraight alliance members, and so on. Girls, for example, will talk more openly about sexual harassment in an all-girls group than in a mixed-gender group.

One high school student wrote the following during a focus group:

> Freshman year I got a reputation for being a "slut." Everyone always asked me about it or commented about it when I was around, and it hurt really badly. It was so unfair because I am not sexually promiscuous. It got to the point where I never went out. I just went home and cried. I started cutting myself. After a while, the rumors dissipated, but I have never recovered the friends I lost during that time, and I still won't go to school parties because I'm afraid of what they say to me.

Another student wrote about a classmate who had recently immigrated to the United States:

> I have a friend who was harassed in school every day because of the color of her skin and her accent. She became depressed, wishing she could return to her home country, but that could not happen. So she started to skip school. All her grades went down from *A*s to *F*s. She felt there was no need to go to a school where she was not accepted for who she was.

After the focus groups, we draft a report and present our findings to faculty members by having them read aloud 25–35 of the student descriptions. Reading these comments together helps teachers develop a shared understanding of the level of harassment and bias. The effects of bullying become very immediate, very real, and very painful.

Information from focus groups is also crucial when working with students. Too often, we talk abstractly about bias, harassment, and bullying. By giving students concrete examples of the words that classmates use in school, we replace the abstract with the harsh reality of what goes on in hallways, cafeterias, and classrooms.

Challenging Stereotypes

Two weeks after a bloody racial fight witnessed by hundreds of students, our center gathered 25 students from the high school in question to discuss racial tension in their school. One-third of the participants were white students who had expressed high levels of hostility to students of color. Another third were students of color who were upset about the racial bias in the school. The final third were students from all races who wanted the school to be safe and respectful.

Students broke into small groups to discuss the use of "the n word." White students asked questions, and students of color provided both history and personal and family experience. Mark, a white student who was angry about the demographic changes in his school, had freely used racial slurs, and was regarded as a leader by many white students, asked to speak. He pointed to Sara, a student of color, and said that her explanation of the history of violence and humiliation surrounding the n word had helped him understood for the first time "how awful that word is." Turning to his white classmates, he said, "We need to change; we need to come together." He looked at Sara, said, "Thank you," and sat down. At that moment, this group of 25 students changed.

The degrading language, slurs, and jokes that students so frequently hear are built on a foundation of stereotypes about gender, race, sexual orientation, body size, religion, disability, and other characteristics. Such stereotyping makes it far too easy for students to depersonalize others who are different and to treat them in degrading and hurtful ways.

Our Controversial Dialogue programs, like the one described above, are intensive facilitated discussions about stereotypes and bias, often including students who have been in conflict. Such dialogues typically include between 18 and 25 students who meet weekly for 90–120 minutes over four to six weeks. These dialogues have been remarkably successful both in reducing conflict and in uniting students from different groups in a joint belief in the importance of preventing bias, harassment, and violence.

Although the dialogue sessions at Mark and Sara's school remained intense even after Mark's comments, the students began listening to one another and talking with their friends who didn't attend the session about the need to end racial animosity. After that first dialogue session, there were no more racial fights for the remainder of the year!

Developing Leadership Strategies and Skills

Recently, racist flyers were distributed to homes in a neighborhood surrounding a high school participating in the Unity Project. People of color living in the neighborhood and students of color attending the school were fearful. The community was shocked. The local press and community members began to suggest, without any basis, that white high school students were responsible for the flyers.

The morning after the flyers were distributed, I was scheduled to meet with 25 students in an ongoing dialogue on race. I asked the students to decide on a response to the incident. Within minutes, the students had decided on two projects. The first was to write a letter to the editor of the local newspaper condemning the flyers and making it clear that this ugly incident did not reflect the values of the school or the community. The letter was typed, signed by all 25 students, and sent to the paper. It was published the next morning.

The second project was to have the school host a community meeting. The students made a large poster sending the message that the high school stood firmly against hate. They sat at a table outside the cafeteria and asked their classmates to consider signing the poster. Eight hundred students signed. At the community meeting, attended by community and elected leaders and by the press, students shared feelings about the flyers, read the letter to the editor, and displayed the poster prominently at the front of the room.

For some people, leadership appears to be innate. Most of us, however, must learn to be leaders. Educators can help students develop leadership skills by talking with them about leadership and by role-playing how they might intervene when they encounter degrading language. But students also need opportunities to actually act as leaders by, for example, speaking at assemblies, presenting to faculty or parents, working on projects in school and in the community to reduce bias and tension, and facilitating discussions with other students. These experiences prepare them to respond effectively when their school experiences a crisis involving bias-motivated violence or threats. The 25 students who responded to the racist flyers turned a hateful incident into one that confirmed school and community values of respect, civility, and diversity.

The Role of Teachers

Although these stories show that students can and do effectively combat harassment and bias, teachers have a critical role to play as well.

Interrupting the Language of Hate

Whether in the hallway or the classroom, teachers must speak up when students use degrading language or stereotypes. In a busy hallway, these interventions can be short. Making eye contact with a student and saying, "I heard that," "We don't talk like that here," or "That word is hurtful" sends the message that bias-motivated slurs and jokes are not acceptable. These low-key interventions break the pattern of escalation and stop some students from continuing to use degrading words. They also model for students what they can do to interrupt hurtful language themselves. And finally, when teachers speak up, they send a message of hope to those students who constantly hear slurs but feel that no one cares.

Responding in the Classroom

Incidents occurring in the classroom present a far better opportunity for learning than the incidents that take place in a crowded hallway. Every incident needs a response from the teacher and, when feasible, a classwide discussion.

When a student uses harsh language or hurtful stereotypes in class, the teacher might demonstrate the need for unity by asking a student for a pencil. The teacher then holds up the pencil and with two hands breaks it in two. Then, the teacher asks five or six students for their pencils. Holding the pencils together, the teacher tries unsuccessfully to break them—there simply are too many to break. The teacher can conclude by saying,

> There is no one student in this class who can't be singled out for mistreatment and bias. And that student can be deeply hurt or, like the pencil, broken. But all it takes is a small group of you to stick together and you become too strong to be broken.

This can be the extent of the exercise, or the teacher might follow up with a longer discussion about the importance of standing up against bias. In faculty workshops, our center provides teachers with a number of similar activities that can serve as prompts to discuss bias, stereotypes, and harassment.

Talking Openly

One Monday morning when I arrived for a session at a school, I learned that a former student had been shot to death by police in the street in front of the school on Saturday night.

That afternoon, I was scheduled to meet with a group of 25–30 students to continue a discussion about racial tensions in the school.

At the meeting, I asked them if they would rather talk about the shooting, and every one of them said yes. I then asked what discussions they had had about the shooting that morning in school. They stared at me blankly until one student said, "No one has mentioned it. Not once!" The students, however, did notice a significant police presence in and around the school. Rumors were flying, and students were anxious. I shared what I knew about the incident.

Students then talked about how they felt. Some were scared, some were angry at the police, and a couple were deeply saddened because they knew the young man who had been shot. The discussion went on for about 20 minutes, and the students then said that they were ready to continue the planned dialogue about racial issues. At the end of the session, the students described how healing it had been to talk about what had happened and learn that they were not alone in their feelings.

Teachers need to talk with students about the major events that affect their lives. These conversations do not need to take an entire class period. Often students want only a few minutes in which an adult validates their experiences. Students cannot focus on academics when they are thinking about traumatic events outside the classroom. Teachers who acknowledge their students' emotional experiences send the message that they understand and respect their students.

"That Assembly"

The Center for the Prevention of Hate Violence has developed an interactive assembly program that combines a candid speech given by someone from our staff followed by small-group discussions facilitated by students. We close the program by asking students to walk from their seats to an open microphone and talk about a time in which they or someone else had done something to create positive change in school climate. Slowly, one by one, and then in twos and threes, students come up to speak about a time when someone broke up a fight, interrupted the use of hurtful language, talked with a teacher about a classmate involved in self-destructive behavior, or reached out to someone who was lonely and sad. Often the line of students waiting to speak seems never to end.

One middle school student wrote this response to the assembly at her school:

"That Assembly"

At the assembly I saw thousands of tears, on the inside and a few on the outside. I heard people tell stories of harassment, stories of sorrow and also apologies. A girl who had made fun of me a year ago had her eyes welled in tears. She turned around and said through a gasp, "I'm sorry." It must have hurt her to keep that incident in her mind for a long year and a half. But it still made some of my pain go away.

Even though some people laughed at first they must know now that it can hurt. And as I left the assembly, I saw the people who had shed tears, surrounded by friends, by strangers, and by teachers. And it made me want to cry. The most beautiful sight in the world is to see someone in sorrow surrounded by reassurance.

As I walked through the halls, I heard something so miraculous. A young girl was telling her friends that she had two fathers, explaining why she had not told her friends. "I love them, but I was so afraid if I told they would get hurt." It makes you want to go up and hug her yourself, not even knowing her name. That one assembly helped her feel safe enough to tell the truth. And when I left that hallway, I realized that assembly changed me, that girl, and so many others.

When we give students the opportunity to tap into their large reservoir of empathy, when we model for students the courage to speak up for someone else, we will often be surprised at their capacity for leadership and their ability to make change.

Stephen Wessler is Executive Director of the Center for the Prevention of Hate Violence, 68 High St., Portland, ME 04101. He is the author, with William Preble, of *The Respectful School: How Educators and Students Can Conquer Hate and Harassment* (ASCD, 2003).

Originally published in the September 2008 issue of *Educational Leadership, 66*(1), pp. 44–48.

Words Can Hurt Forever

James Garbarino and Ellen deLara

Adults in middle and high schools must protect students from verbal harassment and emotional violence.

"Sticks and stones may break my bones, but words can never hurt me." It's an old rhyme from childhood, taught by parents and teachers to generations of children as a tactic for deflecting taunts and teasing. Usually the adult instructs the child to chant it back to the tormentors, like some kind of verbal amulet to ward off the evil spirits of teasing. But the essence of this childhood verse has never really convinced children—not in their hearts. They know that what other children think and say about them does matter. Sticks and stones hurt only for a while, but words can hurt forever.

As children grow into adolescence and enter middle and high school, they continue to suffer the harmful effects of bullying, harassment, and verbal violence. A survey conducted for the National Institute of Child Health and Human Development found that almost one-third of U.S. students in grades 6–10 were directly involved in serious, frequent bullying—10 percent as bullies, 13 percent as victims, and 6 percent as both (Nansel et al., 2001). And the U.S. Department of Education reports that 77 percent of middle and high school students surveyed have been bullied at some point in their school career (1998).

Many students experience bullying and emotional violence, and the majority of students admit to being sexually harassed at school (American Association of University Women, 2001; Garbarino & deLara, in press). In any given specific instance of bullying, however, most students are bystanders (Atlas & Pepler, 1998). Few of them spontaneously intervene on behalf of the victim. Most watch the bullying of their peers with a sense of helplessness, guiltily relieved that it's someone else's turn to be the target. They are frozen in fear and then feel ashamed for doing nothing to help. Warren, a 15-year-old in New York, expresses the bystander's feelings:

> A lot of people . . . they make fun of people. Sometimes they try to push people around. You can get a nervous feeling in your stomach. There are people that it happens to every day. I see a lot of people who are picked on all of the time. I don't know if they feel unsafe. A lot of people just try to ignore it. I think it takes a really mentally strong person to just ignore it and forget it immediately. And I don't think many people do.

We heard Warren's story and many others as we conducted conversations with students throughout the United States to learn about their experiences with bullying, harassment, and school violence. These conversations were part of a research project that gathered information from hundreds of students across the country in grades 9–12, as well as recent graduates, teachers, support staff, principals, and superintendents. We used surveys, semi-structured individual interviews, and focus groups to gather information.

We learned from these students that emotional violence can create a dysfunctional social system that makes it difficult for participants to concentrate on learning. We also found that students want adults in the system to play a more active role in preventing bullying and verbal violence.

Forms of Bullying

Understanding bullying, harassment, and other forms of emotional violence starts with understanding the power of acceptance and rejection in human motivation. Anthropologist Ronald Rohner studied 118 cultures around the world in an effort to understand how the phenomenon of "rejection" works in the lives of children and youth. He found that cultures differ in how they express rejection, but in every culture, rejected young people tend to turn out badly, sometimes by simply failing to reach their potential as a result of self-loathing, but sometimes by growing up to defy cultural norms and become lawbreakers. Rohner (1975) called rejection a "psychological malignancy."

Coopersmith and Feldman (1974) found that young people fear rejection. They crave acceptance, and will go to great lengths to get it. They will desperately try to look and act like "the popular kids." They will become addicted to smoking; shun their parents; and suffer through such painful initiation rituals as being "jumped into" a gang, getting tattooed or pierced, or breaking the law. The need for acceptance runs deep. Most human beings will pay any price to belong.

Although rejection is perhaps the most important and most fundamentally destructive form of psychological maltreatment, other forms also affect adolescents. These include *terrorizing, isolating,* and *corrupting.*

Terrorizing is the use of fear to torment and manipulate. Perpetrators use their victim's fear either to achieve dominance or to obtain specific payoffs, including money or other material items, status with peers, sexual gratification, or power. Bill, a 17-year-old from a large, rural high school in New Hampshire, says,

> I see a fair amount of bullying at my school. There is this one small kid who always gets picked on during lunch by a couple of bullies. I think they are all juniors. One of the bullies will go up to the kid with his fist in the air until the little kid flinches and then the bully starts laughing. It's a regular thing. I'd like to do something. But there is kind of like a social norm to *not* do anything. If it was anything more than verbal bullying and threats, then I would do something.

Isolating involves cutting someone off from essential relationships. As social creatures, adolescents need to be in relationships to flourish. Some students are pushed into a social "no man's land" by the exclusionary efforts of their peers. Once isolated, they can easily become disconnected from the moderating forces of mainstream society. Ironically, this state of isolation may bring together pairs of students who link up in their estrangement from the larger group and begin to develop strange and sometimes dangerous ways of thinking about themselves and their schools.

Michelle, a 10th grader, feels very isolated and lonely at school. Her words give us a direct view into the school day of many students like her:

> *Do you like school?* Not really. I like the classes, but not the people. If I could be home-schooled that would probably be better. The people in school pick on you all the time. Right now, I have a problem with people spreading rumors about me. I don't really like it. Most days I don't want to even come here. The teachers and guidance—they just know I'm here and that's all they really care about. People say that I'm fat, which I know I am but they don't need to pick on me about it. They spread it around that I'm pregnant and I'm not. Just dumb things. My ex-friend, she used to be my good friend but then a couple of weeks ago she started spreading rumors. So now she's not my friend no more.

Michelle's isolation and exclusion from friends and peers unfortunately reflects the experience of many students on a typical school day. These students rarely complain to a parent or to any other adult. They suffer terribly and in silence most of the time.

Corrupting means influencing a student to learn ways of thinking, speaking, and acting that make him or her increasingly unfit for normal or healthy experiences. During the middle and high school years, negative influences are always available to set in motion the process of corrupting. Many parents are shocked when their previously sweet children begin to spout angry and obscene language as they move into the world of adolescent peer groups. Formerly positive students may start to slide toward antisocial behavior when their peers mock those who work hard in school or endorse such negative activities as cutting class.

Adults' Responsibility

Why do students feel powerless sometimes? Their sense of powerlessness flows from interactions with one another, interactions with teachers and other adults in their schools, and an inability to make a positive impact on the day-to-day life of their schools. Teachers and other school personnel often observe adolescent anger, but they typically don't see the profound feelings of helplessness or hopelessness that underlie much of this anger. Students say they will "take it" as long as they can, meaning they will handle difficult and disrespectful behaviors until they can stand it no longer. When they reach that point, they are likely to strike back at someone. Fifteen-year-old Sean comments,

> You hear about kids who get picked on all of the time and they can't take it anymore. That's what happened at Columbine. I don't think it happens that bad at my school, but you never know.

Students in our study often spoke insightfully about adults' lack of awareness of events that happened in the school. We have all heard about the extreme cases of school shooters whose distress signals and hints of homicidal or suicidal intent were missed by school administrators and teachers. In our interviews, students offered many smaller examples of adult inattentiveness and its consequences. One 16-year-old girl says,

> I feel unsafe in the cafeteria because people get in fights and start punching each other and the teachers don't take a strong hand. Lots of times, they don't even seem to notice.

Students believe adults should intervene long before they actually do. Sometimes those in authority delay reacting because they have not determined that a particular interaction among students constitutes a problem. Sometimes the adults have not even observed the upsetting situation. Other times, the delay in intervention arises deliberately from the adult premise that adolescents can work out their own problems, which the adults may consider mere teenage squabbles, scuffling, or repartee. Undoubtedly, some adults choose to remain unaware as a way to avoid doing anything about situations that they believe they can't control.

Students also spoke to us about the importance of teachers as "second parents," as supervisors in their environment, and as mentors for their social and academic growth. When given a chance to say so without the constraints of acting cool or defending a position, these adolescents expressed the need for more supervision and intervention by adults in the school:

> I think if there is enough supervision in areas around and inside the school, many physical and emotional problems could be solved. (boy, age 16)

> There should be more restraints on picking on people. It happens a lot here, and that is why school violence is happening. (boy, age 15)

Every public swimming pool has lifeguards because we know that swimmers need supervision in order to remain safe. Schools are no different in this respect.

Where to Start

One place to start is with concrete and grounded plans for monitoring student and adult activity in the building and on the school premises.

Here are some of the essential components of appropriate supervision in middle and high schools:

- Formulate a uniform plan for when, where, why, and how to monitor and intervene on behalf of students.
- Develop the plan with the cooperation and input of all stakeholders in the school—students, teachers, parents, administrators, counselors, mental health professionals, security personnel, and concerned community members. Make sure that student input comes from every social group.
- Through survey instruments, group discussions, and interviews, solicit students' perceptions of which places and activities are unsafe—in the school, on the grounds, and on the way to and from school. Consider recruiting outside evaluators to ensure anonymity and to capture maximum reliability of student responses.
- Ensure that the adults who will enforce the plan feel committed to it and regard it as purposeful and useful.
- Make it clear to everyone that adults will intervene in interpersonal disputes quickly (for most schools, this means sooner than they currently do).
- Train every adult in state-of-the-art intervention strategies to de-escalate conflicts among students.
- Include in the master plan a uniform policy for intervening with students who come to school under the influence of alcohol or other drugs.
- Avoid the temptation of relying on such technological quick fixes as surveillance cameras and metal detectors; in most instances, these do not help students feel safe.
- Most important, obtain continual feedback from students on the effectiveness of the strategies for supervision that you have implemented.

In addition, schools should provide teachers with inservice training regarding the consequences of allowing bullying and harassment in the school. Any inservice program needs to define forms of bullying and recommend appropriate means of interrupting bullying interactions from student to student and between teacher and student. Several countries already have successful programs from which our schools could make adaptations (see Mattaini, 2001; Olweus, 1993; Smith et al., 1999; Stein & Sjostrom, 1996).

Consequences of Inaction

What does bullying and other disrespectful behavior mean from a systemic perspective? First, our failure to prevent such behavior indicates that the system defines bullying too narrowly, as only physical aggression and extortion. Second, failing to prevent bullying behavior suggests a lack of understanding of the serious and damaging nature of all forms of bullying for many students. Third, our inaction reflects an unwillingness to see bullying as the responsibility of the system. When school personnel do not prevent students from bullying other students, these educators have, in effect, delegated a portion of their authority to the bullies in the system. This situation has many negative consequences, among them the rise of gang behavior in the schools.

When teachers and students participate in bullying activities or witness them and do nothing, they enable the school system to perpetuate this behavior and remain unhealthy and unsafe for all students. If adults do not provide the intervention students need, then students will take matters into their own hands—generally for worse, not better. Caring means demonstrating the will to stay aware and to act in a protective fashion, and in so doing create an emotionally safe school.

Although considered normal by school personnel and many students themselves, emotional bullying and harassment among students exact a high price in terms of the atmosphere of the school. Although student leaders can play a part in reducing bullying behavior within the school, adults must fill a crucial role. We have to ask, What is our responsibility? When it comes to bullying, sexual harassment, and emotional violence at school, the buck stops with adults.

References

American Association of University Women. (2001). *Bullying, teasing, and sexual harassment in school*. New York: AAUW Educational Foundation.

Atlas, R. S., & Pepler, D. J. (1998). Observations of bullying in the classroom. *Journal of Educational Research, 9*(2), 86–99.

Coopersmith, S., & Feldman, R. (1974). *The formative years: Principles of early childhood education*. San Francisco: Albion.

Garbarino, J., & deLara, E. W. (in press). Coping with the consequences of school violence. In A. Goldstein & J. C. Conoley (Eds.), *School violence interventions: A practical handbook*. New York: Guilford Publications.

Mattaini, M. A. (2001). *Peace power for adolescents: Strategies for a culture of nonviolence*. Washington, DC: NASW Press.

Nansel, T. R., Overpeck, M., Pilla, R. S., Ruan, W. J., Simons-Morton, B., & Scheidt, P. (2001). Bullying behaviors among U.S. youth: Prevalence and association with psychosocial adjustment. *Journal of the American Medical Association, 285*(16), 2095–2100.

Olweus, D. (1993) *Bullying at school: What we know and what we can do*. Malden, MA: Blackwell Publishers.

Rohner, R. (1975). *They love me, they love me not: A worldwide study of the effects of parental acceptance and rejection*. New Haven, CT: HRAF Press.

Smith, P. K., Morita, Y., Junger-Tas, J., Olweus, D., Catalano, R., & Slee, P. (Eds.). (1999). *The nature of school bullying: A cross-national perspective*. New York: Routledge.

Stein, N., & Sjostrom, L. (1996). *Bullyproof: A teachers' guide on teasing and bullying for use with fourth and fifth grade students*. Wellesley, MA: Wellesley College Center for Research on Women.

U.S. Department of Education. (1998). *Preventing bullying: A manual for schools and communities*. Washington, DC: U.S. Department of Education. Available:www.cde.ca.gov/spbranch/ssp/bullymanual.htm.

James Garbarino is a professor of human development at Cornell University, Ithaca, New York; jgarbar@luc.edu. **Ellen deLara** is a faculty fellow at the Family Life Development Center, Cornell University; ewj2@cornell.edu. They are the coauthors of *And Words Can Hurt Forever: How to Protect Adolescents From Bullying, Harassment, and Emotional Violence* (The Free Press, 2002).

Originally published in the March 2003 issue of *Educational Leadership, 60*(6), pp. 18–21.

© 2003 James Garbarino and Ellen deLara

Fights Like a Girl

Laura Varlas

How changing what we expect from girls can reduce girl fighting

Whether you're the target or perpetrator of a nasty comment, a socially crippling e-mail, or a public exclusion, girl fighting affects all girls and all schools negatively—and requires structured intervention strategies.

The headlines say violence among girls is increasing: "Are Girls Getting Meaner?" "Ruthless Girlz." "Bad Girls." Some crime statistics say girls are fighting—and being arrested for fighting—more than ever before. Others point out that the incidence of female bullying and violence may be about the same as it ever was, but that authorities are taking the issue more seriously. Regardless, the "mean girl" phenomenon has educators, parents, and students concerned. Innovative programs have begun addressing the problem.

Cruel to Be Kind

Why do girls fight? Girls aggressively act out their emotions for many reasons. Prominent researchers such as Laura Crothers, Julaine Field, and Jered Kolbert have explored the connection between gender identity and relational aggression in girls—the slandering, insulting, or excluding that cause harm by themselves and can precipitate physical violence. The researchers say that girls internalize societal perspectives on gender and that these traditional views of femininity place huge restrictions on how girls can express anger.

To conform to the "nice girl" stereotype, girls often subvert their anger and use more manipulative and covert means to express themselves or gain a sense of personal power. "Girls are doing what we've expected from them. They're rewarded for not being disruptive, and so they do these things behind the scenes," says Lyn Brown, author of *Girlfighting* and professor of education and women's, gender, and sexuality studies at Colby College in Waterville, Maine.

Brown asserts that girls often direct their anger at each other because they are the easiest and most familiar targets. In a society where girls are often narrowly defined through lenses such as cheerleaders, jocks, sluts, or nerds, girls may lash out in frustration at the limits placed on their identity and how they are perceived. For example, Brown notes, if you are the cheerleader, you get the power of popularity and boys' attentions, but often your smarts will be second-guessed.

Do Your Homework

Culturally, girl fighting confounds ingrained beliefs about the so-called nature of girls: girls should be nice, and if they fight, it's cute and trivial. For some, girl fighting is eroticized, which trivializes it even more. Penny Linn, a guidance counselor at Winslow Junior High in Winslow, Maine, agrees that the "assumption is girls start rumors and talk behind each other's back, and that's just the way girls deal with stuff." Girls' fights are often hidden from or invisible to adults.

Educators interested in addressing girls' violence need to deal with the issue in a self-aware and honest way, Brown says. She urges educators to explore their own feelings, speak directly, and refuse to engage in gossip and slander. "It seems common sense that, if we want girls to do these things, then we would model healthier behaviors," she adds. "But we're also part of this culture, and this is hard, personal work." Brown suggests teachers get together to talk about girl fighting and how to model and set high expectations for girls.

Some schools are shifting the girl-fighting paradigm, with the help of passionate guidance counselors and curriculum spun from books such as *The Odd Girl Out, Queen Bees and Wannabes, Girlfighting,* and *See Jane Hit.* Educators in the know are doing more than just armoring their students with adages about sticks and stones.

From Adversaries to Allies

According to Brown, adolescence offers a lot of "openings" to talk to girls about fighting and positive relationships. Adolescent girls give voice to their own outrage, and all that passion is a good thing, says Brown. It's the spark of engagement, and it can be nurtured into a full flame of action toward positive change and identity development.

Capitalizing on those openings, Brown has developed a curriculum called "From Adversaries to Allies" that builds girl coalitions. She has spent the last few years road-testing it in several Maine schools. The curriculum guides small, in-school coalition groups of girls on topics such as sexual harassment, healthy dating relationships, and media literacy—an especially important topic in a world where pop culture often meanly celebrates status and popularity at the expense of the unpopular.

Brown believes a girl-specific curriculum on bullying is necessary because "fighting and bullying is about power, and we give boys and girls different avenues to that power. For girls, the avenue is through their relationships with boys, through their looks and attitude. With boys, it's about physical prowess." The program recognizes this difference and works toward establishing a more complex definition of girlhood and power.

Muses and Hardiness Zones

Coalition groups center around two conceptual frameworks: muses and hardiness zones. Muses are female college students from Colby

College who have studied under Brown. They partner with area middle school guidance counselors to cofacilitate girls' coalition groups. Colby student Jackie Dupont, a muse at Lawrence Junior High, notes that her relationship with the girls in her coalition is "reciprocal in nurturing toward girls' strengths. We're learning from each other." Dupont meets weekly with Lawrence Junior High guidance counselor Angie Lavallee to plan and run Lawrence's coalition groups.

The group itself is meant to be a "hardiness zone," a safe space for girls to talk about their problems and develop hardiness zones of their own—safe places where they can practice and hone their resiliency and apply it to situations where they feel less secure. In addition to meeting weekly, all area middle school counselors involved in girl coalitions meet once a month to talk about their programs.

"We're working toward a common goal," Dupont says, "creating a world where all girls are equal, independent, and safe in their everyday lives."

"And to help them understand that the issues that underlie our fighting are sometimes much bigger than personal issues," adds Brown, "we're trying to help them see that they can move beyond the personal. If they don't like something, they can say it directly; they don't have to do some of these underhanded things."

"Girls in our coalition groups want visibility, they want power, they want to be liked, they want a boyfriend, they want friends—they just have different means of accessing that," says Brown. "What we try to convey in the group is that they really do want the same things, and they're being really hard on each other for wanting those things and doing it in different ways."

Self-Defined, Strong, and Beautiful

Brown is sure educators have the chance to redefine power for girls—"not power over things, but power to effect change, and power to be visible and understood."

In a recent project, Lavallee gave her coalition members cameras and sent them out to take pictures of the women in their lives that they admire. In addition, the students asked these notable women to share their personal definitions of beauty. The coalition members took these definitions and photos, and made collages that were sent out into the Waterville community and posted in stores. When the collages come back, they'll dress the halls of Lawrence Junior High as testaments to strong, beautiful women not found in the pages of *Seventeen*. Lavallee knows that "kids are still frustrated with the way things are, but the girls in the "From Adversaries to Allies" groups are finding new ways to channel their anger—through projects and activities, or through one-on-one counseling sessions."

She adds, "They're less likely to take their frustrations out on each other through fighting, and more likely to come to school with clear heads for learning."

For more on girl fighting—in particular, teaching media literacy as a means to combat stereotypes that can fuel girl fights—as well as a list of resources to complement this article, go to the ASCD Web site at www.ascd.org and link to the April 2006 issue of *Education Update* in the Publications section.

Laura Varlas is a project manager and staff writer for ASCD's Newsletters and Special Publications; lvarlas@ascd.org.

Originally published in the April 2006 issue of *Education Update*, 48(4).

How We Treat One Another in School

Donna M. San Antonio and Elizabeth A. Salzfass

A survey of middle school students' experiences with bullying shows that kids want the adults in school to pay attention and keep them safe.

When rising middle school students are asked to name their biggest worry about going to a new school, they most often answer, "That I will not have any friends" or "That people will make fun of me" (San Antonio, 2004). The prospect of being friendless or getting teased looms large for many students at this age and can profoundly affect their sense of affiliation with school. Students tell us with heartbreaking regularity of the pain and anger they feel when their peers do not see them, include them, or care about them. At the extreme, some students not only are treated with indifference but also become targets of bullying.

Devastating Effects

Olweus (1993) defines bullying as verbal, physical, or psychological abuse or teasing accompanied by real or perceived imbalance of power. Bullying most often focuses on qualities that students (and the broader society) perceive to be different from the established norm, such as expected genderspecific behavior for boys and girls, dress and physical appearance, and manner of speaking. Bullying is connected to diversity, and reducing bullying means taking steps to make the community and the school safe for diversity of all kinds.

Research indicates that bullying—with its accompanying fear, loss of self-efficacy, anger, and hurt—negatively affects the school environment and can greatly diminish students' ability to engage actively in learning (Hoover & Oliver, 1996). Being bullied has been linked with high rates of school absence (Fried & Fried, 1996); dropping out of school (Weinhold & Weinhold, 1998); and low self-esteem, anxiety, and depression (Banks, 1997). A U.S. Department of Education study (1998) found that students who had experienced sustained threats and verbal and physical peer aggression carried out two-thirds of school shootings.

Some researchers and practitioners believe that the impact of bullying is as devastating and life changing as that of other forms of trauma, such as physical abuse. The effects of bullying may linger long into the victims' adulthood (Kaltiala-Heino, Rimpelae, Rantanen, & Rimpelae, 2000). Recent research has documented increased levels of depression and anxiety in adults who had been bullied in their youth (Gladstone, Parker, & Malhi, 2006).

Because of the documented harmful effects of bullying—as well as other forms of social isolation—on school climate and student achievement, educators are taking this problem seriously. Many schools have explored the benefits of implementing schoolwide programs to promote social and emotional learning, prevent bullying, and nurture positive peer relationships. A survey of middle school students that we recently conducted in three schools provides information on bullying behavior that can inform such programs.

A Middle School Survey on Bullying

To measure students' experience with physical, verbal, and relational[1] bullying, we administered surveys in spring 2006 to 211 7th and 8th grade students in three K–8 schools in New England. The three schools differ significantly by race, socioeconomic status, and urbanicity. Rural School,[2] located in a small town, serves a student population that is socioeconomically diverse but is 94 percent white; 25 percent of the students are eligible for free or reduced-price lunch. Big City School is located in a low-income urban neighborhood and serves primarily Latino (65 percent) and black (33 percent) students; 93 percent are eligible for free or reduced-price lunch. Small City School has a socioeconomically and ethnically diverse student body composed of 40 percent white, 36 percent black, 11 percent Latino, and 10 percent Asian students; 30 percent of the students are eligible for free or reduced-price lunch.

We surveyed nearly all the students in each grade, with the exception of 8th graders at Rural School, where we were able to survey only half of the class. The surveys included multiple-choice and open-ended questions. Respondents were evenly split between boys and girls. Most of our findings were consistent with what other research has found and what middle grades teachers know about bullying in the adolescent years. Some of our most significant findings follow.

Extent of Bullying

Most students (76.5 percent) felt safe most of the time. However, students at Big City School reported feeling safe much less often than did their peers at the other two schools (65 percent, compared with 83 percent at Small City School and 81 percent at Rural School). They also feared bullying more, even though students at Rural School reported seeing it occur more often. We believe this reflects the greater incidence of community violence to which Big City School students are exposed.

Rural School was the only school in which a majority of students (about 2 in 3) said that bullying was a serious problem. Many of the respondents from Rural School spoke about the difference between physical and emotional safety. As one 7th grade girl said, "I feel safe physically but my emotions take a blow here."

In terms of grade level, bullying was more common for 7th graders than for 8th graders at the three schools we surveyed, with two notable exceptions: Verbal bullying affected 8th grade girls more than any other subgroup at Small City School, and physical violence affected 8th grade boys and girls more than 7th graders at Big City School.

Finally, across schools, boys and girls experienced physical and verbal bullying to a similar extent, but girls experienced more relational bullying than boys did. Girls at all three schools worried more often than boys that if they did or said something wrong, their friends would gang up on them and decide not to be their friends. This problem appeared to be most dire for girls at Rural School: A full 72 percent of them reported suffering relational bullying either "every once in a while," "often," or "every day," compared with 58 percent of girls at Big City School and 48 percent at Small City School. This finding raises the question of the effect of socioeconomic status and cultural background on the bullying phenomenon. The almost entirely white population of girls at the school with the widest gap between wealthy and poor students was the group most at risk of relational aggression.

Boys were more likely to admit to bullying other students than girls were (which may have something to do with the way bullying is traditionally defined), but no significant gender difference was expressed overall when we asked students whether boys or girls bullied other students more. We also found that boys bullied both boys and girls, whereas girls typically only bullied other girls. We were troubled by girls' graphic narrative responses that demonstrated that boys often bullied girls with demeaning comments about the girls' appearance and demands for sexual interactions, particularly oral sex.

Location of Bullying

In all three schools, bullying happened most frequently in the hallways. When asked how to mitigate bullying at their school, many students suggested putting more adult supervisors in the hallways between classes. The second most common place in which bullying occurred differed across the three schools. At Big City School, bullying tended to happen in the bathrooms, where there was generally no adult supervision. At Small City School and Rural School, bullying happened on the playground and in the cafeteria, both places where adults were on duty.

Reasons Students Are Bullied

Students at all three schools perceived that "being overweight" and "not dressing right" were the most common reasons an individual might be bullied. At Small City School and Rural School, the second most common reason stated was being perceived as gay, which suggests rigid behavior expectations for boys and girls. Many students commented that someone might be a target for bullying if they look or act "different" or "weird."

Students' Reactions to Bullying

The most common strategies students reported using when confronted by bullies were walking away, saying mean things back, hitting back, or telling the bully to stop. The least common strategy was telling an adult at the school. Hitting back was a particularly popular response to bullying at Big City and Small City Schools, particularly among the boys. Given steadily increasing numbers of violent deaths over the last few years in many urban communities, we believe that this finding highlights the importance that urban youth put on maintaining a tough appearance to survive, as well as a perceived lack of options for nonviolent conflict resolution.

Student reactions to bullying also differed according to gender. More boys than girls believed that they had the right to use violence to protect themselves from physical violence or someone hurting their feelings or reputations. Girls reported being more likely to help a victim of bullying than boys did and more often said that bullying is wrong.

Inadequate Adult Response

Most students said they were not confident that adults could protect them from being bullied. Students at Rural School had more faith that their teachers could stop the bullying when they were told about it than did students at the other two schools. However, students in this school agreed with their urban peers that teachers did not seem to notice bullying and did not take it seriously enough. Most students said they wanted teachers to be more aware of all types of bullying and to intervene more often. These findings are consistent with past research in which students reported that most bullying goes undetected by school staff (Skiba & Fontanini, 2000).

When we talk with students in a variety of settings, they have many thoughts about how adults can help to make school safer and stop bullying. They frequently answer with statements like these: "Watch out for us and don't ignore us." "Pay attention." "Just ask us what's wrong." "Talk to the students who have been bullied to see how to stop it." "Start caring more." "Believe us." "Punish the bullies." "Do something instead of nothing." One thing seems certain: Most students want adults to see what is going on in their world and respond to bullying in caring, effective, and firm ways.

What Schools Can Do

The following recommendations for a schoolwide approach to bullying prevention are derived from our review of the literature, our survey findings, and a report generated by Northwest Regional Educational Laboratory (Railsback & Brewster, 2001). All sources agree that schoolwide strategies must complement classroom curriculum. Schools should not frame the issue of how students and educators treat one another as an issue of behavior. Instead, they should opt for a more comprehensive set of goals that address social and moral development, school and classroom climate, teacher training, school policies, and community values, along with student behavior.

Conduct an assessment.

The first step toward creating an effective schoolwide antibullying program is identifying where, when, and how students experience bullying at a particular school. As our study demonstrated, different types of bullying occur with different frequency and magnitude among different populations in different school settings; therefore, a one-size-fits-all approach is not an appropriate solution. Schoolwide bullying intervention programs are more purposeful and relevant when they are informed by students' views. We strongly recommend using a participatory action research approach that involves students in framing a problem statement; constructing a survey; summarizing, analyzing, and reporting the results; and generating ideas for how staff and students can respond to the issues uncovered by the survey.

Create a committee to focus on school relationships.

A committee involving students, parents, and community members along with school staff should focus on schoolwide relationships, not only on student bullying. This committee will assist the school in generating developmentally and culturally sound prevention and intervention ideas.

Implement an antibullying policy.

When asked what teachers could do to stop bullying, many of the students we surveyed said that teachers should be stricter with bullies. An effective policy should be developed through collaboration among students, teachers, parents, and administrators.

Pepler and Craig (2000) say that a whole-school policy is the foundation of antibullying interventions, and they recommend that a policy include the following: a schoolwide commitment to address bullying; a statement of rights and responsibilities for all members of the school community; a definition of bullying, including types and dynamics; the process for identifying and reporting bullying; expected ways for students and staff to respond to bullying; strategies that will be implemented; and a way to assess the effectiveness of antibullying efforts.

Train all school employees.

Bullying can be subtle and hard to detect, making it challenging for adults to intervene effectively. To stop bullying, school staff (including custodians, clerical staff, bus drivers, and lunchroom staff) must first have an opportunity to discuss the various ways and locations in which bullying occurs. From there, they can develop structures for communicating across roles within a school district and decide on an appropriate unified response. Considering that the majority of students in our study did not believe they could count on adults to protect them from being bullied, ongoing training and communication in this area is key. For students to develop positive attitudes toward school, they need to know that all staff members are committed to making it a safe and friendly environment.

Help the bullied and the bullies.

Another step in implementing a schoolwide antibullying program involves providing resources for those most affected by bullying. Many of the students we surveyed who had experienced bullying said that they wanted adults to listen to their stories. Some schools have had success with facilitating groups in which students address issues directly with their peers. The PALS program at Rocky Mountain Middle School in Idaho trains teachers to facilitate these groups, which increase communication and social skills and give stigmatized students a chance to experience a positive interpersonal connection with others and with the school.

Some students who are highly involved in bullying (either as perpetrators or victims) will need one-to-one support. It is important to involve parents and provide referrals for mentoring or counseling. Journaling with a teacher or counselor who reads and replies to concerns and issues may help particularly reticent students. Connecting students to after-school and summer programs will enable them to socialize with their peers outside of the school and form new friendships.

When children have been treated unfairly or violently in their primary relationships, it can be difficult for them to understand why they and their peers should be treated with respect. Nakkula and Selman (1991) describe an effective intervention called *pair counseling* as a way for two children who have difficult peer relationships to come together with the help of a counselor to negotiate differences and learn how to be a friend.

Recognize and name all forms of bullying.

Be aware of the relationships among students and of shifts in cliques and friendships as much as possible. Look for subtle signs of relational aggression that may occur between students, such as whispering, spreading rumors, and exclusion. Let students know that comments and actions against any racial, ethnic, or social group will not be tolerated. Be prepared to explain your ethical position to your students. The students we surveyed suggested that teachers ask students what would benefit them and help students generate realistic and effective ideas. On this topic, one 7th grade girl wrote,

> Teachers do everything, I think, in their power, but if they would just listen to the person who says they're being bullied, instead of just saying "stay away from them" or "ignore it" maybe we would see some change.

Reclaim goodness.

School classrooms and corridors contain a full spectrum of behavior, from countless everyday small acts of kindness to serious acts of aggression. In our effort to mitigate negative student behavior, a commonly overlooked but essential aspect of creating emotionally and socially safe environments is noticing, acknowledging, and actively drawing out acts of kindness. Schools are places of tremendous courage, generosity, and thoughtfulness. Some students risk their own social standing by being kind to an "unpopular" classmate. Some students talk with others who appear lonely and try to offer friendship; they speak up when they see injustice because, in the words of one student, they "don't think it is right to judge people by how they dress." In past research (San Antonio, 2004) and in the survey we describe here, students frequently spoke with admiration about teachers who actively intervened against stereotyping and teasing based on gender, social class, race, and learning needs. Naming and reclaiming goodness in the school community is an important step toward reducing bullying.

Integrate social-emotional education into the curriculum.

An effective curriculum for social, emotional, and ethical learning addresses bullying as a social and moral development issue. Activities in such a program focus on self-understanding, understanding of others, appreciation for diversity, and responsibility to the community. By encouraging empathy, respect, and acceptance and giving students tools for communicating their feelings and confronting conflict positively, an effective social-emotional learning curriculum will likely improve school climate and culture beyond just the mitigation of bullying. (See Choosing a Social-Emotional Learning Curriculum, p. 34, and Social-Emotional Learning Curriculums Online, p. 37.)

Educators Set the Tone

As a primary social environment for young people, classrooms and schools are uniquely good places to learn how to treat others and how to tell others the way we want them to treat us. Dozens of times a day, people in schools negotiate interpersonal exchanges with others from diverse backgrounds, making schools a premier learning environment for social, emotional, and ethical learning. Nel Noddings (2002) has long held that a key purpose of schooling is to educate moral people:

> An emphasis on social relationships in classrooms, students' interest in the subject matter to be studied and the connections between classroom life and that of the larger world provides the foundation of our attempts to produce moral people. As educators we must make it possible and desirable for students to be good. (p. 85)

Of course, students behave in aggressive or submissive ways for a variety of reasons that are not always easy to discern or manage. Some students may posture aggressively because they face violent behavior at home or in their neighborhoods, some have problems reading social cues or controlling their impulses, and some are simply scared. But in our work with schools, we have found that when educators take students' concerns seriously, teach them alternative ways to communicate their needs assertively but not violently, and provide adult guidance, vigilance, safety, good role models, and support, students are more likely to interact positively with their peers.

The findings from the survey we conducted among middle grade students support the concept that educators *can* influence the social and emotional climate of schools. Students' written comments on the survey make it clear that they value fairness, respectful communication, and adults who make them feel physically and emotionally safe and cared for. By implementing an effective social-emotional learning curriculum and addressing the systemic factors that determine school climate, we can create schools where bullying is rare and where all students are ready to learn.

> ### Choosing a Social-Emotional Learning Curriculum
>
> ***Look for a curriculum that***
> - Becomes part of a schoolwide and communitywide discussion (with parents) about values, beliefs about how to treat one another, and policies that reflect these values.
> - Poses developmentally and culturally appropriate social dilemmas for discussion.
> - Challenges the idea that aggression and bullying are inevitable and expected behavior. Demonstrates how people can resolve tensions and disagreements without losing face by giving detailed examples of people who responded to violence in an actively nonviolent manner.
> - Encourages students to express their feelings and experiences concerning bullying and enables students to generate realistic and credible ways to stay safe.
> - Supports critical analysis of the issues and rejects explanations of behavior based on stereotypes (such as the idea that boys will use physical violence and girls will use relational violence).
> - Helps children and teens become critical consumers of popular culture.
> - Addresses all types of bullying.

- Discusses how bullying reflects broader societal injustice.
- Gives ideas for what the adults in the school can do as part of a whole-school effort.

Beware of any curriculum that
- Ignores such issues as injustice, stereotype, and imbalance of power regarding gender, race, social class, and sexual orientation.
- Focuses on the victim's behavior as the reason for being a target of bullying.
- Focuses on student behavior without addressing schoolwide climate.
- Emphasizes having students tell the teacher about the bullying and ignoring bullying assaults.
- Focuses on either bullying only or victimization only.
- Portrays victims or bullies as unpopular misfits.
- Promotes simplistic or trendy solutions (for example, "boys will be boys").
- Promotes good solutions, such as peer mediation, but does not provide clear guidelines for when these strategies should and should not be used.
- Lacks evidence-based, population-specific suggestions for design, implementation, training, and evaluation.

Social-Emotional Learning Curriculums Online

The Collaborative for Academic, Social, and Emotional Learning (CASEL) (www.casel.org) was established to advance the science of social and emotional learning (SEL) and to expand coordinated, evidence-based SEL practice. Resources include the *Sustainable Schoolwide Social and Emotional Learning (SEL): Implementation Guide and Toolkit*.

The Safetyzone (*www.safetyzone.org/index.html*), a project of the Northwest Regional Educational Laboratory, is a clearinghouse for information and material related to school safety. The Web site offers eight school safety technical assistance guides.

The Olweus Bullying Prevention Program (*www.clemson.edu/olweus*) is internationally recognized as a model program for preventing or reducing bullying in elementary and middle schools. It trains not just students, but also teachers, staff, and parents to take a stand on bullying.

Peace Games (*http://peacegames.org*) forms partnerships with elementary schools, families, and young adult volunteers to empower students as peacemakers to create their own safe classrooms and communities.

Committee for Children (*www.cfchildren.org*) provides classroom programs that focus on the topics of youth violence, bullying, child abuse, personal safety, and emergent literacy. Includes information on Steps to Respect, a bullying prevention program shown to be effective in grades 3–6.

References

Banks, R. (1997). *Bullying in schools*. Champaign, IL: ERIC Clearinghouse on Elementary and Early Childhood Education. (ERIC No. ED407154)

Crick, N. R., & Bigbee, M. A. (1998). Relational and overt forms of peer victimization: A multi-informant approach. *Journal of Consulting and Clinical Psychology, 66*, 337–347.

Fried, S., & Fried, P. (1996). *Bullies and victims: Helping your child survive the schoolyard battlefield*. New York: M. Evans and Company.

Gladstone, G., Parker, G. B., & Malhi, G. S. (2006). Do bullied children become anxious and depressed adults? A cross-sectional investigation of the correlates of bullying and anxious depression. *Journal of Nervous and Mental Disease, 194*(3), 201–208.

Hoover, J. H., & Oliver, R. (1996). *The bullying prevention handbook: A guide for principals, teachers, and counselors*. Bloomington, IN: National Educational Service.

Kaltiala-Heino, R., Rimpelae, M., Rantanen, P., & Rimpelae, A. (2000). Bullying at school: An indicator of adolescents at risk for mental disorders. *Journal of Adolescence, 23*(6), 661–674.

Nakkula, M., & Selman, B. (1991). How people "treat" each other: Pair therapy as a context for the development of interpersonal ethics. In W. M. Kurtines & J. Gewirtz (Eds.), *Handbook of moral behavior and development* (Vol. 3, pp. 179–210). Hillsdale, NJ: Erlbaum.

Noddings, N. (2002). *Educating moral people: A caring alternative to character education*. New York: Teachers College Press.

Olweus, D. (1993). *Bullying at school: What we know and what we can do*. Malden, MA: Blackwell.

Pepler, D. J., & Craig, W. (2000). *Making a difference in bullying* (Report #60). Toronto, Ontario: La Marsh Centre for Research on Violence and Conflict Resolution.

Railsback, J., & Brewster, C. (2001). *Schoolwide prevention of bullying*. Portland, OR: Northwest Regional Education Laboratory. Available: www.nwrel.org/request/dec01

San Antonio, D. M. (2004). *Adolescent lives in transition: How social class influences adjustment to middle school*. Albany: State University of New York Press.

Skiba, N., & Fontanini, A. (2000). *Fast facts: Bullying prevention*. Bloomington, IN: Phi Delta Kappa International. Available: www.pdkintl.org/newsroom/newsletters/fastfacts/ff12.pdf

U.S. Department of Education. (1998). *Preventing bullying: A manual for schools and communities*. Washington, DC: Author.

Weinhold, B. K., & Weinhold, J. B. (1998). Conflict resolution: The partnership way in schools. *Counseling and Human Development, 30*(7), 1–2.

Endnotes

[1] *Physical bullying* includes hitting, kicking, or otherwise physically attacking the victim, as well as taking or damaging the victim's possessions. *Verbal bullying* includes name-calling, aggressive teasing, or making insulting comments designed to humiliate the victim. *Relational bullying* includes any behavior that intimidates and hurts the victim by harming or threatening to harm relationships or feelings of friendship and belonging (Crick & Bigbee, 1998). *Cyberbullying* involves the use of information and communication technologies, such as e-mail, cell phone and pager text messages, instant messaging, and Web sites to deliberately harm others (www.cyberbullying.org).

[2] To preserve confidentiality, schools are identified by community type rather than by name.

Donna M. San Antonio is Director of the Appalachian Mountain Teen Project, Wolfeboro, New Hampshire, and Lecturer on Education, Harvard Graduate School of Education, Cambridge, Massachusetts; 617-495-7883; donna.sanantonio@gmail.com.
Elizabeth A. Salzfass is Program and Evaluation Coordinator for Responsive Advocacy for Life and Learning in Youth (RALLY) and Community Service Learning Coordinator with Peace Games, Boston, Massachusetts; lizzie.salzfass@gmail.com.

Originally published in the May 2007 issue of *Educational Leadership*, 64(8), pp. 32–38.

R U Safe?

Johanna Mustacchi

Who better to teach young adolescents about online dangers than other adolescents?

It's not just on the bus or during recess anymore. Bullying can happen the minute our students wake up, can creep in during class time, and can continue after the school day ends—and then follow them home, right into their bedrooms.

My generation was safe from the pressures of peer judgment and abuse once we arrived home from school (the class bully would never actually call your house back then). But cyberspace has no boundaries, and students today have only their wits to protect them from teasing, harassment, and threats that can reach them online anytime.

What I call *cyberabuse* is rampant at school, adding to the old-fashioned face-to-face taunting and power plays that take place among students. (I use the term *cyber* rather than *Internet* to include all mobile communication devices.) Such abuse even goes on as we teach. I once confiscated cell phones from two students who were texting each other during another teacher's class. They showed me the conversation, which was full of insults and vulgar language.

According to a series of studies conducted by the *Journal of Adolescent Health*, more than 80 percent of adolescents own at least one form of new media technology, which they use to communicate with one another, present information about themselves, and share new media creations. The studies examined the relationships among bullying, harassment, and aggression among youth and how these issues translated to electronic media. According to one of these studies (Kowalski & Limber, 2007), which surveyed almost 4,000 middle school students, 11 percent had been electronically bullied at least once in the two months preceding the questionnaire, and 7 percent admitted to being both a bully and a victim. Another study (Williams & Guerra, 2007) showed that electronic bullying peaks in middle school and is inflicted most often through instant messaging, although bullying occurs frequently through text messaging, e-mails, chat rooms, and content on Web sites.

The *Journal of Adolescent Health* research revealed that some state education departments—in Florida, South Carolina, Utah, Oregon, and Washington—have created policies to combat online harassment. (David-Ferdon & Hertz, 2007). But many of the authors agreed that stopping adolescents' use of electronic media in school or installing blocking and filtering software does not adequately address this pervasive problem.

Ideally, we should convince all students to abstain from bullying, and we certainly must try to do so. But it is equally crucial to arm students with the tools they need to protect themselves from bullying, particularly now that bullies take advantage of far-reaching online tools. As a middle school teacher, I've found that a powerful way to arm students against cyberbullying is to have them research some aspect of this phenomenon and then teach others what they have learned—or directly experienced—as they navigate the online world.

Getting Students Talking ...

During my first year teaching media literacy at the Pierre Van Cortlandt Middle School in Croton-on-Hudson, New York, I developed a unit on social networking sites and cyberbullying. For the culminating project, 8th grade students wrote and performed skits portraying a cyberbullying incident, including the motivation for the incident, the consequences, and any resolution the players came to. "Can we curse?" students asked, amazed that I wanted them to show the real deal. My response: Make it realistic.

On the day students presented their skits to their classmates, I called in some reserves: the school psychologist, guidance counselor, student assistance counselor, and our school's drug abuse resistance education officer (a member of our local law enforcement department). The skits raised important issues that captured every student's interest: body image, "stealing" boyfriends and girlfriends, and threats of violence. They also raised anxious questions. My professional colleagues provided advice for students, and the police officer explained legal consequences and how extensively the police will get involved.

Many parents thanked the school for exposing their children to these issues as part of their education. And when school personnel saw how much students had to say—and ask—about online bullying, the seeds were sown for more comprehensive teaching about cybercitizenship. Principal Barbara Ulm had already received numerous requests for help from parents of students in 5th and 6th grades who had been targeted in cyberspace by other students. She asked me to develop a full-blown Internet safety curriculum for the school's 6th, 7th, and 8th graders.

... And Getting Them Teaching

When I began implementing this curriculum the next fall, I noticed how much the 8th graders knew and were eager to impart to one another—with almost desperate urgency. As if riding a roller-coaster, students relayed stories and advice to one another, hitting highs and lows at breakneck speed. They were experts in some aspects of online interaction and risks but complete novices in others. I realized that their knowledge and thirst to exchange information provided a rare opportunity. So I charged my 8th grade students with the job of teaching my 6th graders.

As any middle school teacher knows, there is a vast difference in development between a 6th grader and an 8th grader. The first is a child; the second a young adult. The first wants to emulate the second; 6th graders literally and figuratively look up to their older schoolmates. Most 8th graders realize this and feel a tangible sense of responsibility as role models. These are perfect conditions for motivating older students to present information on a public safety issue—and getting younger students to take it seriously.

Eighth graders first learn *netiquette*—appropriate, courteous online behavior and communication. Students discuss their own definitions of appropriate online behavior. My 8th graders have identified a number of rules, including (1) If you wouldn't say it to the person's face, don't say it online; (2) Be careful with sarcasm—it can be misread; and (3) Be extra careful about what you say online because your audience can't hear tone or see facial expressions.

I then describe certain deviations from appropriate behavior and how to recognize these deviations and safeguard against becoming a victim or perpetrator. I divide 8th graders into groups and make each group responsible for researching one subtopic and creating an engaging 15-minute lesson to deliver to a 6th grade class.[1]

The first year we tried this, students wrote lessons on flaming, phishing, cyberbullying, cyberharassment, cyberbullying or harassment by proxy, and online grooming. They created a list of definitions of these terms followed by succinct advice for coping with each one, which they handed out to 6th graders (see "The Student Guide to Stamping Out Cyberabuse" on p. 79). Students created PowerPoint presentations, SmartBoard drawings, diagrams, and graphics. They incorporated into their presentations online media they found about cyberbullying, such as videos from TeacherTube.com and the group Netsmartz.org. (One powerful resource they found is a British-made public service announcement video available on YouTube called "Think U Know" that shows a young girl reporting a predatory online groomer.) They shared surveys, bookmarks, and a list of Internet safety tips with their peers.

I also infused the unit with instruction in public speaking, and on the day of the presentations, I assessed each student on his or her presentation, including organization, content knowledge, mechanics, delivery, and the quality of visual aids.

As you might expect, every 8th grade student rose to the occasion, even the most traditionally reluctant participants. Their talks, materials, and activities kept the younger students fully engaged. They asked questions and got their peers to think and reflect, sometimes with creative tactics.

For example, one group burst into the classroom in a friendly manner. They handed out lollipops and asked 6th graders to fill out a questionnaire providing their e-mail passwords, addresses, phone numbers, and parents' and siblings' names, explaining that they needed this information for their presentation. The older students handily made their point about how online groomers befriend victims first to gain their trust.

The "teachers" alerted their students to how seemingly innocuous messages can be precursors to harassment and abuse. In addition to showing realistic examples of bullying and aggressive communiqués, they also informed their younger counterparts about protective tools, like procedures that block certain messages or senders, privacy settings, and logistics for reporting incidents to an Internet service provider. In a clever twist, one group included in their PowerPoint presentation the kinds of questions a groomer might send, leaving the victim's answers blank. They asked 6th graders to write how they would respond to the messages.

Some 8th graders later told me they had been very nervous during their presentations, but it wasn't evident at the time. Students displayed a mature understanding of the seriousness of their responsibility. As Dylan noted in his final reflection,

Presenting to the 6th graders helped me realize how easily kids will give out their information for a small prize. ... It's important to always educate kids on Internet safety.

Emily reflected:

I found it really interesting to hear the 6th graders' responses to our questions and to see their faces as they slowly realized the truth with some parts of the Internet. I was glad to see that they took this seriously, and not as a joke. . . . We wanted to scare them, and we did just that. We wanted to show them that this does happen to people all over, and it could very easily happen to them if they are not careful.

6th Graders Reflect and Respond

Following the 8th graders' cybersafety lessons, I asked my 6th grade students to write an article about the experience for our upcoming class newspaper. This fit in well with my 6th grade media literacy curriculum that year, which focused on print media. It was a perfect opportunity to teach "angle" in journalistic writing. I encouraged students to come at the experience from any vantage point that felt relevant to them and to experiment with different types of articles. They had ample material to draw from because they all took notes during the presentations and received handouts from the 8th grade "teachers."

Students rose to the challenge of choosing varied angles and formats: straight news about the fact that students were teaching students, reviews of the lessons and the 8th graders' teaching skills, an Internet safety advice column, editorials on different subtopics, and informational features on how to protect yourself from online dangers. The pieces they created—such as this excerpt from Rita's article "Staying Safe Online"—show that they took in what their older peers imparted to them:

> The most serious of the online dangers is grooming. Grooming usually happens over instant messaging and e-mail. The 8th graders taught the 6th graders that grooming is when someone tries to create an emotional relationship with another person who is usually younger than them. The reason grooming is so dangerous is because the "groomer" potentially wants to meet the victim in person and abuse or kidnap them.

Another 6th grade student, Sean, wrote,

> With the computer age booming, PCs everywhere are catching fire. But it's not because of unsafe wiring; it's the work of one of the most basic forms of cyberbullying: flaming. Flaming is like an emotional bacteria—small, short sentences, sometimes casual, sometimes accidental—that make feelings of anger or depression (sometimes both) spread all through the victim's body.

The 6th graders were unanimously grateful for learning about this issue in the safety of the classroom, where all their questions and concerns could be aired. One student wrote, "I am now so much safer and more aware of the Internet and all the dangers. They pop out at me."

Another acknowledged the positive effect of being taught by the 8th grade students using digital media:

> With all the PowerPoints [on] Internet safety from the 8th graders, I learned more than I normally would. The pictures and everything really got my attention.

Arming Students to Help One Another

As difficult as it may be for us to accept, our students are potentially threatened with bullying and even predation any time they are online or communicating electronically. In a commentary connected to the *Journal of Adolescent Health*'s study, Maria Worthen (2007) writes that educators owe their students education in media literacy—including training that makes them aware of the dangers of cybercommunication.

We must help our students acquire the new literacy skills of recognizing and avoiding aggression in cyberspace. But because this territory is probably more alien to teachers than to students, increasingly students will find *themselves* acting as peer counselors for their friends or fellow students encountering this kind of abuse. We must guide students in how to inform and arm one another. My experience turning 8th graders into peer teachers shows that adolescents are not just up to this task—they will relish it. This new 2.0 world will belong to today's youth. It's our job to help them shape and protect it with courage and wisdom.

The Student Guide to Stamping Out Cyberabuse

The 150 8th grade students at Pierre Van Cortlandt Middle School collaboratively wrote these definitions of aggressive communication practices in cyberspace, as well as tips for handling each one.

Flaming. When someone insults someone else, usually by e-mail, instant message, or text message. To prevent flaming, do not respond, save the messages so you can show a trusted adult, and don't worry if the message is from someone you don't know or recognize; there are ways to track the person down.

Phishing. An attempt to get your personal information by pretending to be a site you are familiar with or trust. Always be sure you know where your e-mails come from. Don't give information over the Internet to sites that don't look valid.

Cyberbullying. A child bullying another child on the Internet. Bullying involves repeated put-downs, insults, and threats, with the emphasis on *repeated*. If you get bullied, tell an adult that you trust. To avoid this situation, do NOT talk to people on the Internet whom you don't know.

Cyberharassment. Harassment through the Internet that involves an adult. An adult can harass a child, a child can harass an adult, and an adult can harass another adult.

Cyberbullying or harassment by proxy. (1) When cyberbullies get someone else (or several people) to do their dirty work, or (2) When a bully intentionally provokes a victim to lash back to get the victim in trouble. If this happens to you, don't lash back. Contact your Internet service provider, talk to an adult, or talk to your friends about it.

Online Grooming. When a predator builds an online relationship with a child by giving compliments or a "shoulder to lean on" or sending gifts until the child trusts the predator. Typical "grooming" lines include

- Where is the computer in the house?
- Are your parents around much?
- You can always talk to me.
- I'm always here for you.
- You don't deserve how they treat you.
- You have a great personality.
- You're beautiful. You should be a model.

To protect yourself from a groomer, (1) always know whom you are talking to online, (2) don't give out personal information, (3) don't post seductive or inappropriate pictures of yourself or others online, (4) never meet up in person with anyone you meet online, and (5) talk with your parents if you feel suspicious about something online.

8th Graders' Top Ten Internet Safety Tips

1. Don't give out personal information.
2. Don't talk to anybody you don't know.
3. Use a secure password.
4. Don't give your password to anybody.
5. Be careful about what you post online.
6. Don't put pictures of yourself online.
7. Tell someone if you get cyberbullied.
8. Be honest.
9. Don't click on pop-ups.
10. Only go to sites you know are safe.

References

David-Ferdon, C., & Hertz, M. F. (2007). Electronic media, violence, and adolescents: An emerging public health problem. *Journal of Adolescent Health, 41*(6), 1–5.

Kowalski, R., & Limber, S. (2007). Electronic bullying among middle school students. *Journal of Adolescent Health, 41*(6), 22–30.

Williams, K., & Guerra, N. (2007). Prevalence and predictors of Internet bullying. *Journal of Adolescent Health, 41*(6), 14–21.

Worthen, M. (2007). Commentary: Education policy implications from the expert panel on electronic media and youth violence. *Journal of Adolescent Health, 41*(6), 61–63.

Endnote

[1] Many Internet safety organizations offer lesson plans, videos, role-playing games, advice, and even school visits. These include Netsmartz Teens (www.netsmartz.org/netteens.htm), SafeTeens.com (www.safeteens.com), Teen Angels (www.teenangels.org), and Web Wise Kids (www.webwisekids.org).

Johanna Mustacchi teaches media literacy at Pierre Van Cortlandt Middle School in Croton-on-Hudson, New York; jmustacchi@croton-harmonschools.org.

Originally published in the March 2009 issue of *Educational Leadership*, *66*(6), pp. 78–83.

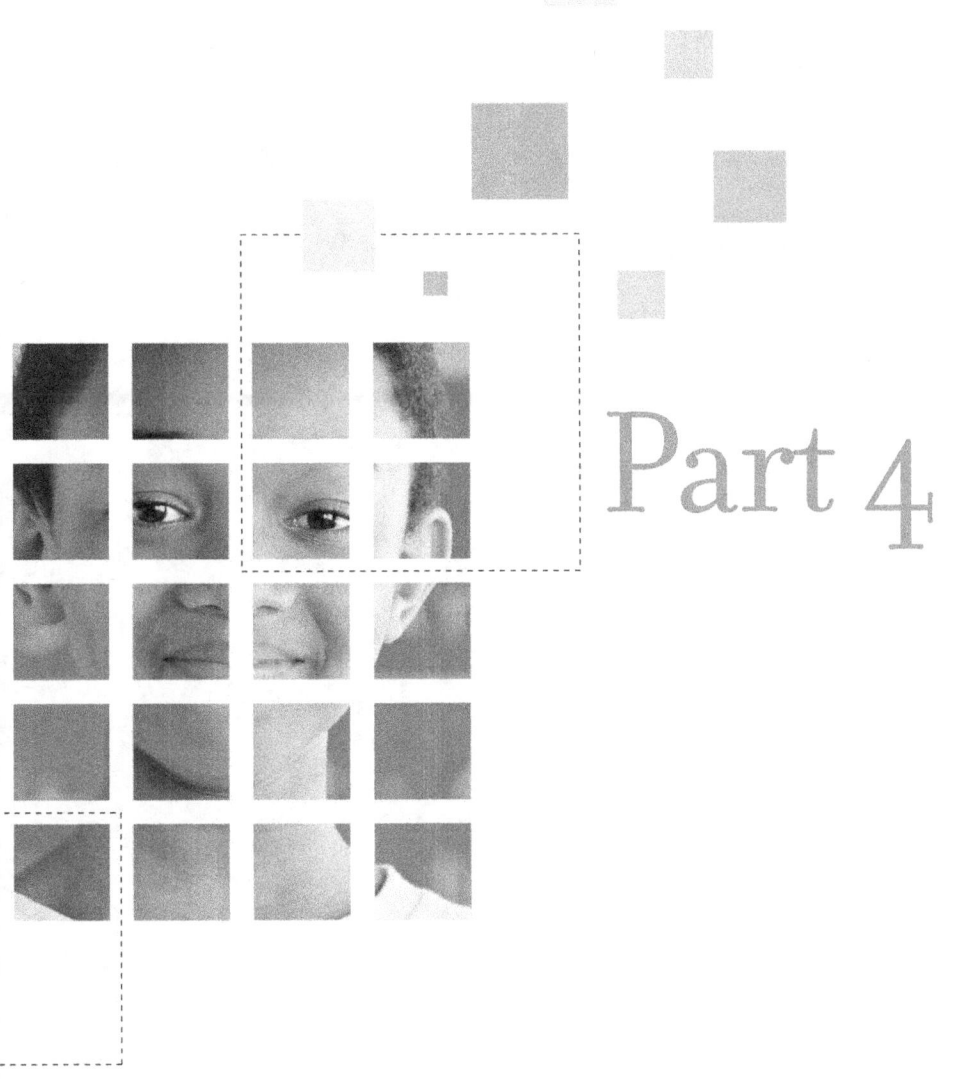

Part 4

Helping Students Cope with Life Challenges

Success with Less Stress

Jerusha Conner, Denise Pope, and Mollie Galloway

Students with high grade point averages often carry an unhealthy load of stress. How can schools help?

The headlines are alarming. Many students who feel the pressure to succeed have been cheating, pulling all nighters to study, becoming depressed, and seeking relief in drug use and self-mutilation. Multiple news reports have directed attention to what some are calling an epidemic of student stress in top U.S. schools (see, for example, Boccella, 2007; Keates, 2007; McMahon, 2007). These headlines are not just media hype; empirical data corroborate the reports.

Our study explored what students themselves said about the causes of their school-related stress and then looked at ways to reduce it. We hoped to find ways for schools to reverse this trend by developing healthier school environments that promote student engagement and well-being.

From 2006 to 2008, we gathered data from 3,645 students, attending seven high-performing high schools in the California Bay Area. These students appear to be exemplars. The vast majority (85 percent) reported a grade point average of 3.0 or higher, and most (63 percent) reported that they often or always work hard in school. They value achievement and care about learning. In addition, 89 percent participate in an extracurricular activity after school, and most aspire to attend a four-year college. By most indicators, these are the kinds of students we would like our high schools to produce.

A different story emerges, however, from our data. Many students reported feeling stressed out, overworked, and sleep deprived. They spoke of the tolls of stress on their mental and physical well-being and on their ability to learn academic material. Ultimately, their comments raise questions about whether a student's grade point average, frequently used as a marker of student success, is a good indicator of what students are actually learning and accomplishing.

Academic Stress and Its Causes

Science has long recognized that some level of stress can be adaptive and even healthy (Seyle, 1956); however, chronic student stress has been consistently associated with negative outcomes (Grant, Compas, Thurn, McMahon, & Gipson, 2004; Kaplan, Liu, & Kaplan, 2005). For the majority of students in this study, academic stress is constant. More than 70 percent of students reported that they often or always feel stressed by their schoolwork, and 56 percent reported often or always worrying about such things as grades, tests, and college acceptance.

Analyses of students' responses to the open-ended question, "Right now in your life, what causes you the most stress?" confirm that academics and schoolwork are major stressors for these youth. Other high-frequency answers included the college admissions process, large projects and assignments, and standardized tests. Students highlighted these school-related factors as causing more stress than other life stressors, such as social issues or family life. Answers such as "family pressure," "divorce," and "parent/sibling illness" did not fall into the top 10 most frequent answers at any school.

Students' responses demonstrated that many feel that schoolwork dominates their day. Certainly, a large share of their time is spent in school, but the demands do not let up after the last bell rings. On average, students in our study reported spending 3.07 hours on homework each night. This does not include time spent online on social activities, such as chatting with friends, or browsing the Internet. One student explained:

> For some reason all teachers love to assign huge amounts of homework on the same nights, which keeps me awake till all hours trying to find the best possible answers because there is a lot of pressure put on us kids to do so well.

Another lamented, "It is not necessarily the difficulty of the work, but the workload itself that causes me the most stress, since the average is about 4–5 hours a night."

On average, these students also spend another two hours each weeknight on extracurricular activities, not including time spent commuting to and from these activities. More than a quarter (28 percent) reported six or more hours of after-school commitments, including homework, each night. These busy schedules leave little room for downtime and rest. In fact, 60.9 percent of the students said that schoolwork or homework frequently keeps them from other things, such as spending time with family and friends; a similar percentage (60.3 percent) reported having to drop an activity they enjoy because of schoolwork and other demands.

Effects of Academic Stress on Learning

While reflecting on their busy schedules and the sources of their stress, several students commented that the pressure is compromising their intellectual development. One student explained:

> I'm stressed because I have so many pointless, mundane assignments that take up large amounts of time, without actually [resulting in] learning anything in class. I don't mind working if I'm actually learning something. I hate wasting my valuable time on assignments that don't accomplish anything for teachers and classes that don't respect me as an intellectual.

Another student wrote,

> If teachers stopped giving out busy work, I'd be able to focus more on important assignments. I always get burnt out when I have to spend a lot of time on useless work.

These students have high grade point averages, but they are frustrated by tedious assignments that hold little meaning for them. Many admitted to copying homework and cheating on tests and quizzes because of the pressure. A full 95 percent of the 11th and 12th grade students in our sample reported that they had cheated at least one time. Even when the work is meaningful, the excessive workload, combined with a busy schedule of outside activities, becomes too much for many of these kids to handle.

Effects of Academic Stress on Student Well-Being

The stress these students feel not only compromises their learning experience, but also takes a toll on their health and well-being. Given the amount of time they spend completing homework, studying, and pursuing extracurricular activities, it is no wonder that the majority of students in our study reported sleeping fewer hours per night than the 9.25 hours experts suggest they need.

On average, the respondents reported getting 6.8 hours of sleep each weeknight. Over one-third (34.6 percent) reported six or fewer hours of sleep each night. Two-thirds indicated that homework or schoolwork often or always keep them from sleeping. Fifty-four percent reported difficulty sleeping, 56 percent reported experiencing exhaustion as a result of academic stress, and quite a few students listed "not getting enough sleep" as a stressor in and of itself. These students' comments reflect the extent of their sleep deprivation:

- "There are times I do schoolwork from 3 p.m. to 3 a.m. even when I don't procrastinate."

- "I just want more time to sleep and maintain a healthy lifestyle, but school keeps inundating me with work and tests at such a fast and constant rate that I'm always tired and stressed."
- "Just this week I had three all-nighters in a row."

In addition to exhaustion, students attributed other physical symptoms, including headaches and stomach problems, to academic stress. Although 19 percent reported experiencing no physical symptoms in the past month due to academic stress, 44 percent reported experiencing three or more physical symptoms in one month alone. For these youth, it becomes hard to maintain the argument that stress can be healthy.

Stress also adversely affects some students' mental health. Nearly one-quarter of the respondents (24 percent) indicated that they frequently felt depressed in the last month, and 252 students (7 percent) had cut themselves during the same time period. These statistics are similar to those in other samples (Nevius, 2005; Ross & Heath, 2002).

Some students turn to stimulants to boost their performance. Twenty-four percent of respondents reported that they had used stimulants such as caffeine or over-the-counter alertness pills to help them stay up to study in the last month, and another 274 students (8 percent) reported using illegal stimulants or prescription drugs for the same reason. Other research indicates that these numbers rise dramatically once students enter college (Johnston, O'Malley, Bachman, & Schulenberg, 2007; McCabe, Boyd, & Teter, 2009).

Students' comments revealed the extent to which some of them are suffering:

- "I get emotionally stressed and have breakdowns, or I go the completely opposite way and stop caring. I wish the administrators would take initiative. I cry all the time!"
- "I was in therapy for anxiety issues last year . . . depression from extreme homework and expectations of my coach."
- "I am stressed to the point of developing chronic insomnia."

- "When I feel especially stressed out, I feel like intoxication is the best way out."

Clearly, these students are experiencing distress. Their grades may indicate that they are meeting or exceeding academic standards, but their words indicate that they are sacrificing their health and well-being.

Strategies for Schools

The schools that participated in this study joined a research-based intervention program known as Challenge Success. This program, based at the Stanford University School of Education, guides school teams of multiple stakeholders as they design and implement site-based policies and practices that reduce student stress and promote greater student engagement, academic integrity, health, and well-being.

Soon after joining the program, these schools administered a baseline survey to a representative sample of their student bodies to determine the extent to which their students experienced academic stress and to examine links among physical and mental health, student motivation, and achievement. The survey data help participating schools not only identify specific problem areas, but also generate community-wide understanding of these problems.

After developing this shared understanding, schools implemented a variety of strategies to reduce student stress and increase well-being. Most schools created more opportunities for students to receive support from staff, developed test and project calendars to help ease students' workload, and revised homework policies. Some also modified college counseling practices, reformed the grading system or grading policies, and created honor codes or new academic integrity policies.

These are the strategies that schools found most helpful:

- Changes to the schedule: Allowing fewer transitions and more downtime or free periods, adding more tutorial time or advisory periods, or going to a block or modified block schedule.
- Staff training and development: Conducting workshops on engagement and alternative assessments.
- Altering exams: Reducing their weight, moving them to before winter break, increasing time between exams, and replacing exams with projects.

At a school where the daily bell schedule and the exam schedule were significantly modified, students reported experiencing less stress. The vast majority of 10th and 11th graders (86 percent and 83 percent, respectively) agreed that adding free periods to the schedule, lengthening the class periods and advisories, and reducing the number of classes each day had effectively eased their workload. More than three-quarters of these sophomores and juniors (77 percent and 76 percent respectively) agreed that rescheduling exams from after the winter break to before the break reduced their stress. Administrators attested to the positive effects of the reforms and commented that student grades, test scores, and college admissions all stayed high, but the stress decreased.

Even seemingly modest reform efforts had positive effects. At another participating school, for instance, some advanced placement (AP) teachers worked to decrease student stress and increase student engagement with learning. One AP Biology teacher cut the homework load in half, eliminated summer work, and encouraged frequent dialogue with students and parents about student well-being. For two years in a row, the AP Biology test scores in his class have gone up, and students have reported higher levels of engagement with the material and less stress. An AP Calculus teacher at another school had similar success when he reduced homework and cut back on the number of problems he had students do each night. His students did less homework than students in other high-level math classes, but they scored as well on the AP exams—with a lot less stress.

The Right Challenge

In response to the overwhelming workload at her school, one student made this plea:

> Don't push students farther than their limit. All my teachers say, "I'm treating you like this because that's how you'll be treated in college." Guess what? I'm not in college; I'm 15 and in high school *for a reason.*

This student is right. The physical and mental health tolls we've depicted are not appropriate for any youth, and educators and parents need to be aware of the problem and attuned to the signs of student stress.

The Challenge Success program is not advocating that teachers water down their curriculums or eliminate homework or even abolish tests and exams. But we see the negative ramifications of a system that pushes students too far, and we know that schools can achieve positive results without the undue pressures.

To be fair, the schools are not the sole source of this problem—parents, students, federal policies, and colleges and universities all play a role. Because the problem is multifaceted, we encourage multiple stakeholders—teachers, students, parents, counselors, and administrators—to work together to formulate plans for change. When everyone recognizes the need for change and has a say in the reform process, schools can indeed foster healthier environments in which student learning and student well-being are mutually reinforcing.

Authors' note: Dot McElhone provided research assistance, and the Lucile Packard Foundation for Children's Health provided support for this project.

References

Boccella, K. (2007, May 21). The year that puts students to the test: As the scramble to get into college intensifies, is it any wonder that juniors feel overwhelmed? *The Philadelphia Inquirer*, p. A01.

Grant, K. E., Compas, B. E., Thurn, A. E., McMahon, S. D., & Gipson, P. Y. (2004). Stressors and child and adolescent psychopathology: Measurement issues and prospective effects. *Journal of Clinical Child and Adolescent Psychology, 33,* 412–425.

Johnston, L. D., O'Malley, P. M., Bachman, J. G., & Schulenberg, J. E., (2007). *Monitoring the future: National survey results on drug use, 1975–2006, Volume II: College students and adults ages 19–45* (NIH Publication 07-6206). Bethesda, MD: National Institute on Drug Abuse.

Kaplan, D. S., Liu, R. X., & Kaplan, H. B. (2005). School related stress in early adolescence and academic performance three years later: The conditional influence of self-expectations. *Social Psychology of Education, 8,* 3–17.

Keates, N. (2007, January 19). Schools turn down the heat on homework. *Pittsburgh Post Gazette.* Available: www.post-gazette.com/pg/07019/755198-28.stm.

McCabe, S. E., Boyd, C. J., & Teter, C. J. (2009). Subtypes of nonmedical prescription drug misuse. *Drug and alcohol dependence, 102,* 63–70.

McMahon, R. (2007, September 9). Everybody does it. Academic cheating is at an all-time high. *San Francisco Chronicle.* Available: www.sfgate.com/cgi-bin/article.cgi?f=/c/a/2007/09/09/CM59RIBI7.DTL.

Nevius, C. W. (2005, April 19). An epidemic that cuts to the bone. *San Francisco Chronicle,* p. B1.

Ross, S., & Heath, N. (2002). A study of the frequency of self-mutilation in a community sample of adolescents. *Journal of Youth and Adolescence, 31,* 67–77.

Seyle, H. (1956). *The stress of life.* New York: McGraw Hill.

Jerusha Conner is Assistant Professor of Education at Villanova University in Villanova, Pennsylvania; jerusha.conner@villanova.edu. **Denise Pope** is Senior Lecturer at Stanford University in Stanford, California; dpope@stanford.edu. **Mollie Galloway** is Director of the Office of Research and Assessment and teaches in the Educational Leadership program in the Graduate School at Lewis and Clark College in Portland, Oregon; galloway@lclark.edu.

Originally published in the December 2009/January 2010 issue of *Educational Leadership,* 67(4), pp. 54–58.

Helping Self-Harming Students

Matthew D. Selekman

Schools can reduce the likelihood of self-harming epidemics and manage student difficulties when they occur by following a few practical guidelines.

Student self-harming is one of the most perplexing and challenging behaviors that administrators, teachers, nurses, and counseling staff encounter in their schools. Approximately 14 to 17 percent of children up to age 18 have deliberately cut, scratched, pinched, burned, or bruised themselves at least once (Whitlock, 2009), with 5 to 8 percent of adolescents actively engaging in this behavior (J. Whitlock, personal communication, September 27, 2009).

Self-harming behavior is not a new phenomenon among adolescents. Mental health and health-care professionals have typically viewed such behavior as a symptom of an underlying psychological or personality disorder as a possible suicidal gesture suggesting the need for psychiatric hospitalization or as a symptom of post-traumatic stress disorder caused by sexual or physical abuse.

However, both research and practice-based wisdom indicate that the majority of self-harming adolescents do not meet the criteria for diagnosable DSM-IV[1], psychological or personality disorders, have never had suicidal thoughts or attempted to end their lives, and have never experienced sexual or physical abuse (Selekman, 2009). Most self-harming adolescents use the behavior as a coping strategy to get immediate relief from emotional distress.

Preteens and adolescents today are growing up in a highly toxic and materialistic world. They are bombarded daily by violent, sexualized, and self-destructive media messages and themes that encourage them to grow up rapidly and become junior adults. They also have too many daily choices regarding specific material "must-have" possessions, extracurricular activities, dressing and fitting in with popular peers, possible college attendance, and so forth. Several stressors play a major role in fueling self-harming behavior among adolescents today.

Fitting in with Peers

In adolescence, being rejected by your peers is the equivalent of social death. The peer group is much more demanding today than it used to be, and it changes at a frenetic pace. Adolescent students who lack strong social skills often struggle to stay afloat and may resort to extreme behaviors endorsed by more popular and powerful peers; they may experiment with cutting as their entry ticket into the high-status, inner-circle clique. Adolescents who can't afford highly prized popular possessions like the iPhone or designer clothing may resort to stealing them.

Many adolescents and children also spend far too much time online, communicating with their peers on Facebook or on MySpace—or "Mean Space," as some people now call it. Some adolescents have been victimized by peers who play the on-and-off befriending game or spread terrible rumors about them as a form of underground psychological warfare. I have worked with a number of adolescents who were the victims of these vicious and emotionally devastating character assaults. Fitting in and staying connected to socially well-positioned and popular peers become more challenging because of the intense politics of these social networking sites.

Overloaded Stress Circuits

Another frequent complaint I hear from both self-harming and other adolescents is feeling overwhelmed by multiple life stressors. In addition to juggling their social connections, the students are trying to manage massive homework loads and are often pressured by their parents to perform at a high academic level. Some adolescents are growing up in achievement-oriented families, in which the parents put undue pressure on them to get straight As. In addition, the parents often push their adolescents to schedule too many extracurricular activities to make them as attractive as possible to top colleges and universities. To cope with the stress, some of the more emotionally vulnerable adolescents turn to self-harm, resort to eating-distressed behaviors like bulimia, or engage in substance abuse.

Quick-Fix Solutions

Adolescents are growing up in a media world where one of the most popular messages is that we must obliterate stress and other problems as quickly as possible. What better way to get rid of all your problems than to take a pill, which many advertisements on TV suggest is the ultimate solution for physical, psychological, and behavioral difficulties.

In some cases, adolescents may witness their parents abusing prescription medications, smoking, and drinking for stress relief. The message they receive is that stress is a bad thing—that people can't channel it into constructive activities but must quickly eliminate it.

Self-harming adolescents have discovered that their brain chemistry can serve as a 24-hour pharmacy (Plante, 2007). When adolescents self-harm, their bodies immediately secrete naturally manufactured endorphins into their bloodstreams to protect them from physical pain. These endorphins rapidly numb the emotional distress they may be experiencing. As with drug addiction, longtime self-harming adolescents not only report feeling loss of control, compulsion to engage in this behavior, and physical tolerance of the pain but also experience mild withdrawal symptoms like anxiety and irritability when they abstain from self-harming (Selekman, 2009; Whitlock, Muehlenkamp, & Eckenrode, 2008). Thus, self-harming has become one of the most popular painkilling and sedative drugs for youth today.

Emotional Disconnection and Invalidation

In families of self-harming adolescents, emotional disconnection and invalidation are common family dynamics. For whatever reason, one or both parents are not emotionally and physically present to comfort their adolescents when they are emotionally distressed. When the parents are present, they tend to respond in invalidating ways, such as by yelling, threatening, becoming hysterical, dishing out extreme consequences, distancing themselves, or not listening. So some adolescents take matters into their own hands—they self-harm to soothe themselves.

Further, extreme emotional disconnection from their parents often leads self-harming adolescents to gravitate toward other disconnected and often unsavory peer groups, an affiliation that tends to reinforce their self-harming behavior. Adolescents may feel that they belong and are respected in these groups. However, their involvement may expose them to other self-destructive behaviors, such as bulimia, substance abuse, and risky sexual behaviors.

Another factor that contributes to emotional disconnection in families is the computer screen. Developing emotional intimacy by means of a screen of some sort has become much more important to some adolescents than having human contact. Brazleton and Greenspan (2000) found that children and adolescents spent, on average, five and one-half hours a day in front of a screen. On the basis of what I hear from adolescents and parents in my private practice, this figure has gone up. Close to 70 percent of 8- to 18-year-olds have a TV in their bedroom (Taffel, 2009); laptops or personal computers have most likely replaced many of these.

Parents often do not provide firm guidelines for screen usage and do not regularly monitor the Web sites their children visit. There are many toxic Web sites and so-called online support groups for self-harming individuals where adolescents can witness people brutalizing their bodies, see other graphic images, read poetry and stories with self-harming themes, and learn new methods for self-harming.

Fears About the Future

Some of the self-harming adolescents with whom I work are anxious about whether they'll get into college or be able to pursue certain career paths, especially given the current grim economic situation. Some have seen their parents lose their jobs as well as their retirement savings. Some have had difficulties finding part-time jobs because few places are hiring.

Those whose college attendance depends on getting a scholarship may experience high levels of anxiety about not letting their parents and themselves down with their academic and extracurricular performance. Self-harming and other equivalent behaviors can give some students temporary relief from these anxieties and fears.

Signs and Symptoms

On the basis of what we know from clinical experience and research as well as from the adolescents themselves, most adolescents who self-harm tend to cut or burn themselves on their arms, legs, abdomens, or the bottoms of their feet, all places they can cover up. Many self-harming adolescents wear pants and long-sleeved shirts even when the weather is warm to cover up their scars, fresh cuts, or burn marks.

We have to worry most about those who cut or burn themselves around their eyes and on their necks. These students—as well as those who deliberately display the scars, cuts, or burn marks on their arms and legs—are often waving a red flag, indicating they're in emotional trouble. In many cases, a friend or peer will become alarmed and seek out a teacher or other school staff member to share his or her concerns.

Many self-harming adolescents have difficulty managing their depressed, anxious, and angry feelings. In some cases, they cannot articulate their feelings, possibly because of repeated invalidation in their interactions with their parents. Self-harming, bulimia, and substance abuse are adolescents' solutions. Anthony Favazza, a leading authority on self-harming, found that close to 50 percent of his female patients had concurrent problems with bulimia (Favazza & Selekman, 2003).

On a cautionary note, tattoos, body piercings, or dark Goth-looking makeup and clothing may not indicate self-harming. There is a difference between self-decorating to be cool—as a symbol of peer group tribal connection—and engaging in these behaviors to rid oneself of emotional demons.

What Schools Can Do

School personnel need to be familiar with the territory of adolescent self-harm. They need to understand the common causes, signs, and symptoms; the difference between self-harming behavior and suicidal behavior; constructive and empowering ways to respond; and effective treatments.

Schools can provide two major interventions on the junior and senior high school levels that can help reduce the likelihood of self-harming epidemics.

Intervention 1: Create a Support Group

Once you have red-flagged self-harming students, you can refer them to an on-site intervention group that capitalizes on their strengths to teach them how to become more resilient, effectively cope with stress, and take on leadership responsibilities in their schools and communities.

I have developed one such model that improves students' coping skills—the Stress-Busters' Leadership Group.[2] Over nine sessions, students look at their strengths and "protective shields"; learn skills related to mindfulness, meditation, loving kindness, and compassion toward self and others; focus on finding balance and harmony in their lives; learn how to navigate family minefields; and acquire effective tools for mastering school stress. Ideally, a male-female cotherapy team of school social workers, psychologists, or counselors is best for gender balance. However, one counseling professional can also effectively run the sessions. (See p. 50 for a description of a session.)

Students who have completed the program often stay involved in prevention work in their schools and communities. Graduates serve as ideal gatekeepers for identifying self-harming students and for getting them to see a counselor or participate in a new group. Finally, groups like these can reverse self-harming and other self-destructive behavior epidemics in schools by accentuating at-risk students' strengths and honing their leadership abilities.

Intervention 2: Educate Responding Adults

Adult inspirational others serve a major protective function for at-risk children and adolescents (Anthony, 1984; Selekman, 1997, 2005, 2009). These can be teachers, coaches, extended family members, family friends, neighbors, clergy, and community leaders. Adult inspirational others are often compassionate, possess strong social skills, and are good at identifying and accentuating the strengths in children and adolescents. They consistently make themselves available to young people for connection, support, and advice. In every school, some staff members have served this role for at-risk students without even knowing it.

Eight practical guidelines can help adults effectively respond to self-harming students.

1. Because teachers and school nurses are often the first responders, it is crucial that they be respectful listeners to

self-harming students; validate the students; build trust; and serve as a bridge to get the students to a school psychologist, social worker, or counselor for further help. If the self-harming student has a strong relationship with the teacher, it may be useful for the teacher to sit in on counseling sessions. Teachers and school nurses should ask the student these questions:

- How can I help you?
- How has the cutting helped you?
- How does cutting fit into your life right now?
- I'm happy to be there for you, but I also need to connect you with one of our social workers because of our school policy. Would you like to see a male or a female social worker (when the option is available)?
- If I can arrange it, would you like me to sit in on your first meeting with your social worker?

2. At all costs, school personnel need to avoid responding to self-harming students with disgust, anxiety, or fear. They must not lecture the students about the dangers of this behavior, play detective and ask to see their cuts or burn marks, or interrogate and further invalidate them. Instead, they should strive to understand the meaning of this behavior *for the student*, how the behavior has been helpful, and how they can now be helpful to the student. It is important to remember that each self-harming student's story is unique. Self-harming students need to know that teachers and other school personnel care about them and are available for emotional connection, support, and advice when needed.

3. Once a referral is made to the school counseling staff member, the counselor needs to determine in conjunction with his or her supervisor and the student whether the school can successfully counsel the student on-site or whether parent

involvement is required. For students who have just begun experimenting with self-harming or who have engaged in this behavior only intermittently, a trusting relationship with a school counselor may generate alternative coping strategies. I recommend that the student also participates in an on-site intervention group, such as the Stress-Busters' Leadership Group.

4. If the student has been self-harming regularly and is engaging in other self-destructive behaviors like bulimia, substance abuse, and risky sexual activity, the school needs to contact the parents immediately for referral to a private practitioner or community-based program for family therapy that specializes in treating these adolescent behavioral difficulties. Concurrent participation in an on-site intervention group is also recommended.

5. For students who have been self-harming regularly; who are cutting themselves more deeply; or who are cutting or burning themselves around their eyes, necks, and private parts, this is a medical/psychiatric emergency. These students should be taken immediately to the nearest hospital emergency room for evaluation.

6. Although only a small percentage of self-harming students become suicidal, if these students have not responded well to both on-site and outside counseling, struggle to cope with multiple life stressors, and clearly voice suicidal thoughts, they need to be immediately taken to the nearest hospital emergency room.

7. Identified school personnel who have been serving as inspirational adults for other disconnected at-risk students can provide added support to self-harming students who are trying to reduce or stop engaging in this behavior. These adults can closely collaborate with the involved counseling staff members for guidance and back-up if necessary.

8. Graduates of intervention groups who are interested in schoolwide prevention work help identify at-risk students who are self-harming, get them to counseling staff, and spark their interest in participating in a new group for added support. The school can ask these graduates to cofacilitate new intervention groups and get involved in the school peer counseling program.

More Than Just a Problem

As provocative and perplexing as this behavior may seem, we must not lose sight of how bright, creative, and talented many self-harming students are. With compassion, guidance, and support, we can empower self-harming students by being respectful listeners and accentuating their natural gifts.

A Look Inside a Stress-Busters' Leadership Group Session

In the initial session in the Stress-Busters' Leadership Group—called What Are My Strengths and Protective Shields—the group leaders get to know the participants by having them discuss their key strengths, talents, hobbies, and interests as well as any important positive changes that have recently occurred. After discussing group rules and confidentiality, leaders ask members what they would like to get out of group participation and what they would like to change in themselves. The leaders negotiate with each group member some doable and measurable goals and ask each participant to track his or her progress.

In a 15–20 minute presentation on resiliency, leaders describe the major protective factors that have helped at-risk children and adolescents overcome adversity. Group members discuss which of these protective factors they are already using and how such factors helped them manage specific stressful events. Group members learn about positive psychology research, which focuses on strengths and virtues (Peterson, 2006), and take the Values in Action Inventory of Strengths for Youth (available online at www.viastrengths.org). Group members will discuss the results in the next group session.

Participants then engage in an exercise called *visualizing movies of success*. Group members close their eyes and picture a blank movie screen. Using all their senses, they project on the screen a movie about something they accomplished that pleased them and made them feel proud. This can include doing a good deed, handling a difficult family situation well, performing well with their band, doing something that surprised them about their abilities, and so on. Participants then share their movies with the group.

As a conclusion, participants acknowledge the various strengths of group members. Students also create *victory boxes* out of old shoe boxes, which they decorate in any way they wish. Each day, they write down on slips of paper personal victories or accomplishments, along with the thinking and actions that helped them pull off each victory. They share with the group at least one of their most meaningful personal victories that occurred during the week.

—*Matthew D. Selekman*

Endnotes

[1] DSM-IV refers to the *Diagnostic and Statistical Manual of Mental Disorders*, published by the American Psychiatric Association. The DSM-IV includes all currently recognized mental health disorders.

[2] For a more in-depth blueprint for running Stress-Busters' Leadership Groups, see my book, *The Adolescent and Young Adult Self-Harming Treatment Manual: A Collaborative Strengths-Based Brief Therapy Approach* (Norton, 2009).

References

Anthony, E. J. (1984). The St. Louis risk research project. In N. F. Watt, E. J. Anthony, L. C. Wynne, & J. Roth (Eds.), *Children at risk for schizophrenia: A longitudinal perspective* (pp. 105–148). Cambridge, UK: Cambridge University Press.

Brazleton, T. B., & Greenspan, S. I. (2000). *The irreducible needs of children: What every child must have to grow, learn, and flourish.* Cambridge, MA: Perseus.

Favazza, A. R., & Selekman, M. D. (2003, April). *Self-injury in adolescents.* Annual Spring Conference of the Child and Adolescent Centre Department of Psychiatry, University of Western Canada, London, Ontario.

Peterson, C. (2006). *A primer of positive psychology.* New York: Oxford University Press.

Plante, L. G. (2007). *Bleeding to ease the pain: Cutting, self-injury, and the adolescent search for self.* Westport, CT: Praeger.

Selekman, M. D. (1997). *Solution-focused therapy with children: Harnessing family strengths for systemic change.* New York: Guilford.

Selekman, M. D. (2005). *Pathways to change: Brief therapy with difficult adolescents* (2nd edition). New York: Guilford.

Selekman, M. D. (2009). *The adolescent and young adult self-harming treatment manual: A collaborative strengths-based brief therapy approach.* New York: Norton.

Taffel, R. (2009). *Childhood unbound: Saving our kids' best selves: Confident parenting in a world of change.* New York: Free Press.

Whitlock, J. (2009, May/June). Self-injuring adolescents on the rise. *Psychotherapy Networker*, 13–14.

Whitlock, J., Muehlenkamp, J., & Eckenrode, J. (2008). Variation in non-suicidal self-injury: Identification and features of latent classes in a college population in emerging adults. *Journal of Clinical Child and Adolescent Psychology, 37*(4), 725–735.

Matthew D. Selekman is a licensed clinical social worker (LCSW) and an addictions counselor. He is Codirector of Partners for Collaborative Solutions (www.partners4change.net), 1007 Church Street, Suite 515, Evanston, IL 60201; 847-226-4219; ms@partners4change.net.

Originally published in the December 2009/January 2010 issue of *Educational Leadership*, 67(4), pp. 48–53.

Reaching the Fragile Student

Sue Zapf

Students who are battling tough odds on the home front need a clear invitation to learn.

If you had visited my classroom last September, you would have observed 8th and 9th grade students struggling with school in typical ways. Michael would have been straining to remember his math facts, Steven balking at getting his thoughts down on paper, Elizabeth staring out the window unaware of the assignment I'd just given her, and Amy sighing heavily in response to another failed test. Javier would have been sitting with his arms stretched across his notebook, not doing anything—and not planning to do anything soon.

Although the academic struggles of these students are typical and obvious to any observer, the nonacademic struggles each one faces are less obvious. Michael's mother had left him in the "custody" of his 16-year-old sister, and he had become homeless. Steven—who had a single parent, six siblings, and a history of violence—had been regularly harassed in his mainstream school because of his small size. Elizabeth had repeatedly used methamphetamine, Amy was three months pregnant, and Javier had been skipping school and often spending all day isolated in his room playing video games.

These portraits are composites of students in the Compass program for 8th and 9th graders at Independent School District #194's Area Learning Center, an alternative public school in Lakeville, Minnesota. For eight years, my coteacher John Cates and I have worked with

20 students each year in this alternative setting, which we designed. Administrators from the surrounding middle schools refer to Compass students with a history of academic failure and life circumstances that put them at risk. Twenty-five percent of our students are minorities, and 50 percent qualify for free or reduced-price lunch.

John and I have realized one truth about the students we teach who face serious academic and life battles: A thread of emotional pain runs through each of our student's stories. Until we reach each of them at an emotional level, their academic problems will continue.

Compass: An Inviting Environment

Realizing this truth, we have forged a positive environment that nourishes, rather than depletes, each learner's spirit. Compass draws on the insights of William Purkey and John Novak (1978/1984), who maintain that many traditional teacher practices—such as punishing students or judging student work with the goal of winnowing out low performers—are "disinviting." Often unintentionally—and sometimes even intentionally—such practices exclude struggling youth from the learning community.

A better way to reach students is to proactively cultivate "intentionally inviting" practices that welcome all students into the culture of learning. Typical inviting practices include greeting students at the classroom door or immediately acknowledging a student asking for help—even in your busiest moments—and providing assistance as soon as feasible.

When I first read Purkey and Novak more than 20 years ago, I realized that my actions as a teacher were largely *unintentionally* inviting: I was successful in motivating students, but I didn't know why my tactics were working, so I couldn't replicate them. Learning to actively welcome students into the learning process—even through simple things like asking about their interests—transformed me as a teacher.

It also served me well when I began working with fragile students who needed powerful invitations to learn.

In Compass, John and I stay with our 20 students most of the day, providing a high level of consistency regarding rules and expectations. We teach English, social studies, and a course in life skills and study skills. Specialists teach math, science, and physical education. Mike, a paraprofessional, works in our classroom part of each day, supporting both students and teachers.

Building Trust and "Ball Talks"

For the first three weeks of the school year, John and I spend a great deal of time being intentionally inviting as we build community and trust. I do things large and small that I know will send students a strong message of acceptance, such as checking in with them about personal concerns they've shared or keeping a supply of gum at my desk and offering students some when they get fidgety.

We talk about the "bag" each of us carries that contains our life experiences and how those experiences affect not only how we react to others, but also how we learn. We help students understand that all people are different, that each of us has a different way of thinking and a personal set of strengths and weaknesses (Levine, 2005). Students reflect on their individual strengths and deficits and on what "hot button" emotional issues may get in the way of their personal interactions and learning.

To continue building that sense of community, we host "Ball Talk" every Friday. John, Mike, and I talk among ourselves for five to seven minutes in front of the students, allowing them to eavesdrop on our conversation as we discuss how things are going (we call this "Ball Talk" because we sit on exercise balls in front of the classroom). We might comment on our delight with students' behavior during a special presentation or our frustration with their inability to meet deadlines.

When we teachers have finished, we open up the floor for students to offer comments or suggestions. For this practice to work well, we require respect from all students and staff. A sign hangs above our classroom door: "No putdowns by anyone for any reason at any time." We discuss this expectation at length at the beginning of the year, and students frequently repeat it to one another—and even to adults whom they consider to be guilty of put-downs.

In addition to Ball Talks, John and I meet individually with each student every Friday to discuss that learner's progress and concerns. Before this meeting, students reflect on what went well that week, what did not go well, and what goals they have for the coming week. No matter what conflict arose during the week, what personal challenge each particular student faced, or what assignment the student may have neglected, John and I use this meeting to remind the student in question that the three of us are a team working toward the student's success.

An Inviting Grading System

Two years ago, John and I realized that although we had become intentionally inviting in our relationships with students, our grading system awarding As through Fs was disinviting. Most of our students had been receiving Fs in school for years; when we used traditional grading, they just resigned themselves to getting Fs from us as well. So we changed to the "A, B, C, or Do It Over" system, adapted from the work of Rick Wormeli (2006). Students must keep improving any assignment until the work reaches at least C level.

We were hesitant to make this change, unsure how our students would respond to a demand for quality work. However, what could be more intentionally inviting than telling students that they *can't* fail, that all of them can get Cs or above? John and I believe all our students can earn an A, B, or C on every assignment. And they do, even if it takes them seven tries, even if they miss the first and second deadlines, and even if they have to seek help outside the school day. We build in a period in the day during which students can get extra help from teachers, and John and I stay after school two days a week to provide help to any student who requires it. When a student is late with an assignment, we have that learner complete a form that explains why the work was late, when it will be turned in, and what that learner will do if he or she misses the next deadline. When students see only *C*s and above on their report card, they feel proud, knowing they earned those grades.

Bumps in the Road

Bumps in the road inevitably come up when working with students who have life and school histories fraught with instability. We try to look at problems as opportunities for learning rather than occasions for punishment. Our students would tell you that we try to "heal the wound, rather than put a Band-Aid on it." For example, if two students have a verbal confrontation, we work to mediate it and repair the relationship rather than punish them for arguing. If students use inappropriate words, we remind them to use language and a tone more fitting for the setting instead of sending them to the office.

Although punishments might provide short-term solutions, creating an inviting learning situation is more likely to result in long-term changes. One of our students was an angry young man who reacted with incivility to any provocation. Brett's stepfather was abusive, and Brett's distress over this spilled into school. When someone in class spoke out of turn, Brett would get up and walk out without permission. He snapped back disrespectfully to even simple requests.

It would have been easy to punish these behaviors; instead, John and I taught Brett and his classmates the skill of compartmentalization, or how to keep different areas of life from competing or interfering with each other (Levine, 2005). Brett learned that if he could focus on school when he was at school and leave his home conflicts at home, he would have more success. During the two years Brett attended

Compass, his grades improved significantly, and his inappropriate behaviors decreased.

Signs of Success

The outcomes we see show us our inviting environment is working. Between September 2006 and June 2008, Compass students' grade point average (averaged among all Compass students who stayed in the program two years) increased from 1.67 to 3.20. Discipline referrals are virtually nonexistent now. The power of our approach is also evident from the reflective comments we receive on our twice-yearly surveys, such as these words from a student and a parent:

> I am learning a lot, and my grades are better. At my other school, I was failing all my classes. After I saw I was failing, I just gave up and didn't do anything. Coming here was a new beginning for me.

> The change in my daughter's attitude has been staggering. She has gone from having a total disregard for attending school to getting up at 4:30 a.m. . . . and facing each day with confidence. Where she once was filled with anxiety, there is now self-assurance.

John and I observe our students' increased self-assurance at our annual Deans' Day, a time when students invite the deans or counselors who recommended them to the Compass program to spend an hour with us. The students create invitations, help prepare food, explain their classes, and lead the administrators in "Are You Smarter Than a Compass Student?" as John and I watch, amazed at the transformation that has taken place in each learner.

If you visit my classroom this fall, you will see that Michael, who has moved in with a friend's family, has finally memorized his math facts. You will see Steven interact positively with peers as he revises his writing, notice Elizabeth engaged in her work, admire Amy's social studies project, and hear Javier contributing to discussions and asking for help. And you'll hear John and me talking about the new students who have joined our community, students we trust who will accept our invitation to learn.

References

Levine, M. (2005). *Ready or not, here life comes.* New York: Simon and Schuster.

Purkey, W., & Novak, J. (1978/1984). *Inviting school success: A self-concept approach to teaching and learning.* Belmont, CA: Wadsworth. (Original work published 1978)

Wormeli, R. (2006). *Fair isn't always equal: Assessing and grading in the differentiated classroom.* Portland, ME: Stenhouse.

Sue Zapf is a core teacher in the Compass program at Independent School District #194's Area Learning Center in Lakeville, Minnesota; 952-232-2080; sczapf@aol.com.

Originally published in the September 2008 issue of *Educational Leadership, 66*(1), pp. 67–71.

Peers Helping Peers

Margo A. Mastropieri, Thomas E. Scruggs, and Sheri L. Berkeley

With support from their peers, students with special needs can succeed in the general classroom.

The Individuals with Disabilities Education Improvement Act of 2004 requires schools to include students with disabilities in the general education curriculum to the greatest extent possible, and the No Child Left Behind Act requires educators to hold these students to the same academic standards as their classmates. How can teachers achieve these goals? One strategy is having students help one another (Slavin, Hurley, & Chamberlain, 2003). Peer assistance, cooperative learning, and classwide peer tutoring are three effective methods for improving learning for all students.

Peer Assistance

Peers can assist students with disabilities by helping them read directions for classroom assignments and gather classroom materials or by transcribing lecture notes for them. They can also open doors or move furniture to accommodate a wheelchair and act as a buddy during emergencies or fire drills. The specific tasks will depend on the disability of the student in question and the nature of the classroom. When help is unnecessary, students with disabilities should function as independently as possible (Cushing & Kennedy, 2003).

Peer assistance does not need to be burdensome for the assistants. The assistants generally perform many of the activities anyway, and the tasks usually are not time-consuming. Peer assistance can actually benefit the assistant because it promotes social responsibility and a stronger understanding of others' needs. Students who appear to work well with others would most likely make excellent peer assistants.

To implement peer assistance, the teacher needs to identify the situation that requires assistance and train both students involved in the necessary procedures, reminding them to use appropriate social skills when interacting. It is important to continually monitor the progress of peer assistance and make changes as needed. Appropriately implemented, peer assistance can greatly improve the efficiency and collegiality of the classroom.

Cooperative Learning

For years, teachers have used cooperative learning to raise classroom achievement among diverse groups of learners (Johnson & Johnson, 1986; Slavin, 1991). In cooperative learning, students work in small groups on such activities as solving math problems, collaborating on science experiments, preparing group presentations in social studies, or even resolving interpersonal conflicts. Effective cooperative learning includes several important components.

First, teachers should specify the content objectives and the interpersonal and small-group skills necessary for the activity. It is also important to define the group parameters. Cooperative groups usually include four to six students; however, smaller numbers may be necessary in the lower grades, and higher numbers may sometimes be possible. Teachers can assign students randomly to groups when all students are likely to work well together. But when teachers gauge that students will have difficulty staying on task or behaving appropriately, it's best to deliberately plan groups with a balance of student skills and interests. It's preferable to have only one student with a disability in a group. When a class has high absenteeism, the composition of a group can vary daily, but groups need to be stable for certain activities, such as ongoing science projects.

Giving a specific role to each student in a group can promote cooperation and group efficiency. A group might include a summarizer (to summarize the group's conclusions); a checker (to make sure all students meet the activity objectives); an accuracy coach (to correct or verify responses); and an elaboration seeker (to relate the present activity to other situations) (Johnson & Johnson, 1986). All students, however, should be responsible for all these tasks. For example, all students, not just the accuracy coach, need to know the correct responses to questions the group worked on.

Teachers can assign group roles on the basis of their knowledge of student strengths. For example, they might choose students with strong comprehension skills to be accuracy checkers, good writers to be summarizers, and students with strong verbal skills to be elaboration seekers. Whatever their role, students are usually more successful when teachers explicitly train them to interact appropriately and negotiate individual differences (Gillies & Ashman, 2003; Jenkins & O'Connor, 2003).

Despite the success of cooperative learning, students with special needs may not always benefit from this approach (McMaster & Fuchs, 2002, 2005). The advantages of cooperative learning might be limited when typically achieving peers complete all the tasks for students with disabilities or when students are not held accountable for learning.

While students are in groups, teachers need to ensure that they all stay on task and interact appropriately. At the end of the activity, teachers can provide closure by restating the objectives, summarizing major points, asking students to provide ideas or examples, and answering any final questions. Each student should be evaluated on the group product and on his or her own learning, as well as his or her contribution to the final product and the group dynamic.

We saw cooperative learning at work in a study of three 4th grade classes engaged in a seven-week science unit on ecosystems (Mastropieri et al., 1998). Each class had approximately 25 students. One class worked in cooperative groups to create vertical "ecocolumns" using two-liter soda bottles and to study the effects of such variables as road salt, fertilizer, and acid rain on control and experimental ecosystems. This class included five students with disabilities (two with learning disabilities, one with mild mental retardation, one with emotional disabilities, and one with physical disabilities). Each student with a disability was in a group with two typically achieving students, with one exception. Because the student with emotional disabilities was more volatile, he was in a group with only one partner. All typically achieving students in these groups were selected because they could work well with peers with special needs.

All students took multiple-choice pre- and post-tests and performance-based post-tests and were measured on their attitudes toward science. At the end of the unit, students in cooperative-learning groups substantially outperformed students in the comparison classes who had studied the same content from textbooks. The students with disabilities performed near the middle of their own class and well above the average of the comparison classes.

Classwide Peer Tutoring

Another technique for increasing achievement and addressing diverse learning needs is classwide peer tutoring (Delquadri, Greenwood, Whorton, Carta, & Hall, 1986). The following examples show how classwide tutoring can support student learning.

Classwide Peer Tutoring in Reading

In the Peer Assisted Learning Strategies (PALS) program developed at Vanderbilt University (Fuchs, Fuchs, & Burish, 2000), which has been used with students from kindergarten through high school, teachers pair each student with a partner for about 35 minutes a day, three days a week. Pairs usually include one strong and one less strong reader ("a coach and a player" or "an admiral and a general"), and pairings are changed routinely. The stronger reader first reads the passage aloud to the tutoring partner for five minutes. Then the weaker reader reads the same passage aloud for five minutes. While one partner is reading, the other follows along and corrects errors as needed.

At the end of the reading session, students engage in a two-minute Retell session in which both readers ask each other, "What did you learn first?" followed by, "What did you learn next?" In the next segment (Paragraph Shrinking), each partner (1) names the most important person or thing (the "who" or "what") in the passage; (2) states the most important thing about the who or what; and (3) explains the main idea of the passage in 10 or fewer words. If a student makes an error, the partner says, "No, that's not quite correct" and encourages the student to skim the passage for the answer. The last segment (Prediction Relay) has four parts: (1) predicting what will happen next, (2) reading the next half-page of material, (3) checking whether the prediction came true, and (4) addressing the items from the Paragraph Shrinking step.

The PALS program can be a successful strategy for accommodating students with diverse learning needs and increasing the achievement of the entire class (Fuchs & Fuchs, 2005; Sáenz, Fuchs, & Fuchs, 2005). Educators have successfully implemented similar approaches on the secondary level, including math (Calhoon & Fuchs, 2003); world history (Mastropieri, Scruggs, Spencer, & Fontana, 2003); and middle school English (Mastropieri et al., 2001).

Differentiated Curriculum Enhancements

Differentiated instruction involves modifying curriculum, tasks, or approaches to address diverse needs (Gartin, Murdick, Imbeau, & Perner, 2002). In a model we call Differentiated Curriculum Enhancements, students work on instructional materials differentiated by (1) practice time, (2) embedded strategic information, or (3) levels of difficulty.

Differential practice time. We implemented classwide peer tutoring in four middle school history classes (Mastropieri, Scruggs, Marshak, McDuffie, & Conners, 2006). Of the 55 students involved, 15 had disabilities. We carefully matched students with disabilities with typically achieving peers on the basis of teachers' perceptions of students' abilities to work together. The assigned pairs worked together for the duration of the project.

In collaboration with teachers, we identified important content that would appear on the end-of-year high-stakes tests and developed practice sheets to help students review this content. Tutors asked tutees questions from the practice sheets and laid aside those that the tutee correctly answered. When students had difficulty recalling the information, tutors put the sheet in a separate file for later review. Tutoring pairs moved on to a new set of fact sheets when the tutee mastered the previous set. Tutoring pairs worked on each set of fact sheets for different amounts of time, depending on how much practice the tutee needed.

Unit tests revealed that students in the peer-tutoring classrooms significantly outperformed students in comparison classrooms in which students reviewed the same content independently. Students with learning disabilities in the tutoring classroom were more likely to achieve scores that were similar to those of normally achieving students than were their counterparts in the comparison classes.

Embedded strategic information. When we employed classwide peer tutoring in inclusive high school chemistry classes, we suggested several strategies that peer tutors were to use only if tutees needed help (Mastropieri, Scruggs, & Graetz, 2005). The two classes studied consisted of 39 students, 10 of whom had disabilities. Students questioned their partners on important content (for example, What is a mole? [a unit of weight]) and prompted each other to provide more elaborate responses (What else is important to know about moles?). If tutees knew the correct answers, the tutors provided feedback and proceeded to the next set of questions. If students had difficulty, tutors provided a strategy to help them remember the content. For the mole example, the tutor displayed a picture of a mole (the animal) sitting on a scale and said, "Think of the word *mole*. Then, think of this picture of a mole on a scale looking at his weight in grams. It will help you remember that a mole is the atomic weight of an element in grams." When the tutee provided the correct information, the tutor moved on to the next question. Tutoring supplemented regular classroom instruction, taking up about 15–20 minutes of a 90-minute class.

Students took pre- and post-tests consisting of factual and comprehension items. Although students without disabilities significantly outperformed those with disabilities, all students who participated in tutoring significantly outperformed those who did not. Gains were particularly strong among students with disabilities. They outperformed nontutoring students with disabilities by 42.5 percent (compared to only a 16.2 percent difference between tutoring and nontutoring students without disabilities).

Increasing levels of difficulty. Teachers can also differentiate materials according to level of difficulty, as we saw in our study of inclusive middle school science classes (Mastropieri et al., in press). This study included 13 8th grade classes containing a total of 213 students, 14 of whom were classified as having disabilities and 35 of whom were English language learners.

Student pairs studied charts and graphs, measurement, independent and dependent variables, and qualitative and quantitative research methods. We developed materials at three levels of difficulty for each topic. At the least difficult level, students identified science concepts (for example, independent and dependent variables) with the help of prompts included in the materials. The middle level contained prompts that tutors were to share only as needed. The third and most difficult level of materials required students to respond without prompts. All students with disabilities and most English language learners started working with materials at level one and progressed to subsequent levels after mastering the previous level. Both students in the pair worked on the same level.

We implemented these procedures with 13 classes randomly assigned to experimental or control conditions over 12 weeks. Most pairs were able to successfully complete the activities. Pairs in close proximity sometimes helped one another, but students could ask the teacher for help if they encountered a challenge they couldn't solve.

All students took pre- and post-tests consisting of multiple-choice and open-ended items, along with end-of-the-year high-stakes tests. Overall, the average student in a tutoring class outperformed the average control-group student by 10 percent. The advantage was similar for students with and without disabilities.

Meeting Diverse Needs

Today's teachers face significant demands, including the need to increase achievement and respond to diverse learning needs. Enabling students to help one another is an important strategy for creating an effective and efficient inclusive classroom. With careful planning, monitoring, and evaluation, teachers can use these techniques to ensure that their classrooms accommodate students with a variety of learning needs.

References

Calhoon, M. B., & Fuchs, L. S. (2003). The effects of peer-assisted learning strategies and curriculum-based measurement on the mathematics performance of secondary students with disabilities. *Remedial and Special Education, 24*, 235–245.

Cushing, L. S., & Kennedy, C. H. (2003). Facilitating social relationships in general education settings. In D. L. Ryndak & S. Alper (Eds.), *Curriculum and instruction for students with significant disabilities in inclusive settings* (pp. 206–216). Boston: Allyn and Bacon.

Delquadri, J., Greenwood, C. R., Whorton, D., Carta, J. J., & Hall, R. V. (1986). Classwide peer tutoring. *Exceptional Children, 52*, 535–542.

Fuchs, D., & Fuchs, L. S. (2005). Peer-assisted learning strategies: Promoting word recognition, fluency, and reading comprehension in young children. *Journal of Special Education, 39*, 34–44.

Fuchs, D., Fuchs, L. S., & Burish, P. (2000). Peer-assisted learning strategies: An evidence-based practice to promote reading achievement. *Learning Disabilities Research and Practice, 15*, 85–91.

Gartin, B. C., Murdick, N. L., Imbeau, M., & Perner, D. E. (2002). *How to use differentiated instruction with students with developmental disabilities in the general education classroom.* Arlington, VA: Division on Developmental Disabilities of the Council for Exceptional Children.

Gillies, R. M., & Ashman, A. F. (Eds.). (2003). *Co-operative learning: The social and intellectual outcomes of learning in groups.* New York: Routledge Falmer.

Jenkins, J. R., & O'Connor, R. E. (2003). Cooperative learning for students with learning disabilities: Evidence from experiments, observations, and interviews. In H. L. Swanson, K. Harris, & S. Graham (Eds.), *Handbook of learning disabilities* (pp. 417–430). New York: Guilford.

Johnson, D. W., & Johnson, R. T. (1986). Mainstreaming and cooperative learning strategies. *Exceptional Children, 52*, 553–561.

Mastropieri, M. A., Scruggs, T. E., & Graetz, J. (2005). Cognition and learning in inclusive high school chemistry classes. In T. E. Scruggs & M. A. Mastropieri (Eds.), *Cognition and learning in diverse settings: Advances in learning and behavioral disabilities* (Vol. 18, pp. 107–118). Oxford, UK: Elsevier.

Mastropieri, M. A., Scruggs, T. E., Mantzicopoulos, P. Y., Sturgeon, A., Goodwin, L., & Chung, S. (1998). "A place where living things affect and depend upon each other": Qualitative and quantitative outcomes associated with inclusive science teaching. *Science Education, 82*, 163–179.

Mastropieri, M. A., Scruggs, T. E., Marshak, L., McDuffie, K., & Conners, N. (2006, April). *Peer tutoring in inclusive history classes: Effects for middle school students with mild disabilities.* Paper presented at the annual meeting of the American Educational Research Association, San Francisco.

Mastropieri, M. A., Scruggs, T. E., Mohler, L., Beranek, M., Boon, R., Spencer, V., & Talbott, E. (2001). Can middle school students with serious reading difficulties help each other and learn anything? *Learning Disabilities Research and Practice, 16*, 18–27.

Mastropieri, M. A., Scruggs, T. E., Norland, J., Berkeley, S., McDuffie, K., Tornquist, E. H., & Conners, N. (in press). Differentiated curriculum enhancement in inclusive middle school science: Effects on classroom and high-stakes tests. *Journal of Special Education.*

Mastropieri, M. A., Scruggs, T. E., Spencer, V., & Fontana, J. (2003). Promoting success in high school world history: Peer tutoring versus guided notes. *Learning Disabilities Research and Practice, 18*, 52–65.

McMaster, K. N., & Fuchs, D. (2002). Effects of cooperative learning on the academic achievement of students with learning disabilities: An update of

Tateyama-Sniezek's review. *Learning Disabilities Research and Practice, 17,* 107–117.

McMaster, K. N., & Fuchs, D. (2005, Spring). Cooperative learning for students with disabilities. *Current Practice Alerts, 11.* Available: www.teachingld.org/pdf/alert11.pdf

Sáenz, L. M., Fuchs, L. S., & Fuchs, D. (2005). Peer-assisted learning strategies for English language learners with learning disabilities. *Exceptional Children, 71,* 231–247.

Slavin, R. E. (1991). Synthesis of research on cooperative learning. *Educational Leadership, 48*(5), 71–82.

Slavin, R. E., Hurley, E. A., & Chamberlain, A. (2003). Cooperative learning and achievement: Theory and research. In W. M. Reynolds & G. E. Miller (Eds.), *Handbook of psychology: Educational psychology* (Vol. 7; pp. 177–198). Hoboken, NJ: John Wiley and Sons.

Margo A. Mastropieri is a Professor of Special Education in the College of Education and Human Development at George Mason University, Fairfax, Virginia; 703-993-4136; mmastrop@gmu.edu. **Thomas E. Scruggs** is a Professor of Special Education at George Mason University; 703-993-4138; tscruggs@gmu.edu. **Sheri L. Berkeley** is a graduate student at George Mason University; 703-993-3850; sberkele@gmu.edu.

Originally published in the February 2007 issue of *Educational Leadership, 64*(5), pp. 54–58.

Silence Is Golden

Judith Gaston Fisher

Leading students in weekly mindfulness meditation helps them learn to calm their emotions and focus their thoughts.

It's Monday morning, a time when many students and teachers might exhibit lethargy. But the faces of my students don't reflect dread of the coming week. They greet one another with smiles that say, "Yes! It's Monday!"

To begin their school week, students turn their chairs to face the wall, put their hands on their knees, and wait for the music to commence. This action signals their readiness to begin Monday morning meditation. We all sit up straight, relax our muscles, and focus on deep "belly breathing." For the next 10 minutes, we settle into silence and a reprieve from external pressures.

My students, participants in a program called the Learning Center at the Community School in St. Louis, Missouri, need this reprieve. Selected students from the school's 3rd through 6th grades come to the Learning Center four times a week for 30- to 40-minute help and enrichment sessions. My room is full of students needing extra attention. Before I initiated a meditation routine, many of these learners lacked both calm and focus. Some have an official diagnosis like ADHD, some need help with a particular topic or project, and others struggle with organizing academic tasks or even their backpacks. ("I can't find my planner." "I *know* I turned in that missing assignment.") A few come to my classroom because of social issues: They feel left out or even angry that they aren't accepted by their peers.

Educators are familiar with the challenge of teaching students with widely different strengths and problems. During my years of teaching, I have benefited from many helpful methods for tailoring teaching to diverse students. I've planned lessons and activities that touch on Howard Gardner's nine intelligences (1991), and I've followed Carol Ann Tomlinson's approach of differentiating content, process, and assessments according to student readiness and interest. (Tomlinson & McTighe, 2006).

Still, for many years I felt that a sense of readiness, of wholehearted participation, was missing. I wanted my students to be engaged, but like many teachers, couldn't identify what was standing in their way.

Overscheduled and Overwhelmed

As I considered this question, I observed my students' lives. I saw hurried children caught in a fast-forward pace. Wake up, grab breakfast, get dropped off at school, travel from one class to another, jump in the car, go to your tutor, hit horseback riding before dinner, and in the evening practice soccer (or tennis, singing, or piano). Add in homework, elaborate birthday parties, keeping up by e-mail and text message, and—for some kids—shuttling between mom's house and dad's house.

I considered pediatrician Mel Levine's (2003) claim that many children today are exhausted, even sleep deprived. What I perceived as my students' lack of motivation was instead, I concluded, a response to stress that was sapping their attention.

Scientific research has increasingly focused on the visceral experience of stress. The Social Readjustment Rating Scale (SRRS) identifies and assigns value points to 43 common stressors occurring in adult life, ranging from death of a spouse (100 points) to receiving a traffic ticket (11 points). An individual subjected to a stressor rated as low as 25 points will undertake coping strategies (Harrington, 2008).

We don't have the equivalent of an SRRS scale for children, but surely stress affects them, too. If we were to construct such a scale focused on students' worlds, I imagine it would include the following events:

- Moving
- Changing schools
- Parental pressure to perform in school or in an extracurricular activity
- Lack of sleep
- Losing a pet
- Parents getting divorced
- Being bullied
- Social isolation

Knowing that my students experience such pressures—and suspecting that packed schedules aggravate the punch that each event packs—I pondered the consequences. I wondered if students might feel perpetually overwhelmed. Some young people with alternative learning styles seem to be particularly susceptible to getting overwhelmed by internal and external stimuli in a way that causes focusing problems.

The human body is meant to experience the physical components of stress—pounding heart, racing pulse, a surge of cortisol and adrenaline, and a rise in insulin and blood pressure—as warning symptoms in emergencies. But on a day-to-day basis, these symptoms are harmful (Benson, 2004). Many adult health problems—stomach ulcers, insomnia, and migraines, to name a few—are connected to stress. What if the pressures many children feel also hurt their health—and sap their ability to think and learn well?

My question became, How can I get my students to relax? Although I couldn't make their lives stress-free, I thought a weekly meditation session might help them experience the physical, emotional, and social benefits of stepping back from constant activity and calming their minds. So, tentatively, I began teaching them the art of silence.

Guiding Meditation

I instruct students in a meditation approach called mindfulness, focusing on four components: awareness of the present moment, conscious deep breathing, visualizations, and affirmations. To begin, I guide students in positioning their bodies to be relaxed and alert and to focus on rhythmic breathing. I read aloud meditative passages I have created that help them get into this relaxed, alert state or visualize pleasant and empowering scenes, such as the following:

> Place your hands on your knees. Close your eyes. Imagine a string connected to the ground, moving up your spine, and emerging at the top of your head. Feel the pull of the string causing your back to become straighter, your shoulders to drop, and your chest to push forward.

> Relax your eyes. Let your jaw open as you let go of the tension in your mouth. Relax your neck and shoulders. As they relax, your shoulders will drop into your torso. Let the tension go from your chest. . . . As your stomach relaxes, it will push forward just a bit. Relax your buttocks, your legs, and your feet. Now scan your body for any sign of tension and let it go. Your body is as heavy as lead.

As students turn their focus within, their minds stop jumping around. Meditation is about training oneself to live in the present instead of dwelling on the past or worrying about the future. Focusing on your breath or concentrating on a sound or phrase helps achieve this awareness of the present:

> Begin slow and deep breathing. To the count of six, bring in a slow, steady breath of fresh air into your belly and lungs. Let go of the breath to the count of six, releasing the impure air that has been trapped in your pores and cells. In the next breath, imagine the air as a color. Watch the color slowly move to all

parts of your body. As you release the air, see the impurities disappear into the surrounding sky.

What's Happening As Students Meditate

According to research, getting into a meditative state not only relaxes people, but also counters the negative physical effects—and the barriers to learning—that chronic stress produces (Benson, 2004). It may even improve the emotional state. University of Massachusetts researchers Richard Davidson and Jon Kabat-Zinn have reported that individuals with high levels of brain activity in the left prefrontal cortex exhibit overall feelings of enthusiasm, joy, energy, and alertness, whereas individuals with more activity in the right prefrontal cortex feel greater tension and stress and are more prone to depression and disease (Goleman, 2003). In one study involving 41 adults, after subjects practiced mindfulness meditation for eight weeks, their brains showed increased activity in the left prefrontal cortex and they reported a happier state of mind than did control subjects (Kalb, 2004).

I sometimes lead students in guided visualizations designed to increase their focus and positive mood:

> You are in the desert. The sky is blue with only wisps of clouds on the horizon. The sun is bright. You feel the wind on your face and through your hair as you lift your eyes and inhale the freshness of the day. Small and giant cacti are in full bloom. . . . You are struck by the stark beauty of the desert as sagebrush blows from one place to another.

Meditation often gives students the ability to shift thoughts into a more positive state. They use these new habits of mind to avoid self-defeating thoughts that once impeded their potential. We've experimented with using *affirmations*, positive thoughts and words that can lead to positive feelings and, in turn, better actions.

Each student selects an affirmation—such as "I pay attention in class" or "I complete my homework." We create bookmarks containing these affirmations, and I urge students to recite them to me as they enter the classroom. They repeat key words from their affirmations and repeat them during our meditation sessions. Amazingly, their behavior often comes into line with their affirmation.

For example, Susannah often struggled with anger and self-control in our classroom. She chose as her affirmation, "I am a calm and beautiful person." As she continued to declare this phrase to herself—and at times to the whole class—she indeed became more calm and considerate.

Observable Benefits

My observations, brief surveys, and comments from students, teachers, and parents tell me that my students are benefitting vastly from doing morning meditations and using personal affirmations. My students have become more accepting of themselves and others, more focused, and more in control of their emotions. I have seen students identify "triggers"—emotions or behavior that in the past might have sent them spiraling into anger or fear—and avoid responding negatively to them.

My 6th grade boys were the first to share with me how meditation was affecting their daily lives. They'd say, "Mrs. Fisher, I know it's Friday, but can we meditate? I need to prepare for my baseball game tonight." Another boy reported that before a secondary school entrance interview, he asked his parents if he could sit in the car alone to calm himself.

One Friday, the 6th grade boys noticed that I was agitated and anxious. As I began to teach, they asked me to stop and confidently stated, "Mrs. Fisher, you seem like you need to get calm. We need some silent time so we can all be more able to learn. Can we meditate?"

But it was Susannah who let me know how significant this work was for her life. After three years of participating in Learning Center, she stopped me in the hall, a wide smile replacing the scowl that had once been her signature expression. "You know, Mrs. Fisher," she said. "These affirmations really work!" Susannah hugged me and skipped down the hall to join her classmates.

References

Benson, H. (2004, September 27). Brain check. *Newsweek*, 45–49.

Gardner, H. (1991). *The unschooled mind: How children think and how schools should teach*. New York: Basic Books.

Goleman, D. (2003). *Destructive emotions: A scientific dialogue with the Dalai Lama*. New York: Random House.

Harrington, A. (2008). *The cure within: A history of mind-body medicine*. New York: Norton.

Kalb, C. (2004, September 27). Buddha lessons. *Newsweek*, 48–51.

Levine, M. (2003). *The myth of laziness*. New York: Simon and Schuster.

Tomlinson C., & McTighe, J. (2006). *Integrating differentiated instruction and understanding by design*. Alexandria, VA: ASCD.

Judith Gaston Fisher teaches in the Upper Elementary Learning Center at the Community School in St. Louis; 314-503-7966; www.twitter.com/education_beat; jfcs900@aol.com.

Originally published in the December 2009/January 2010 issue of *Educational Leadership, 67*(4).

When a Student Dies

Michael Jellinek, Jeff Q. Bostic, and Steven C. Schlozman

An intervention mindful of the grieving process can help schools cope with the loss of a student.

Principals, teachers, and guidance counselors often feel ill prepared to address a student's death. The following guidelines can help a school meaningfully respond to an event that can profoundly affect the school and community.

Initial Response: The Crisis Team

The principal or an experienced school counselor should gather initial information about the death and discuss with the deceased student's family members which facts they wish to share with the school community. The focus of the communication with students and staff should be strictly factual, not speculative. Acknowledging exactly what is unknown is better than trying to fill in the gaps. To forestall possible negative behaviors, the message should publicly acknowledge the possibility of self-destructive reactions among students, such as having suicidal thoughts, or of undesirable actions, such as retaliating toward the driver if a student has died in a car accident. Suggest ways that staff members and students can address these concerns, include a promise for ongoing communication, and encourage questions and feedback.

A crisis team is a good starting point for planning communication (Kline, Schonfeld, & Lichtenstein, 1995). The team usually consists of the principal (the team leader), assistant principal, school psychologist/ social worker, guidance counselor, and one or two senior teachers. Include school nurses early in the planning process (Lohan, 2006), and ask a pediatrician or mental health consultant to take an advisory, not leadership, role. This team crafts the initial announcement; decides how to disseminate information; and alerts essential staff regarding schedule changes, meetings, setting up a crisis center, and so on. Initial planning may be as simple as a communication strategy, or it might be more complex if there is a threat of ongoing danger, multiple deaths, or public health concerns. If the deceased student's siblings attend other schools in the community, the crisis team should advise their principals.

It is preferable to notify staff members individually, perhaps through the faculty phone chain, to allow them initial privacy to contend with the death. The crisis team can then meet with faculty members, who typically need to address their own reactions before sharing the information with students. The principal or school counselor should lead this meeting in a smaller group setting rather than make an announcement in a large assembly or over a public address system. It is important to share information about the death with faculty, students, and parents in a timely manner before leaks and rumors spin out of control. Holding faculty meetings before and after school for several days can help monitor the school community and provide support.

How the School Reacts

The needs of students and staff members will depend on their relationship to the deceased, their coping mechanisms, and the circumstances surrounding the death (Thompson, 1990).

Student Reactions

Initially, the deceased student's closest friends will need support from a school counselor. The school might offer students repeated opportunities to talk together, in group lunches or after-school meetings, for example. If several students were directly exposed to the accident or suicide, they may need group opportunities to discuss their reactions. Students with a history of trauma and loss (for example, the death of a parent) or with a history of depression or other mood disorders will require frequent monitoring. In one case on which we were consulted, a classmate was particularly distraught after a 13-year-old girl died of cancer. A guidance counselor learned that this classmate's mother had died of breast cancer three years earlier. The guidance counselor sought the student out and contacted the family to alert them to the likely rekindling of grief and to the warning signs of depression.

Students and faculty respond on their own time lines, so the individual pace of denial, anger, despondency, or acceptance will vary widely (Ramer-Chrastek, 2000). As a result, school administrators must rely on students and staff as daily barometers to help them monitor how rapidly the school should resume a regular routine and how much time students and staff need to collectively grieve the loss. Generally, the structure of school helps the grieving process. A return to classes, homework, and routine activities is usually indicated within a few days (Noppe, Noppe, & Bartell, 2006).

Survivors each experience the loss in a different way, with unanticipated emotions often overwhelming their rational understanding of the death. Typically, *elementary students* worry most about the effect of the death on their immediate lives; they tend to benefit from reassurance that they are safe and their family life will not substantially change. *Middle grades students* are usually concerned about how they might have foreseen or even prevented this death, so they may benefit from a discussion of the facts surrounding the death and a clarification of their lack of responsibility (usually) in the death. *High school students* often worry about the finality of this person's death, and they will probably benefit most from a discussion of the meaning of the student's life and what will persist following the funeral.

Staff Reactions

Staff reactions will influence how teachers present information to students. An administrator or counselor should maintain ongoing communication with teachers and staff members who worked directly with the deceased student. This can help clarify which staff members are having the most difficulty and suggest additional interventions. In one instance, a teacher was particularly overwhelmed when a student died in an alcohol-related traffic accident. When the principal reached out to speak with him, the teacher described a family history of alcoholism that contributed to his brother's death in a car accident. The principal was then able to understand the teacher's reaction and encouraged outside counseling so the teacher could separate, but address, both events.

Why and Who's to Blame?

The death of a child or adolescent unleashes strong emotions. People often try to soothe themselves by searching for an answer or relief from the feelings of loss and risk. Many find temporary relief by focusing intense feelings of anxiety, blame, anger, and guilt in the form of an attack on some individual thought to be responsible. The tone and content of communication from the crisis team can anticipate some of these reactions and redirect students back to grieving and a reasonable discussion of life's risks.

Accidents

Accidents are particularly difficult because of their suddenness, but also because of the perception that someone might have been able to prevent them. Blame may settle on a teacher who didn't notify the principal's office about a student who skipped a class and later died in a car accident. People may blame other students who survived the accident but encouraged the driver to skip, drink, or look away from the road. In accidents in which some students survive and others do not, educators should anticipate and attempt to prevent students from taking action against surviving students out of a sense of misguided loyalty (Twemlow, Fonagy, Sacco, O'Toole, & Vernberg, 2002). This is particularly important, given the increased risk of violence in students who have been bullied at school (Anderson et al., 2001). In such cases, schools need to indicate to students how they may express their loyalty in more meaningful ways.

Suicide

The suicide of a child or adolescent occurs more frequently during the spring semester ("Temporal Variations," 2001). Because details of the suicide frequently become a focus of attention, it is important to provide brief, accurate information that has been cleared with the family (for example, "Tracy died from a gunshot wound"). Posing such questions as, What do you think Tracy would want us to be talking about? or, How will it be helpful for us to talk about these details? can redirect students' efforts to obtain more details or personal information. Those close to the student often believe that they missed or failed to respond to signs from the student. In addition, faculty and students often believe they may have said or done something that contributed to the suicidal act (for example, assigning too much homework).

The anger following a suicide is frequently displaced from the victim toward other students or staff (Newman, 2000), increasing the likelihood of assaults or additional self-harming acts. Contacting students close to the victim and examining their reactions privately may reveal the role they perceive themselves to have played in the suicide or any thoughts they may harbor about engaging in self-destructive behavior out of loyalty to the victim. A suicide also increases the risk of self-destructive behavior in those suffering from depression or who have attempted suicide in the past (Weinberger, Sreenivasan, Sathyavagiswaran, & Markowitz, 2001).

The closeness of the suicide makes the act a more realistic option in the minds of some adolescents. Some students, especially those feeling unpopular or isolated, may be drawn to suicide because of the community reaction, which can seem to glorify the deceased student. Guidance counselors often feel under pressure to prevent the contagion of suicide and monitor all vulnerable students. In a high school of 1,000 adolescents, statistically 100 or more are particularly vulnerable. It is helpful to tell the guidance staff the truth: Predicting suicide is practically impossible; the most school counselors can do is monitor the students at risk.

Chronic Illness

Chronic illness resulting in a student's death is sometimes less traumatic to a school, particularly if surviving students were prepared and had opportunities to say good-bye. Still, some staff members and students may not have believed that the student would really die; they may feel cheated by God because their prayers went unanswered. Students of all ages sometimes fear they might "catch" whatever caused the chronic illness and then feel guilty for having avoided that student. Discussions should acknowledge student guilt and fears as well as address how people can contend with severe or chronic illnesses (Ramer-Chrastek, 2000).

Student deaths from chronic illness are often more difficult for adults, who experience a different version of survivor guilt as they question the meaning of death for someone who will never experience the joys of childhood, adolescence, or adulthood. Such adults may need help recollecting the joys the dying student already has experienced; focusing on the joys the student can still experience while he or she is still sufficiently healthy (for example, Make-A-Wish programs); and recognizing that these students may not have "missed" certain joys that they never thought about.

The Timetable of Grief

Grieving is a process, not an event (Brock, 2001). Unfortunately, administrators may sometimes prematurely attempt to reestablish the normal routine. This often comes off as lacking in compassion, so it is helpful for administrators to talk with those who knew the student best to assess the mood of the school. Staffing a designated room with clinical personnel can be helpful for at least five days after the death. Schools sometimes decide to stay open on the first weekend after the death to provide a supervised place for those who wish to gather there.

Schools should also provide a book in a designated office where students can come in and write to the deceased's family. This is preferable to placing pictures or newspaper articles about the death in prominent places where students must confront their feelings every time they walk by. Such a book should usually be available to students for about four weeks. Appropriate staff members can monitor writings to ensure they will be helpful to the family and to spot students who may be experiencing more-than-usual difficulty with the death. Similarly, encouraging a student to commemorate loss through some form of participation, such as drawing pictures or planting a tree, promotes inclusion in the process and provides a meaningful ritual (Gibbons, 1992).

Because it is normal to respond initially with denial and avoidance to an overwhelming event, posttraumatic debriefing should be available between 24 and 72 hours after the event. One should never force a discussion, but rather provide open conversation and exploration of the powerful feelings that shared traumatic events create.

The crisis team should gather information from the faculty meetings, counseling staff, nurse, message book, parents association, and their own conversations. The team can then plan letter and e-mail communications to students, faculty, and parents regarding such matters as the school's schedule, funeral arrangements, memorials, and meetings.

Someone on the crisis team also needs to take responsibility for managing the large number of well-intentioned parents, volunteers, and mental health experts who may appear at the school to offer help. The designated person should organize the efforts so they are compatible with the crisis team's plans and check credentials of any grief counselors, thus maintaining control. Students need protection—at least at the school—from intrusions by the media and inquisitive others.

Initial and Long-Term Memorials

A memorial, the formal acknowledgement and lasting recognition of someone's death, is a vital aspect of how we grieve. Planning a memorial can productively channel energy, be profoundly educational, and communicate key values.

The crisis team should define the location and likely duration of the initial memorial. For example, having flowers and notes at the school entrance; alerting students that the press will have access to the memorial outside of the school (not inside); and deciding how long the memorial will stay in place (usually several days) help organize students and staff. The principal should designate a site inside the building, such as a large bulletin board, for notes and pictures. The deceased student's locker and desk are often painful, personal sites and are thus less appropriate.

Placing memorials in areas where they serve as constant reminders of the death can be problematic. It is often helpful for the principal or school counselor to meet with the deceased student's friends to talk about the scale and duration of memorials, especially if they are in public corridors or classrooms. Contact with the family to clarify and respect their wishes facilitates community cohesion.

Grieving students or faculty should take their time before deciding on longer-term memorials, such as scholarships. They need to address such questions as, How will we keep this student's name alive in the school? How will we honor this person's memory? What life lesson does this student's life—and death—provide? How can this death lead to expansion of helpful choices for all future students? The most effective memorials connect generations of people by illuminating cherished principles or aspects of the deceased person's life that remain meaningful for us all.

What We Can Learn

Each tragic death offers a window into the school's culture. Any problem in that community—a poor relationship between faculty and administration or too much emphasis on a single aspect of the school's goals (on academics or sports, for example)—will come to the fore and complicate the school's coping with the death.

Each death also kindles a reexamination of the vital teachings of the school. An anniversary ceremony is the final step in the recovery plan and reflects the school's values in terms of remembering, doing, repairing, preventing, and learning.

Authors' note: The authors wish to acknowledge the assistance of Faye Kurnick, Jodi DiNatale, and Judith Bygate in reviewing clinical strategies to address student deaths.

References

Anderson, M., Kaufman, J., Simon, T. R., Barrios, L., Paulozzi, L., Ryan, G., et al. (2001). School-associated violent deaths in the United States, 1994–1999. *Journal of the American Medical Association, 286*(21), 2695–2702.

Brock, S. E. (2001). *Suicide postvention.* Sacramento: California State University. Available: www.csus.edu/indiv/b/brocks/Workshops/NASP/Suicide%20Postvention%20Paper.pdf

Gibbons, M. B. (1992). A child dies, a child survives: The impact of sibling loss. *Journal of Pediatric Health Care, 6,* 65–72.

Kline, M., Schonfeld, D. J., & Lichtenstein, R. (1995). Benefits and challenges of school-based crisis response teams. *Journal of School Health, 65*(7), 245–249.

Lohan, J. A. (2006). School nurses' support for bereaved students: A pilot study. *Journal of School Nursing, 22*(1), 48–52.

Newman, E. C. (2000). Group crisis intervention in a school setting following an attempted suicide. *International Journal of Emergency Mental Health, 2*(2), 97–100.

Noppe, I. C., Noppe, L. D., & Bartell, D. (2006). Terrorism and resilience: Adolescents' and teachers' responses to September 11, 2001. *Death Studies, 30*(1), 41–60.

Ramer-Chrastek, J. (2000). Hospice care for a terminally-ill child in the school setting. *Journal of School Nursing, 16*(2), 52–56.

Temporal variations in school-associated student homicide and suicide events—United States, 1992–1999. (2001). *Morbidity and Mortality Weekly Report, 50*(31), 657–660. Available: www.cdc.gov/mmwr/preview/mmwrhtml/mm5031a1.htm

Thompson, R. (1990). *Post-traumatic loss debriefing: Providing immediate support for survivors of suicide or sudden loss.* Ann Arbor, MI: ERIC Clearinghouse on Counseling and Personnel Services. (ERIC No. ED315708). Available: www.ericdigests.org/pre-9214/post.htm

Twemlow, S. W., Fonagy, P., Sacco, F. C., O'Toole, M. E., & Vernberg, E. (2002). Premeditated mass shootings in schools: Threat assessment. *Journal of the American Academy of Child and Adolescent Psychiatry, 41,* 475–477.

Weinberger, L. E., Sreenivasan, S., Sathyavagiswaran, L., & Markowitz, E. (2001, July). Child and adolescent suicide in a large, urban area: Psychological, demographic, and situational factors. *Journal of Forensic Sciences, 46*(4), 902–907.

Michael Jellinek, MD, (mjellinek@partners.org) is Professor of Psychiatry and of Pediatrics and **Jeff Q. Bostic, MD,** is Assistant Clinical Professor of Psychiatry, Harvard Medical School. **Steven C. Schlozman, MD,** is Assistant Professor of Psychiatry, Harvard Medical School, and Lecturer in Education, Harvard Graduate School of Education.

Originally published in the November 2007 issue of *Educational Leadership, 65*(3), pp. 78–82.

Part 5

Teaching Values, Building Character

Democracy at Risk

Deborah Meier

School's most pressing job is to teach the democratic life.

Just because ancient Greece was a democracy doesn't mean that just anyone could sit in on Plato's seminars or Socrates' discourses. Or in the early days of America, that just anyone could vote for the U.S. Constitution. In democracies like these, only a tiny proportion of the population was eligible for full citizenship.

The small elite usually included white males with inherited incomes or members of the so-called "leisured classes." Only the leisured had time for the tough intellectual work—and networking—that democracy rests on. Only males were included because women were presumed not to think well outside of hearth and home. And only whites were represented because people of color were slaves and could hardly have leisure time, not to mention a vote on their own enslavement. Working people who weren't property owners were also not included.

From this societal structure followed certain ideas about schools and education. The 5–10 percent of the population who were privileged to vote were recipients of a special education—different from vocational apprenticeships—that focused on providing the ruling class with the special knowledge that it alone required.

Times have changed. Today, approximately 90 percent of all those 18 years old and older in the United States are eligible to vote. When 90 percent of all adults are presumably rulers, 90 percent should be getting that same "special" education. Or so it seems to me.

Schooling for Ruling

When democracy operated directly—more like old-fashioned New England town meetings—and the voters were all members of an esteemed network of adult males who knew one another face-to-face, much education of the elite occurred informally. This elitism in education remains true today. Only 10–20 percent of Americans receive the formal and informal education intended to produce a ruling class. As elite private and public schools boast, "We're here to educate the leaders of the future." They're not so interested in the followers.

Self-governance, so the rhetoric claims, refers to a governing body that is chosen of, by, and for the people. In modern times, although we've changed who "the people" are, we have not changed the road to peoplehood.

That's what schools ought to be doing—schooling for ruling. That's their singular public responsibility. There is no other place in modern life where ordinary people learn the trade of democracy—its particular body of knowledge, its particular skills, its "habits of mind."

Few and far between are the communities in which our young people witness democratic discourse, with its complex set of trade-offs. Seldom do young people see the justice system at work or how juries debate, except in glamorous TV shows. Few have heard of Robert's Rules of Order—unless they served on student governments. Most would find it startling that there are no constitutions governing democracy in many long-standing democracies, such as Great Britain. Most U.S. schoolchildren have been taught that "the majority wins" is the basic premise of democracy, although our own system breaks that rule over and over again. (Only one of the five central governing institutions in the United States—the House of Representatives—honors majority rule.)

Am I calling for more civics courses, and perhaps more attention to U.S. history? No. We remember about as much from those courses as we do from those in algebra and trigonometry or physics and ancient history. If we're lucky, information sticks with us until the final exam, and then gradually (or for some of us, quickly) it drops out of sight. Unless we are part of a community, club, or profession in which we continually practice such knowledge and skill, they never become habitual.

Moving Beyond Dependency

We need to create settings in which the young learn democracy firsthand, as we learn most things—by observation and imitation—and then gradually by more formal apprenticeships. This should include time to reflect on practice, read what others have thought, and develop alternative ideas.

Schools are uniquely suited environments for this. Who better than adult, well-educated teachers to practice and, by their example, teach democracy? If we don't trust teachers to make decisions about their own craft, how can we possibly claim to trust ordinary citizens to make decisions about matters far beyond their daily experience or skill? When we deprive teachers of a voice and vote—as we are doing today—we teach a lesson, but perhaps not the one we intended to teach: This hierarchical, top-down world that our young people encounter suggests that democracy is not an appropriate form of governance.

Parents and communities used to have a decisive voice through local school governance, but that was some time ago. When I was born, there were 200,000 school boards for a population one-third the size of the United States today. Now there are fewer than 20,000 school boards, and in the large population centers, these are chosen by the mayor, if they exist at all.

Today, few teachers or parents, let alone young people, are in a position to make authentic choices with real consequences. They often depend on decisions that are made far removed from them in ways they little understand. It's hardly surprising, then, that researchers and college faculty complain about students' lack of initiative in their own education. We've taught students the habits of dependency and compliance, with the apparent alternative being rebellion, not independence and thoughtfulness.

This is reversible. We need to scour the school day for choices that ought to belong to the learner, not just to the teacher, and for choices that ought to belong to the teacher, not just to the principal, school board, or state authorities. As students grow older, they can play apprenticeship roles in the governance of various aspects of school life. The same is true for preservice and new teachers.

Honing a Democratic Citizenry

Like many other members of the Coalition of Essential Schools, Mission Hill School in Boston, Massachusetts, follows this path from novice to full participating member. The school day is filled with options and strives to increase accountability for the wise use of such powers. Once a week, staff members meet to review any needed decisions—and no decisions are beyond their purview. These include matters as petty as establishing dress codes and revising schedules and as momentous as selecting overarching school themes and hiring teachers and leaders. At these meetings, staff members also present their curriculum plans to their colleagues and discuss breakthrough research.

Students are equally involved in school governance. At the end of 7th grade, students elect representatives to the School Governing Board, which consists of five students, five staff members, five representatives from students' families, and five members of the broader community. The board's most crucial decisions have to do with approving the school budget and selecting and evaluating the principal. Decisions require the approval of the majority of each of the four constituencies. In addition to this practice of decision making at the wholeschool governing level, all meetings—including staff meetings—are open to everyone, as are the minutes.

Even more important, we have designed all our courses to focus on the habits of mind that we think are most central to an informed and intelligent democratic citizenry, whether it's math, history, literature, science, or the rules that govern us in our hallways. Our five habits of mind include questions that we believe are at the heart of any discussion about policy, and they define a well-educated person:

- *Evidence:* How do we know what we know, and what's the evidence?
- *Viewpoint:* Could there be another point of view?
- *Connections/Cause and Effect:* Do you see any patterns? Has this happened before? What are the possible consequences?
- *Conjecture:* Could it have been otherwise? If even just one thing had happened differently, what might have changed?
- *Relevance:* Does it matter? Who cares?

Students need sufficient time in class to ponder such questions. For example, in our physics courses, instead of trying to cram all of physics into students' heads in a single year, we instead take a few central ideas and spend two years on them. Given this time frame, it becomes sensible to ask students to explore the controversies that these ideas produced in the setting in which they were discovered—as well as the ideas they replaced.

These five mental habits are not "taught" or memorized. But both teachers and students practice them over and over as we study our subject matter and live and work together. For example, when our faculty members select professional development, they must demonstrate to one another how the subject matter fits such habits. When students graduate, they must present evidence of such habits in all their work, showing that they are aware of other viewpoints and arguments and that they are resting theirs on evidence considered valid in the field. And when faculty members present their proposed curriculum to their colleagues, they must show that students will have ample opportunity to read and learn about different viewpoints, have access to a wide range of evidence, and be called on to look for patterns and make conjectures.

There are habits of work and heart, too, on which decisions rest regarding who "belongs," who gets left out, and what rules to honor most. When someone is hurt, for example, are we more concerned with punishing the wrongdoer or with helping the wronged?

And we talk, talk, talk. As adults, we share with students the way we negotiate the world, in more detail as they become closer to adulthood themselves. The school's central shared space—our "office"—is open to all; there, students may hear me arguing with someone from the central office or overhear collegial discussions. Instead of endlessly reminding students about how best to handle the mistakes they inevitably make, we often use ourselves as examples—how, for instance, I dealt with the police officer who stopped me for speeding and why what works for me might not work for them. We avoid saying things like, "It's not my decision" and "I had no choice." We look for opportunities to say, "Yes, we decided that." We want kids to become accustomed to taking responsibility for their choices, so we try to model that attitude as adults.

Our family conferences include the student—and we do not try to avoid disagreements in those conferences. Our aim is to reach agreement even if it takes time, even if it means more meetings. It's an attempt to use democratic-style thinking to live by. But above all, it's just a stab at doing what few of us have had an opportunity to experience before—being full members of an important membership-based community.

Living Democracy

Schools can foster these habits by teaching both basic academic subjects and specialized classes—like our schoolwide course on the electoral system—in ways that get to the heart of specific democratic dilemmas. Schools can teach these habits by the way they organize themselves into classrooms and structure school governance—and by the way they teach all members how to deal with restrictions that are beyond our control. When I am "caught" breaking a rule—for example, when a police officer motions me over for speeding—I share with my students my dilemma: I didn't make that rule, but I am responsible for how I handle having broken it.

Democracy is embedded in the work of living in a socially shared space, and it becomes a habit as we go back and forth between living it and studying it, over and over, and then passing on our accumulated wisdom to the young.

Democracy, as Winston Churchill reminded us, is a flawed and at times absurd idea, until one considers the far more flawed alternatives. From the viewpoint of students, most of life *is* that flawed alternative. For many students, schools are the only place where they might come to grips with why democracy may not be quite so absurd.

Deborah Meier is Senior Scholar and Adjunct Professor at New York University's Steinhardt School of Education; deborah.meier@gmail.com.

Originally published in the May 2009 issue of *Educational Leadership*, *66*(8), pp. 45–49.

"Hobo" Is Not a Respectful Word

Sarah Hershey and Veronica Reilly

Middle school students seemed blind to the homelessness and poverty in their own community. A well-designed service learning unit opened their eyes.

First-time visitors to San Francisco are often struck by the prevalence of homelessness. On a morning walk to work, it's common to pass by people requesting change, pushing shopping carts piled with all their possessions, laying out randomly collected items to sell, or curling up under a blanket atop a tattered piece of cardboard. For many San Franciscans, homeless people are just another piece of the city's fabric. Their high visibility renders them almost invisible.

Although homeless people could be found one block in every direction from the Chinese American International School (a K–8 school serving about 400 students, many from middle- and upper-class backgrounds), our students rarely seemed to notice them. We frequently challenged student comments like, "Why would you give someone change? They're just going to use it to buy drugs," or "You're dressed like a hobo!"

We were also concerned that so many students complained about having to participate in the school's community-service day. As a language arts teacher and a social studies teacher at the school, we wanted to help our students understand the realities and causes of homelessness and gain an appreciation for the value of service work. We decided to take a risk: to put aside the "traditional" curriculum for the last six weeks of 7th grade and substitute a service learning unit on homelessness and poverty.

Getting Started

Several elements distinguish *community service learning* from *community service*. The Web site of Learn and Serve (www.servicelearning.org), a program of the Corporation for National and Community Service, explains that

> service-learning combines service objectives with learning objectives with the intent that the activity change both the recipient and the provider of the service. This is accomplished by combining service tasks with structured opportunities that link the task to self-reflection, self-discovery, and the acquisition and comprehension of values, skills, and knowledge content.

To achieve these goals, we implemented the homelessness and poverty unit in a 90-minute daily block combining our 7th grade language arts and social studies classes. In language arts, students read short stories from the Junior Great Books anthology and analyzed them for details that might indicate the socioeconomic class of major characters, read oral histories of homeless Americans from Steven Vanderstaay's book *Street Lives*, and participated in minilessons on relevant skills in grammar and writing research papers. In social studies, they examined social, political, and economic factors that contribute to poverty, analyzed the concept of "class," and received minilessons on citations and bibliographies. We brought all 40 students together for such activities as the unit launch, introduction of research and oral presentation projects, speakers, field trips, culminating reflections, and planning an ongoing 8th grade service project.

We designed a pretest that incorporated national and local statistics about homelessness and poverty. The pretest countered stereotypes and piqued students' interest, and it also provided a basis for their first small-group project, "Myth vs. Fact" posters. Each poster challenged a stereotypical belief: All homeless people are drug users, homeless people don't have jobs, the only reason people are homeless is that they made bad choices, and so on. We displayed the posters throughout the school, and the following year we were delighted to discover that many students remembered seeing them as 6th graders and even recalled some of the myths and facts.

A week into the unit, we divided the students into small groups to choose research topics from a list of topics related to homelessness and poverty; these topics included mental illness, domestic violence, physical disabilities, housing, youth/families, health care, veterans, Hurricane Katrina, employment/minimum wage, the paths out of homelessness, societal attitudes and media portrayal, and global connections. Individual students then developed their own more specific research questions, such as,

- How accurate are the media's portrayals of homelessness?
- When do homeless victims of domestic violence seek help, and if they don't, why not?
- How has the Iraq war spurred veteran homelessness? Is there a significant difference between veterans returning from Iraq and from Vietnam?
- How does the health care system in the United States compare to those of other countries in terms of the effectiveness of services provided for homeless and poor people?
- Do states with a lower minimum wage have more homeless people than other states? Why or why not?

Experiential Learning

The unit included two major field trips. Students first visited the San Francisco Food Bank, where they learned about hunger in the city and packed thousands of pounds of food for distribution. The experience was so powerful in building community among the students and in developing a sense of making a real difference that one class elected to return to the food bank four times during 8th grade. With each visit, they set and met a goal of surpassing their previous foodpacking totals.

The second field trip was to a place familiar to the students: the supermarket. During the week before the trip, the students kept a record of the food they ate. On the day of the trip, they were assigned a hypothetical family of four, told that family's income and expenses, and asked to buy enough food for a week's worth of meals. Both hypothetical parents had full-time, minimum-wage jobs with full health benefits, excluding dental care. However, after deducting the costs of health insurance premiums, dental cleanings, braces, rent, car insurance, gas, taxes, utilities, clothes, and miscellaneous expenses, the family was left with only a small amount of money for food.

What students recorded in their ongoing unit reflection journals revealed that this exercise produced deep learning. Although some of our students came from families that experienced tight budgets similar to the hypothetical family, most lived in middle- and upper-class homes.

Students in the latter groups developed genuine empathy: "That was *so* stressful! It must really take a toll on parents who have to do that every week," or "I never realized how much food costs! I usually just go to the supermarket with my mom and throw stuff in the cart. I'll never think about the supermarket in the same way again." All the students learned about nutrition, how diet affects short- and long-term health outcomes, and the complicating factor of lack of access to affordable health care.

Conducting In-Depth Research

We invited three speakers: Jason Albertson, a clinical psychiatric social worker for the San Francisco Department of Public Health's Homeless Outreach Team; Clifford Sarkin, a Children's Defense Fund lawyer whose work focuses on expanding health care access for children in California; and Lisa "Tiny" Gray-Garcia, a poverty scholar, author of *Criminal of Poverty: Growing up Homeless in America*, and cofounder of *POOR Magazine/Poor News Network*. Collectively, the speakers gave students a deeper understanding of what it means to be homeless, what services are available to poor and homeless people, and how they can help end homelessness and poverty.

In tandem with field trips and speakers, students began to research their topics. We started them off with packets of information, including articles we gathered and materials from the National Coalition for the Homeless Web site (www.nationalhomeless.org).We also provided an annotated list of Web resources. Students researched their topics during class time, which enabled us to give them one-on-one guidance. The small-group setup facilitated student-to-student sharing; students often came across information that was not directly relevant to their own research question but that proved useful to a member of their group who was researching a different aspect of the same topic.

Because we allowed students to choose their general topic and specific research question, they were able to pursue subjects that were meaningful to them as well as relevant to the unit. Many students who were previously unengaged in class writing projects became engaged in this research.

One student who was researching how people qualify for government-funded health insurance printed out pages and pages of Medicare regulations, read them carefully, and asked us such specific, targeted questions that we had to recruit a lawyer familiar with health policy to help answer them. Previously, this capable student had done the minimum for many projects. Another student who normally struggled tremendously to get simple assignments done on time chose to research the major factors contributing to youth homelessness; this student spent hours poring over personal accounts of how different youth became homeless.

The research culminated in an individual research paper as well as an oral presentation by each small group. This allowed for a balanced combination of personal responsibility and group cooperation.

Publicly Sharing the Learning

After all their hard work, many students were eager to share what they had learned with others. The audience for the oral presentations included not only other students but also families, school administrators, and other interested community members. We encouraged students to be creative, to use at least one visual aid, and to have each group member speak for an approximately equal amount of time. Before the day of the presentation, each group gave a dress rehearsal to their own class to get teacher and peer feedback. This helped them troubleshoot and build confidence before their public performance.

Finally, on the appointed day, we gathered together. Students used PowerPoint, handmade posters, skits, movie clips, and quizzes to bring their presentations to life. Each group's presentation was about 10 minutes long and was followed by questions from the audience. This was sometimes the most difficult part of the presentation, but again and again students rose to the challenge. It was satisfying to see the pride and relief on students' faces when they stepped off the stage, because, almost invariably, they had performed incredibly well.

One group compared and contrasted clips from the South Park episode "Night of the Living Homeless" and the movie *The Pursuit of Happyness* as part of their media analysis. They also presented results from a survey they had created to assess the 6th–8th grade students' perspectives on homelessness. In observing that the 6th graders' views were overwhelmingly more negative and stereotypical than that of the 7th and 8th graders who had completed the homelessness and poverty unit, one group member concluded that the curriculum was responsible for the difference.

Taking Action

The research papers and oral presentations served as a springboard for the next step: action. Our school had traditionally made community service a graduation requirement, but the type of service was not specified or integrated into the curriculum. One of our major goals in this project was to transform the community-service requirement into thoughtful, engaged community service learning.

After the presentations, we sat down with both classes and discussed what action they wanted to take in response to their research. Through brainstorming and discussion, we narrowed our options down to a handful of possibilities and voted on a final action project.

During the first two years of the project, students chose to return to the San Francisco Food Bank multiple times to volunteer. Last year, students decided to follow the whole process of distributing food to hungry people in San Francisco: They made one return trip to the food bank in the fall, and they also planned to volunteer at a garden that grows food for the food bank and at a soup kitchen where food is distributed from the food bank in the spring.

Because we had the same students in both language arts and social studies for two consecutive years, we implemented the action project in the students' 8th grade year, following the research project year. (Schools where this is not the case could simply conduct the research project earlier in the year, leaving time to carry out the action project during the same year.)

The difference between student attitudes toward community-service activities before and after the unit was amazing. Previously, many students complained that their school community service was "child labor" and had "no point." Since launching this curriculum, students eagerly inquire about when we will be starting our planned action project, and they are dedicated and enthusiastic while working on it. The complaints about community service have disappeared.

Lasting Benefits

We initiated the homelessness and poverty unit in 2005 and have repeated it every year. Although only one of us is still working at the school, the curriculum persists. The short-term effects of the unit have been significant. Every year, we have seen students' attitudes and knowledge transform. Stereotypes and misinformation have changed into deep understanding and compassion. At first, some people were skeptical, fearing that the students would not acquire necessary academic skills through this unit. They soon saw, however, that students benefited academically from the critical thinking, academic rigor, student-centered instruction, and project-based learning that were at the unit's core.

Perhaps even more important, the project has had a lasting effect on many of our students. Several school alumnae who participated have told us that they continue to be involved with community service. Many students talk about an ongoing, increased awareness and concern about homelessness and poverty in their community and in the world. Some have said they now make sure to acknowledge people begging on the street (even if they don't give money); others have organized their families to give away unneeded clothing to homeless people living near their homes. One student even resurrected her religious community's food drive, which had virtually come to a halt.

The project has also had lasting effects on us as teachers. Like many people, we entered education because we wanted to make a difference in others' lives. There is no greater joy than seeing our students want to make a difference, too. We learned from our students and their research projects and were inspired again and again by their enthusiasm. To be sure, taking curriculum in new, uncharted directions involves challenge and risk—but this experience has reinforced our belief that some risks are worth taking.

Sarah Hershey is a middle school English teacher at the Bentley School and a diversity consultant with in Vision Consulting in Oakland, California; sarah@invisionconsulting.org. **Veronica Reilly** is a middle school language arts teacher at the Chinese American International School, San Francisco, California; very23@gmail.com.

Originally published in the May 2009 issue of *Educational Leadership, 66*(8), pp. 64–67.

No More Haves and Have-Nots

Joyce A. Huguelet

A North Carolina elementary school makes sure no students are left out of school activities.

At Winter Park Elementary School, the ice cream is free! This Wilmington, North Carolina, school's free ice cream is one of the many ways it puts the needs of the whole child first.

It all began with a change in plans. After 35 years in public education, I was preparing for retirement in 1997 when the opportunity to become the principal of a small school in an old building was more than I could resist. In the years previous, the Winter Park building and additional mobile units had housed almost 700 students. Everyone dreamed of the new building that was slated to open for the new school year. However, between the planning for and completion of the new building, the student body had already outgrown the new facility. Consequently, 300 disappointed students were left behind at the old Winter Park.

Although the building was old, the staff would be entirely new. A carefully selected panel of parents and educators looked for teachers with a passion for lifelong learning and a commitment to students.

Establishing Our Beliefs

Summer sessions before school began gave parent representatives and staff members an opportunity to explore our basic values and beliefs. We found commonalities that bonded us into a cohesive force for re-creating Winter Park Elementary. Making learning meaningful, addressing individual learning styles, and meeting the social and emotional needs of children emerged as the basic principles of the school mission statement: To provide an emotionally safe environment and meaningful learning experiences to develop joyful and productive lifelong learners.

Creating Equity

To provide an emotionally safe learning environment, we needed to level the playing field so students could focus on interacting and learning. We are a Title I school with approximately 45 percent of our students qualifying for free or reduced-price lunch. Our school district includes several trailer parks, one housing project, and several middle-class communities. We occasionally have homeless families in our district. Several practices soon came under scrutiny because they created haves and have-nots.

One the first school practices that we began to understand as unfair was the selling of ice cream in the cafeteria on Fridays. Parents managed the ice cream box, selling ice cream to students who could buy it. They began to tell me about the problem of students with no money wanting ice cream. Initially, the parents bought ice cream for those who did not have the 50 cents. That practice, however, proved unacceptable—not because of the financial burden on parents, but because of the discomfort it caused some students. A few parents got so upset that they refused to work at the ice cream box. (Good for them!) I considered cutting ice cream totally, but on investigation I learned that the Food Service Department needed the revenue from ice cream sales. The solution was to purchase ice cream for all children on two Fridays a month. Buying ice cream for all children twice a month generated enough funds to satisfy Food Service, and all students got to enjoy the treat.

We paid for the ice cream in several ways. Individual parents, businesses, or families made significant donations. One time we collected spare change to help pay for it. But the most support came from our parent teacher association (PTA), which began to include ice cream as a standard item in its yearly budget.

As we continued to look at our practices, we realized that our somewhat typical school often made students painfully aware of their lack of money. At the end of our second year, I began to question the practice of selling anything at school. One experience made a big impression. On the last day of school, students received their yearbooks, and small groups of students would bring their yearbooks to the office for me to sign. A student in one group said to me, "Mrs. Huguelet, I would like you to sign my yearbook, but I left it at home today." I knew very well that she had not bought a yearbook and that she was covering this fact up so the other children would not know that she could not afford one.

When I discussed this incident with parents and staff, they unanimously agreed to change another practice. Since that time, the PTA has provided yearbooks free to every student. The PTA keeps the yearbook simple and fairly inexpensive, but everyone gets the same free yearbook.

We also began to think about school supplies, book fairs, contests, and fundraisers. As we revised policies and practices, we always considered the socioeconomic levels of our families. Again, actual experiences often sparked action. One fall just before school started, a parent said to me, "I need to start looking at sales and going to different stores to find the best buys on school supplies." I asked her how much she paid for supplies for each of her children, and she said, "About $85." This parent was well able to buy supplies for her children, but I wondered about the parents who did not have that much money.

As we examined the situation, we found that by using funds allocated from federal, state, and local budgets the school could provide supplies for all the students. There were even some advantages for teachers. They could specify exactly what supplies students needed for their classes and know that all students would have them. I know that many schools find a way to provide supplies for students who cannot afford them, but the issue was not just whether students had supplies. It was about whether students could concentrate on learning and making friends instead of being distracted by the embarrassment of having less than their classmates.

Financial Support

You may ask how we pay for all the extras we provide for all students. Amazingly, when our school began to focus on practices that match our beliefs about children and public education, we were able to find the money. Funds from the state and district support some activities. The PTA, individual parents, and local businesses provide additional funds.

Our PTA established a fall "Make It Happen" campaign, during which the PTA asks each family that can to donate $35. Parents know they will not be asked to buy school supplies or participate in any other fund-raisers. The PTA tries to get as much participation from families as possible, realizing that some parents are financially unable to participate.

Additional Practices

The free ice cream, yearbook, and school supplies are only a few ways that Winter Park strives to promote equity among students. These are some of the other policies we've established:

- All field trips are free to all students.
- The T-shirts the school designs about every two years are free to all students.
- We never collect money from students for gifts for anyone.
- The school provides all supplies for required projects.

- When parents or any adults come to school for lunch, they eat cafeteria lunches. (Some working parents cannot bring fast-food lunches for their children; therefore, we ask all parents to refrain from bringing fast-food lunches to school.)
- Book fairs are held after school hours to avoid putting children in a situation of seeing books they want and not being able to buy them.

We also turned our attention to forced competition. Winning may have value for winners, but the negative effects on the losers makes competition in elementary schools questionable. Instead of promoting contests, we focus on celebrations, performances, and events that display and celebrate the talents of all our students. Recognizing that some students enjoy competition, we make contest information available to interested students. Pervasive competition has given way to a more collaborative and creative atmosphere.

From Philosophy to Practice

During my eight years at Winter Park, there was a major emphasis on professional development. Staff members formed study groups to read, discuss, and apply ideas from the best educators. The ideas of Alfie Kohn became very important to us. We studied *Punished by Rewards* (1993) and *Beyond Discipline* (1996), and we implemented his basic ideas.

We also spread the word by printing the following statement in our school and parent handbook:

> Staff and parents of Winter Park have a very specific philosophy about creating an emotionally safe learning environment at our school. We strongly believe that all children at our school should have access to all the benefits and activities that the school offers. No one should ever feel uncomfortable because he/she can't participate in whatever is happening at school.

Therefore, we do not ask students to bring money to school to buy anything or to pay for any activities. We provide everything free—from school supplies to field trips and yearbooks. The benefit to the school as a whole is that all children feel emotionally comfortable for learning and forming social relationships. Every person in our school community is equally respected and valued. All students and all adults are winners!

In the handbook, this statement is followed by a list of the specific practices we've implemented to ensure equity among our students.

An Emotionally Safe Learning Environment

A 1st grade teacher related a story of a student who recently transferred to Winter Park from another school. He said, "The day is so much shorter at this school." The length of the day is the same at both schools. Winter Park's focus on an emotionally safe learning environment is the basis for its success, and students such as this one have noticed the difference.

There are not many places in our society where children from diverse backgrounds have the opportunity to learn and interact without feeling uncomfortable. Our communities, our country, and the world need citizens who are educated, confident, and valued. We need citizens who have learned to value others from different economic, social, and ethnic backgrounds. Winter Park is making strides toward developing such citizens.

References

Kohn, A. (1993). *Punished by rewards*. New York: Houghton Mifflin.
Kohn, A. (1996). *Beyond discipline*. Alexandria, VA: ASCD.

Joyce Huguelet is former Principal of Winter Park Elementary School, Wilmington, North Carolina; huguelet@bellsouth.net.

Originally published in the May 2007 issue of *Educational Leadership*, *64*(8), pp. 45–47.

Waging Peace

Robert Blair

In violence-ridden Bogotá, Colombia, students are learning conflict-resolution skills in the elementary grades.

When Andrés is angry, he clenches his teeth and balls his hands into tight fists. The pose is familiar to both his teachers and peers—it means someone is about to get punched. Today, however, Diego grabs him by the elbow. "Use *Tuga la Tortuga*," he says. Andrés pauses, sits down on the floor, wraps his arms around his knees, and tucks his chin to his chest—a self-control strategy dubbed Tuga the Turtle. He breathes deeply. His rage is so strong that it takes him a minute to calm down. He stands up and returns to his seat. The class resumes.

Andrés and Diego are two 2nd graders with chronic aggression problems in the *Aulas en Paz* (Classrooms at Peace) program in Bogotá, Colombia. Aulas en Paz (AeP) is a primary school project designed to promote what the National Ministry of Education calls "citizenship competencies"—the basic skills we human beings need to interact constructively, democratically, and peacefully with one another (Chaux, Lleras, & Velásquez, 2004). By combining in-class lessons with workshops for teachers and home visits for parents, the project aims to integrate those skills into every arena of student life.

For 18 months, in 2006 and 2007, I worked with AeP as a Fulbright Fellow, helping to design, observe, and evaluate curriculum; train aspiring teachers; and disseminate the model to other cities in the region. The program is now being implemented in 50 schools in four conflict-torn areas.

In Colombia, the need for this type of program is undeniable. Nearly 50 years of armed conflict among leftist guerrillas, rightist paramilitaries, and drug traffickers has left in its wake a culture of generalized violence (Zuluaga, 2002). Students grow up surrounded by the tragic realities of civil war: massacres, assassinations, and forced displacement. Political and urban-youth violence reinforce each other, perpetuating the cycle of bloodshed (Chaux, 2003). If the armed conflict is ever to end, the new generation must learn to clamor for peace.

But AeP isn't applicable only in Colombia. The problems that the project addresses are universal. In the United States, violence in schools diverts limited resources to security and psychological services, disrupts the learning process, and claims dozens of lives every year. When teenagers are expelled or drop out, many end up in gangs or in jail. If we want to make our cities safe, we have to begin with our schools.

Most schools aren't able to muster the time and money needed to implement a program as intensive as Aulas en Paz, which involves several components: "citizenship competencies" courses for the whole class, workshops for select groups of students, and weekly visits and occasional phone calls to the families of students with the most severe aggression problems. AeP's multicomponent approach differentiates it from many other conflict-resolution programs, but it also tends to make the program time-consuming and expensive.

However, several lessons learned from the Colombian experience don't require any new resources—just a bit of effort and flexibility. Four lessons in particular can help transform the atmosphere of schools.

Lesson 1: Start Early

"My students can't do this," María says. She is a teacher in training in one of the more politically and geographically isolated barrios of Bogotá. In a few months, we will begin implementing one component of the AeP program in her public school. We've asked her and her fellow teachers in training for feedback, and some are decidedly skeptical. "These kids barely know how to read, and you want them to learn conflict-resolution skills?" she asks. "They're just too young."

María's doubts are understandable. Our experience, however, has taught us never to underestimate the capacity of children to grasp concepts and skills they can apply to their daily lives. The story of Andrés and Diego is instructive: Once kids recognize the relevance and effectiveness of conflict-resolution strategies, they typically internalize these strategies and begin to use them to resolve their own disputes. Describing emotions in specific terms ("excited" or "angry" rather than simply "good" or "bad"); using "I" statements; breathing deeply and counting backwards to control anger; showing simple gestures of affection to console a hurt classmate—these are techniques that students can learn as early as 2nd grade.

Research confirms what we have discovered through practice. Richard Tremblay, director of the Montreal Prevention Experiment, has found that children as young as 7 years old are capable of learning control of violent impulses and basic interpersonal skills, the building blocks of more sophisticated conflict-resolution techniques (Tremblay, Masse, Pagani, & Vitaro, 1996). Intervening early is especially essential if we want to curb aggressive behaviors before they become irreversible. According to Leonard Eron (1990), these behaviors "crystallize" by age 8. This finding is alarming, but it offers an important insight for intervention. Many of the teenagers who end up fighting, abusing drugs, and dropping out at age 15 were already hitting, biting, and calling one another names when they were 6 years old. We often wait to intervene until an adolescent gets into serious trouble. But by then it may be too late.

Lesson 2: Create Opportunities to Learn from Peaceful Peers

At a public school in a small suburb of Bogotá, teachers tackled the discipline problem by establishing a "time-out trailer": an unused storage shed adjacent to the playground where teachers send habitual rule-breakers to sit and do homework while they wait for the day to end. This practice follows the same seductive logic behind detention and in-school suspension in U.S. schools. At the expense of a few rough hours for the one unlucky teacher chosen to supervise the trailer, the rest of the faculty enjoys a productive day.

The problem with this system is that aggressive students encourage one another through a process known as *behavior modeling*. Grouped together in the same room for hours at a time, aggressive students tend to get *more*, not less, aggressive. They may even learn some new tricks. Teachers in Bogotá have told me stories of bullies teaching other bullies deviously creative ways to pick on their peers. Time-out trailers, detention, and in-school suspension are perfect set-ups for this negative kind of behavior modeling to occur.

As an alternative, AeP uses a model pioneered by Tremblay in Montreal called *heterogeneous groups*. Groups of six students—two identified as "aggressive" and the other four as "prosocial"—are picked to participate in after-school workshops. The small size of the workshops permits us to do a wide variety of activities with the kids, from role-playing games to art projects. We hope to achieve the reverse of the behavior modeling taking place in a time-out trailer: The aggressive students observe how their prosocial peers act in the classroom, and with a lot of coaching from the facilitator, they begin to adopt some of those positive behaviors.

The intimacy of the heterogeneous groups also helps the aggressive students build new relationships. This is important for the simple reason that friends usually don't bully friends. At the beginning of the year, we survey all the students who participate in the program, asking them to name their friends. The results are sad but unsurprising: Aggressive students tend to identify only a few of their classmates as friends, and those few are usually other aggressive students.

The effect of the heterogeneous groups is remarkable. Students who reported having only two or three friends at the beginning of the year identify as many as 20 or 30 by Christmas break. These gains are impressive even when compared with a control group.

But how can teachers replicate these successes in a regular classroom, where time and space don't always permit such individualized attention? They can begin by identifying the most aggressive and most prosocial pupils in the class. Most teachers do this instinctively. Those who are unsure can simply ask the students in anonymous surveys which of their classmates most often tease and bully (or help and defend) their peers. Students' answers almost always coincide with the assessments of teachers and school psychologists. The students know.

Teachers can use the answers to these surveys to organize lesson plans. For example, if the teacher notices that some of the most aggressive students in the class are also some of the best athletes, he or she might design lesson plans that help students analyze problems of aggression on the playing field. Or the teacher might intentionally pair an aggressive student with several prosocial students in group projects that demand a lot of communication among group members (analyzing a short story, for instance). Teachers can also use the information they have learned from student surveys to change the layout of the classroom. In the partner work, group projects, and seating arrangements, even a big, busy classroom offers many opportunities for aggressive students to learn from their prosocial peers.

Lesson 3: Give Students Ownership of the Rules

In Melisa's classroom, Miguel is galloping around the room while the rest of the class reads a short case study of a conflict between two friends. Camila notices and says, "*Kanorakú! Kanorakú! Kanorakú!*"

This is a mnemonic for *Cartelera de Normas y Acuerdos* (Rules and Agreements), the name the group has given to the rules they established for themselves on the first day of class. Miguel finally hears Camila, sees that the other kids are waiting for him, and returns to his seat.

Students are more likely to follow rules they define themselves. Even young children are capable of recognizing and creating rules to curtail behaviors that obstruct learning. The rule-making process begins with a brainstorming session; the students come up with several ideas, discuss them as a group, and pick a handful that will become the official classroom rules.

The rules are generally pretty basic at the start: Ask the teacher for permission to leave the room; clean up after yourself when you're finished with your snack; obey the teacher's hand signal that calls for silence. Rules are added or clarified as needed throughout the semester. For example, the students in one heterogeneous group would groan whenever someone made a point with which they didn't agree. With their teacher, they made a rule against groaning; the students would have to come up with another way of expressing their frustration.

Classroom rules should be specific and tailored to address discipline problems that the kids have observed in school. For example, a better alternative to "Be respectful" would be "Don't snatch things from other students." The kids should also decide on the consequences and punishments associated with breaking the rules. To do this, they must first be able to distinguish between these two concepts. A *consequence* is the effect of a lack of discipline on the entire class; a *punishment* is a sanction imposed on a particular student. The class might decide, for example, that students should raise their hands before they speak. They should be able to identify the consequences of breaking the rule—if they don't raise their hands before they speak, they won't be able to hear their classmates' comments—and define an appropriate punishment—the teacher won't call on a student who violates the rule the next time, even if that student knows the answer.

The list of rules hangs on the wall of Melisa's classroom as a visible reminder of the commitments that students made to one another as peers and friends. The students follow the rules because the rules are *theirs*.

By telling one another to "*Kanorakú*," students routinely call attention to these rules, thus regulating their own behavior. For many students, this is the first time they've been asked to reflect on the rules that govern their behavior and to decide for themselves whether or not those rules are worthwhile. They learn this process in time, with coaching from the teacher. The teacher consciously refrains from reminding students of the rules so that students will remind one another instead. However, if the kids seem to be using *Kanorakú* to gang up on a student who has trouble following the rules, the teacher will take control.

One strategy that we have found tremendously effective is giving the rules a catchy name. As in Melisa's classroom, naming the rules helps students appropriate them as their own. It also encourages them to view the class as a special club with its own unique language. At Melisa's school, we have heard students remind one another to "*Kanorakú*," even on the playground. We hope that students will apply the strategies we teach throughout the day, both inside and outside the classroom.

Lesson 4: Practice Is Key

One of the most basic instincts of teachers everywhere is to suppress conflicts in the classroom. Conflicts interrupt lesson plans, damage relationships, and threaten the physical safety of students and faculty. In the classroom, the need to maintain control can feel urgent, even desperate. Conflicts represent a threat to that control, so we try to smother them before they ignite.

By stifling conflicts, however, we forfeit one of the richest opportunities we have to coach students in the delicate skills of peacemaking. When quarrels arise, students too often defer to an adult who resolves the dispute for them. What the students don't realize is that they are capable of managing their own conflicts. All they need is practice.

This is the single most important principle underlying every AeP activity. Encouraging students to be respectful, tolerant, and well behaved is important, but it isn't enough. Neither is just discussing conflict-resolution techniques in class. Students need opportunities to put those techniques into frequent and conscious practice.

Often, students only get the chance to rehearse conflict-resolution skills when quarrels arise. These are volatile moments when emotions run wild. Students often let their anger, sadness, or embarrassment take over; in response, teachers often force an artificial reconciliation to prevent the dispute from spiraling out of control. Emotional outbursts, improvisation, and the need for a quick if superficial solution cheapen the learning process.

Students can effectively practice conflict-resolution skills during simulated disputes—through role-playing games, for instance. These usually involve conflicts between two or more fictional characters; students have to resolve the conflict themselves or with the help of a mediator. For instance, one role-play might involve two characters, one of whom promised to visit the other but never showed up. One character is angry because he purchased supplies for his friend's visit; however, the friend had a family emergency and was unable to go. The purpose of the game is to get both students to communicate how they're feeling and to understand why the other character acted the way he or she did. This can better equip them to implement those skills to resolve real conflicts.

Lessons for Us All

These simple lessons have proven invaluable to the success of the AeP curriculum. They cost nothing and require no new staff or materials. But they work, judging from the results I saw when using this 8-month program with 2nd graders. The number of observed "aggressive" events in the classroom and on the playground declined to one-fifth of their initial frequency. Prosocial behaviors (such as helping, consoling, and cooperating) increased ninefold. The frequency of interruptions in the classroom decreased threefold. Students who identified few friends at the beginning of the year identified many by the end. Most impressive, the program was implemented in a school located in the most violent neighborhood of Bogotá. By waging peace in schools like that, Colombian teachers can show us how to wage peace everywhere.

References

Chaux, E. (2003). Agresión reactiva, agresión instrumental y el ciclo de la violencia. *Revista de Estudios Sociales, 15*, 47–58.

Chaux, E., Lleras, J., & Velásquez, A. M. (2004). *Competencias ciudadanas: De los estánderes al aula.* Bogotá: Ministerio de Educación Nacional.

Eron, L. (1990). Understanding aggression. *Bulletin of the International Society for Research on Aggression, 12*, 5–9.

Tremblay, R., Masse, L. C., Pagani, L., & Vitaro, F. (1996). From childhood physical aggression to adolescent maladjustment: The Montreal Prevention Experiment. In R. D. Peters & R. J. McMahon (Eds.), *Preventing childhood disorders, substance abuse, and delinquency* (pp. 268–298). Thousand Oaks, CA: Sage.

Zuluaga, J. (2002). Guerra prolongada, negociación incierta: Colombia. In Roberto Briceño-León (Comp.), *Violencia, sociedad y justicia en América Latina* (pp. 339–367). Buenos Aires: CLACSO.

Robert Blair worked with the *Aulas en Paz* (Classroom at Peace) program in Bogotá, Colombia, as a Fulbright Fellow in 2006–07. He is currently a doctoral candidate in political science at Yale University; rblair82@gmail.com.

Originally published in the September 2008 issue of *Educational Leadership, 66*(1), pp. 32–37.

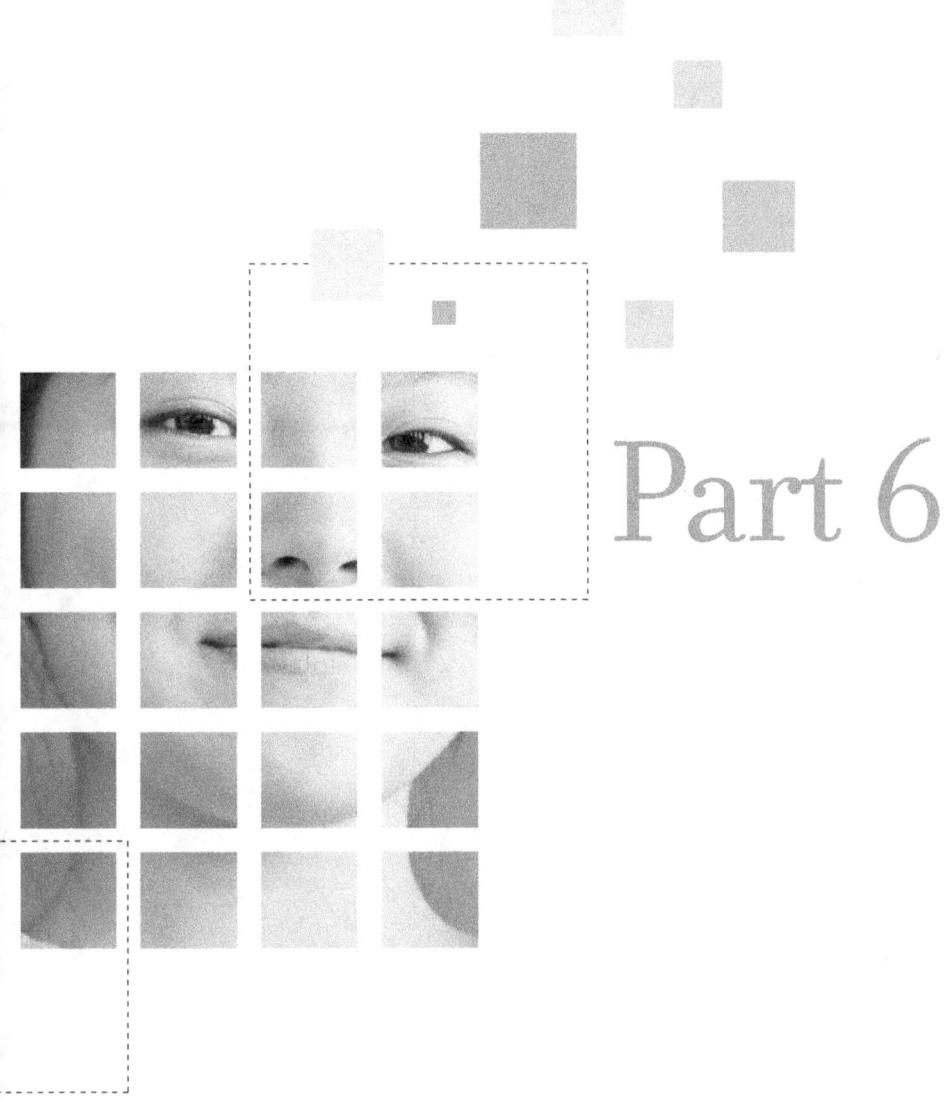

Part 6

Creating Healthy and
Safe Schools

Centers of Hope

Joy G. Dryfoos

Full-service community schools can improve the lives of children in poverty.

Schools are often blamed for the ubiquitous achievement gap between low-income children and their wealthier peers. But schools alone cannot fix a society that allows poor children to fail. To address the achievement gap in a meaningful way, we need to reach beyond the traditional school boundaries, involving the community in combating the effects of poverty on children and their families.

Full-service community schools are designed to do just that. According to Jane Quinn, Director of the Children's Aid Society's community schools effort, "Community schools *are* a poverty program" (personal communication, October 20, 2007).

A full-service community school remains open for extended hours, weekends, and summers, welcoming families and community members into the building for an array of services and activities provided by community agencies. Needs related to physical and mental health, dentistry, social services, after-school activities, and educational enrichment are addressed on-site. Usually, one community agency takes the lead and acts as the school's partner. A full-time coordinator from that agency works closely with the principal and the school staff to coordinate the services community agencies provide with what goes on in classrooms.

Growth of a Movement

The community-school concept is not really new. One hundred years ago in Chicago, John Dewey and Jane Addams were promoting collaboration and community involvement. Dewey believed that

> the significant thing is to make the school. . . . a centre of full and adequate social service [and] to bring it into the current of social life. (Dewey, 1978, p. 80)

The popularity of Dewey's model of the school as a "centre of social service" has varied during the 20th century. The latest wave of community schools started in the early 1990s. Between 3,000 and 5,000 full-service community schools are now in operation across the United States, according to one estimate (Wolfe, 2007).

My own discovery of community schools took place in 1992 at the Salome Urena Middle Academies (Intermediate School 218) in the Washington Heights area of New York City (Dryfoos, 1994). My work on high-risk behavior had led me to conclude that specialized prevention programs addressing such issues as drugs, sex, and violence were not sufficient to change the prospects for many children and youth at risk of failure (Dryfoos & Barkin, 2006). Along with enhanced educational opportunities, disadvantaged children also needed stronger supports. I was looking for an approach that would bring together all the health and social services disadvantaged children need and integrate them with instructional interventions and family involvement. I heard about the Children's Aid Society model at a meeting of the Carnegie Foundation's Task Force on Youth Development and wasted no time in arranging a visit.

Washington Heights had all the conditions typical of a poor innercity community: many new immigrants, low-wage jobs, two or three families sharing one apartment, substance abuse and trafficking, and high rates of teen pregnancy. In response to these problems, the Children's Aid Society, a large social agency, had created a community school model in partnership with the New York City school system (Moses, 2005).

Intermediate School 218, serving students in grades 5–8, was open for extended hours and offered a wide range of services. It had a health clinic with dental care (and later, mental health and eye care); an extensive after-school and evening program; significant parental involvement; and community-service projects that linked the classroom with the neighborhood. When I visited, I was impressed by the quality of the after-school program and amazed at the number of parents involved in school activities.

This design was replicated in a number of schools in the city, and the Children's Aid Society developed a technical-assistance capacity that has served hundreds of schools and communities in the United States and abroad.

At about the same time, similar programs were popping up across the United States, all designed to address the problems of disadvantaged youth and their families by extending school hours and bringing partners into the schools (Dryfoos, 1994). These initiatives included Full-Service Schools in Florida; Healthy Start sites in California; Beacons in New York City; United Way's Bridges to Success in Indianapolis; the C. S. Mott Foundation in Flint, Michigan; the Center for Community Partnerships at the University of Pennsylvania; and many others. In 1998, all this activity led to the formation of a national organization—the Coalition for Community Schools—within the Institute for Educational Leadership. Today more than 150 organizations are partner-members of the Coalition and are developing districtwide and statewide strategies to promote full-service community schools.

The Chicago Story

Chicago Public Schools, one of the largest school systems in the United States, serves more than 400,000 students in 613 schools. The district has become home to the largest community schools initiative in the

United States and is emerging as "the testing ground for the community schools concept" (Wolfe, 2007, p. 3). Superintendent Arne Duncan articulated the school system's rationale for creating community schools:

> Our schools are absolutely safe havens. . . . So what better place to engage the entire community and to get families working together, learning together? . . . As our schools become community centers, we're convinced that it is going to be extraordinarily beneficial to our students long-term. (Duncan, 2003)

Although various foundations and nonprofit organizations had been promoting community-school efforts in the city for many years—ever since the Polk Brothers Foundation implemented its Full Service Schools Initiative in 1966—it wasn't until 2002 that Chicago Public Schools formalized its efforts at the district level by establishing the Community Schools Initiative. By fall 2007, 115 community schools had opened their doors, and 25 more were in the works; 83 percent were elementary or middle schools, and the rest were high schools. These public schools have been transformed into centers of their communities, where families have access to medical and dental care, children take music and art lessons in enriched after-school programs, and parents receive job training.

Each school partners with at least one nonprofit organization, such as a Boys and Girls Club, the YMCA, or Hull House. The school building remains open in the afternoon and evening, on weekends, and into the summer. Each community school establishes a representative oversight committee or advisory board that is responsible for monitoring the programs that take place in the building. This group surveys students, parents, and teachers to find out what they would like to see offered at the school. A full-time site coordinator facilitates communication and coordination. The community school must link the social support programs to the school's academic program.

Funding

When Chicago launched its Community Schools Initiative in 2002, about $2 million was made available by the district and several foundations. Each selected school received $130,000: $50,000 for programs, $65,000 for the community partner, and $15,000 for evaluation. Today, the district supports its community schools with a diverse set of funding sources totaling approximately $16 million for the most recent year, 2007. These sources include federal grants, private foundation funds, public funds, and corporate gifts.

Evaluation

Now in its sixth year of implementation, the Community Schools Initiative is demonstrating the power of community schooling to bring about positive changes for students, families, schools, and communities. A number of indicators have improved, including grades, test scores, quality of homework, class participation, class behavior, and parent participation. According to one report, 81 percent of community schools are showing improvement in academic achievement, compared with 74 percent of regular schools (Blank & Berg, 2006).

The University of Chicago conducted a three-year evaluation of the Community Schools Initiative that documented best practices, examined patterns of participation, and evaluated outcomes for students and families (Whalen, 2007). All of the school buildings in the study are open until at least 5:00 p.m., about 43 percent are open until 7:00 p.m., more than half open several hours before school, and half provide programs on Saturdays. Almost two-thirds offer summer programming. More than 400 external partner organizations are involved in providing assistance with health and social services, youth development, arts and culture, recreation, and business. Several of these organizations are the lead partner agency in five or more school sites.

The report found that "students are receiving a balanced exposure to academic supports such as tutoring; academic enrichment in math, science, and literature; arts and cultural experiences; and recreational opportunities" (Whalen, 2007, p. 2). It concluded that the community school process is improving achievement levels, the quality of instruction, and the climate for learning, and that these effects are strongest among community schools that have been in operation the longest.

Lessons Learned

Chicago is well along on the road toward its ultimate goal—transforming all 600-plus public schools in the district into community schools with working partnerships. Of course, Chicago enjoys some unique advantages. The superintendent is unusually committed to the concept of community schools and is articulate and determined in the pursuit of this goal. In addition, Chicago benefited from the groundwork laid by major funders who had supported community schools in the city even before the Community Schools Initiative, creating models and evaluations that could be replicated.

But Chicago's experience also offers lessons that apply to other districts. It demonstrates what can happen in a large district when everyone gets on board and sticks with the goal. The mayor's office, major universities, foundations, community organizations—all have responded to the concept and joined forces within the schools.

Another significant lesson is the importance of the school principal in implementing a community school. Chicago principals receive ample orientation and learn how to bring much-needed services into their schools. Success in implementing the complex community-school model depends on relationships, starting with the principal's ability to communicate with partner agencies and negotiate policies—for example, who will take responsibility for keeping the school building open for extended hours?

The principal can also take the lead in integrating after-school enrichment with classroom activities. This essential integration requires that teachers and after-school providers spend time together linking after-school activities to the in-school curriculum. Because improved achievement is the goal, all the support services must be shaped to remove barriers to learning.

In some community schools, the services provided by existing school personnel (such as nurses and social workers) have not been coordinated with those provided by outside service agencies (for example, a clinic brought in by a community health center). Lack of coordination can create *silos*—support-service units that are not connected with one another or with the school's personnel. The school principal can help avoid this problem through careful planning at the start and continuous communication throughout the effort. He or she should also ensure that working teams include both school personnel and outside-agency personnel.

It would help the community-school movement if education schools would pay attention to the importance of collaboration, teaching school administrators how to work with community agencies. At the same time, social-work schools should make sure that social workers have the requisite skills to relate to educators.

Although research has documented various benefits of community schools, it has also found that student test scores are slow to improve. First, the school has to be transformed into an effective learning community, which requires at least several years of hard work on the part of teachers, administrators, service partners, and the broader community. The transformation process is labor intensive; it requires open communication, endless meetings, and a lot of patience. And even with all the extra supports provided by community schools, experience has shown that the quality of instructional leadership and professional development is still the key determinant of student academic achievement.

Hope for the Future

Our education system is not equipped to take on the responsibility for solving all our societal problems. Unless we change our approach, the achievement gap will continue to grow and poor children will fall further and further behind. That is why the concept of community schools needs to gain greater visibility among parents, school boards, school administrators, city administrators, major professional organizations, and schools of education and social work.

At the federal level, the outlook is positive. Much of the discussion around the renewal of No Child Left Behind indicates that future efforts will include parts of the community-schools framework. Senator Ben Nelson and House Majority Leader Steny Hoyer have introduced the Full-Service Community Schools Act, which calls for $200 million in new funding for community schools (Nelson, 2007). While citizens await action on that act, the Appropriations Committee has directed that $5 million be used for establishing full-service community schools. These funds will be allocated on a competitive basis to consortiums of local education agencies and community-based organizations. (See http://communityschools.org for further information on appropriations.)

Community schools offer hope. They bring together in one place an array of helping hands. They integrate social and health supports with educational enrichment. They teach low-income parents how to help their children do better in school and connect families to the resources they need, such as welfare, help with income taxes and citizenship processes, and even assistance in creating small businesses. In this process, the school becomes a hub, improving the safety and stability of the neighborhood. Those concerned with the improvement of education outcomes and the reduction of poverty would do well to take an interest in community schools.

Author's note: Adeline Ray, Community Schools Initiative, Office of Extended Learning Opportunities, Chicago Public Schools, provided information about community schools in Chicago for this article.

References

Blank, M., & Berg, A. (2006). *All together now*. Alexandria, VA: ASCD.

Dewey, J. (1978). The school as social centre. In J. A. Boylston (Ed.)., *The Middle Works of John Dewey 1899–1924, Vol. 2* (pp. 80–93). Carbondale: Southern Illinois University Press.

Dryfoos, J. (1994). *Full service schools: A revolution in health and social services for children, youth, and families*. San Francisco: Jossey Bass.

Dryfoos, J., & Barkin, C. (2006). *Adolescence: Growing up in America today*. New York: Oxford University Press.

Duncan, A. (2003, May 13). Remarks at the Coalition for Community Schools press briefing, Washington DC. Available: www.communityschools.org/CCSDocuments/ADuncan.pdf

Moses, C. W. (2005). History of the CAS model. In J. Dryfoos, J. Quinn, & C. Barkin (Eds.), *Community Schools in Action* (pp. 13–24). New York: Oxford University Press.

Nelson, B. (2007, May 15). Nelson and Hoyer introduce legislation to foster development of full-service community schools [Press release]. Available: www.bennelson.senate.gov/news/details.cfm?id=274370

Whalen, S. (2007). *Three years into Chicago's Community Schools Initiative: Progress, challenges, and lessons learned (executive summary)*. Chicago: University of Illinois. Available: http://cpsafterschool.org/CSI_Three.Year.Study_Dec_06_07_ES.pdf

Wolfe, F. (2007, July 23). Capitol Hill watch: Legislation could increase community schools' push. *Education Daily, 40*(135), 1, 3.

Joy G. Dryfoos is a researcher, writer, and lecturer who resides in Brookline, Massachusetts; jdryfoos@verizon.net. She is a founder of and advisor to the Coalition for Community Schools at the Institute for Educational Leadership, Washington, D.C. (www.communityschools.org).

Originally published in the April 2008 issue of *Educational Leadership, 65*(7), pp. 38–43.

A Full-Service School Fulfills Its Promise

Eileen Santiago, JoAnne Ferrara, and Marty Blank

*An elementary school gathers community partners
to alleviate the effects of poverty.*

Full-service community schools represent a promising education approach that improves learning by addressing students' overall social, emotional, physical, and intellectual needs. Ten years ago, Thomas Edison Elementary School in Port Chester, New York, took on the challenge of creating a full-service K–5 community school. By adopting this model, we have been able to raise the quality of teaching and learning in a school with a largely poor, immigrant population—and to improve the lives of students and their families. Our experience has shown us that schools can play a crucial role in helping students and their families overcome the challenges of poverty.

Although Port Chester is surrounded by affluent areas of Westchester County, our community is far from wealthy. More than 80 percent of Thomas Edison's students receive free or reduced-price lunch, and nearly 50 percent are English language learners. The majority of our families are recent immigrants from Hispanic countries.

Although community schools are more typically found in urban settings, the term *urban* has come to be associated with poverty as much as with geographic location.[1] With the influx of immigrants into suburban areas, poverty and its concomitant problems have steadily extended beyond the inner city into suburban areas like Edison's.

Many of Edison's students enter school with problems that affect their readiness to learn. Their families struggle to afford adequate housing, child care, nutrition, and health care. They also face the stresses that accompany immigration: worry about legal status, the difficult process of acculturation, language barriers, frequent moves and disrupted schooling, separation from family members, and school expectations very different from those in their home countries. Edison provides a range of services—including school-based health care, family counseling, parent outreach and education, and after-school enrichments—delivered right at the school.

Divining Community Concerns

In the late 1990s, teachers and administrators at Edison could see that the struggles of neighborhood families were affecting students' safety and well-being and contributing to low academic achievement. In 1999, only 19 percent of Edison's 4th graders passed New York State's English language arts assessment, and only 75 percent passed the state mathematics assessment.

That year, Edison began the process of becoming a full-service community school. Edison faculty and community stakeholders first sought a deeper understanding of the conditions that were influencing student learning. We conducted focus groups, individual interviews, and surveys in which we asked school practitioners, parents, students, and representatives of community-based organizations what concerns they had about Edison's students' lives and schooling.

Teachers' frustrations included the fact that parents sent children to school sick—expecting the school nurse to provide primary health care—and the difficulty of communication with parents. Parents, in turn, expressed needs for child care, help overcoming language barriers, and guidance on school involvement. Community groups recognized how often emotional and physical stresses were handicapping students.

We drew on these concerns to design a school in which the school district and community-based organizations combined resources to meet students' needs. We created a community-school advisory board that represented key constituents. Manhattanville College volunteered to serve as one of our first partners, fulfilling its own mission of becoming more actively engaged in the community. The Coalition for Community Schools was instrumental in providing a conceptual framework for how community schools can support students' families.

Our advisory board met once a month during our first year, planning and putting in place the community-school framework and developing goals and measurable objectives. We hired a community-school coordinator to help secure funds, coordinate partnership activities, and serve as a liaison between Edison and the partner agencies.

Partnerships in Action

Our School-Based Health Center

A review of the school's health records confirmed teachers' observations that many students were coming to school sick. We discovered that fewer than 23 percent of Edison students had health care coverage. The school shared this data with the Open Door Medical Center, an organization providing medical care to poor and underserved families in Port Chester, and initiated a partnership with them. Open Door secured federal grants and other funding to establish a school-based health center.

At the health center, the Edison school nurse and the Open Door nurse practitioner coordinate health care initiatives involving students and their families. The nurse practitioner provides primary care to students at the school. Common colds and other illnesses, which were previously often left untreated, now receive prompt medical attention. This reduces the number of student absences. A weekly visit from Open Door's dentist provides much-needed dental care for Edison's students.

In the past, the only source of relief from a toothache had been a bottle of pain reliever carried in a student's backpack.

All Edison students can receive health care at the center, including screenings, vaccinations, and prescription medication. We refer students needing more complex medical care to Open Door's main medical facility in the community. Open Door staff members provide nutrition and wellness education to parents and help families obtain federally funded medical insurance.

Health-center staff often uncover more serious illnesses, which might also have remained undetected until serious symptoms or complications appeared. For example, while screening a 10-year-old student, school health personnel diagnosed the boy with diabetes. The nurses developed a treatment plan for him that included parent education. This early diagnosis should ensure that this boy receives ongoing monitoring and care so that his illness will not pose barriers to his learning.

As a result of the health center's services, 94 percent of Edison's students are now medically insured and receive ongoing medical and dental care. The success of this model has led the district and Open Door to expand this kind of program to other schools.

Therapy and Family Casework

To complement the work of teachers and health-center staff in addressing the developmental needs of the whole child, Edison set up a partnership with the Guidance Center, a local mental health facility. A bilingual family caseworker meets with families in distress and helps parents realize their roles as their child's first teachers and primary advocates. The caseworker both helps families in crisis and supports the general parent population at the school, sometimes by facilitating communication between school staff and parents who do not speak English and providing new families with school supplies and clothing, if needed. A social worker provides therapeutic counseling for students in crisis and teams up with the family caseworker to ease the stresses on students' families. These services help Edison establish links with the families that are hardest to reach.

For example, when a single mother from Mexico recently enrolled her child in Edison, it became clear that this student had special needs and that domestic violence was a problem in this family. The caseworker immediately invited the mother to participate in parenting classes and referred her to a county agency for legal advice and protection, assistance with securing legal residency, and help obtaining a work permit. When her child was diagnosed with Asperger's syndrome, we provided counseling to both parent and child. In typical schools, families with these kinds of burdens often become invisible. This mother now speaks publicly about domestic abuse and helps other women in similar situations.

Parent Education and Capacity Building

Edison has hosted a weekly bilingual gathering for parents at the school throughout the past six years, facilitated by the caseworker from the Guidance Center. Parents participate in workshops, seminars, and discussion groups about topics of interest to them. We call this weekly event "*La Segunda Taza de Café*," a Spanish phrase that means "A Second Cup of Coffee." We look on these gatherings as a cordial invitation to parents to come and chat. Discussions have helped parents understand state standards and assessments, exercise their rights and responsibilities in schools, discover strategies to help their children learn, and gather information on citizenship and naturalization. One goal behind this parent program is to develop parents' leadership capacity. Edison's immigrant parents are now visible in the school and active with the Parent Teacher Association.

After-School Enrichment

Services, Education, and Resources of Westchester, a nonprofit organization, was instrumental in creating Edison's after-school program. This program now serves 130 students daily and meets the twin needs of homework help and child care that parents and teachers identified in our initial community survey. The after-school program offers students martial arts, photography, chess, tennis, computer-assisted instruction, and the opportunity to produce a literary magazine. Through professional and nonprofessional staff members, including many bilingual workers, we both support students' growth in English and offer them enrichment experiences in their native languages. We validate the rich Hispanic heritage of our students by bringing in artists to teach arts and crafts reflecting the culture and styles of indigenous Hispanic people and by inviting them to join a folk dancing troupe that performs frequently.

Partnership with Manhattanville College

Edison's long-standing professional development relationship with Manhattanville College is an important resource for improving teaching and learning. Edison hires many teachers trained at Manhattanville, which helps us find enough qualified teachers willing and prepared to work in a school confronting the conditions of poverty.

The majority of our new teachers have participated in structured preservice learning experiences through Manhattanville, ranging from facilitating small-group instruction with Edison students to student teaching at Edison. All our new hires participate in a two-year induction program coordinated by the college liaison, with Edison teachers serving as mentors. This formal guidance has increased the school's retention of new teachers; 30 percent of Edison's teachers are Manhattanville alumni. Veteran teachers continue to refine their practice by taking courses in English as a second language, literacy, and content-area instruction at the college for free or at reduced cost.

Ten Years of Whole Child Education

In June 2007, Edison celebrated its 10-year anniversary as a full-service community school. The changes we made have led to dramatic achievement gains. In 2006, 93 percent of Edison's 4th graders passed the New York State Assessment in English Language Arts, and 89 percent passed in mathematics. We have continued to survey parents, students, and faculty about how well Edison's initiatives are supporting their needs and creating an inclusive culture. Seventy-five percent of our families now participate in schoolwide events. The New York State Education Department has recognized Thomas Edison for its innovative practices and achievement gains.

Through 10 years of growing into a full-service community school, Edison has had some insights. We believe that to successfully create a community school, educators must

- Take a broad view of developmental growth and learning, beyond a narrow focus on test scores.
- Hear the perspectives of all stakeholders—both within and outside the school—about the needs of local children and families. Directly engage all community members in creative problem solving.
- Redefine their mission as ensuring the overall developmental growth of children.
- Realign programs and services to meet the needs of children and families in a comprehensive, integrated manner.
- Combine community and school resources.

A key feature of our design is the fact that community-based partners provide services right on the school site and cultivate interagency cooperation. Reshaping ourselves as a community school has enabled our faculty to focus more on teaching and learning, has given families direct access to resources that improve their lives, and has expanded our partners' ability to reach children and families. We are now educating the whole child at Edison.

Endnote

[1] Noguera, P. A. (2003). *City schools and the American dream: Reclaiming the promise of public education.* New York: Teachers College Press.

Eileen Santiago (esantiago@pcschools.lhric.org) is Principal at Thomas Edison Elementary School. **JoAnne Ferrara** (ferraraj@mville.edu) is Chair of Curriculum and Instruction at Manhattanville College in Purchase, New York. **Marty Blank** (blankm@iel.org) is Director of the Coalition of Community Schools in Washington, D.C.

Originally published in the April 2008 issue of *Educational Leadership*, 65(7), pp. 44–47.

A Coordinated School Health Plan

Pat Cooper

McComb School District in Mississippi supports the fundamental needs of all students—with outstanding results.

In September 1997, the McComb School District in Mississippi hired me as the new superintendent of schools and gave me a mandate to improve academic performance, working within a framework of caring and inclusion. McComb is a small city of about 13,300 residents located in rural southwest Mississippi. Of the 3,000 students who attended the community's seven public schools, approximately 85 percent were eligible for free or reduced-price lunch, and more than 30 percent were living below the federal poverty line.

The school system had become fractious in terms of race relations, the "have and have not" syndrome, and private school competition. Public support was waning. In a community whose population was 50 percent white, McComb School District had a white student enrollment of only 15 percent.

A Community Comes Together

In undertaking the challenge of turning around this struggling school system, McComb's district leaders identified three questions that we needed to answer:

- What do community constituents not like about the school district?

- What do they want their school district to be like?
- How do they want us to get there?

To address those questions, we turned to the community. At the beginning of the 1997–1998 school year, we sent out notices to clubs, organizations, and churches, and we published invitations in the local newspaper encouraging people to take part in restructuring the school district. Respected and knowledgeable citizens and education leaders jointly facilitated the meetings. The 350 participants were divided into five groups according to their interests: health and wellness, facilities, technology, public relations, and academic opportunity. Each group met once or twice each month from September through May, and all groups participated in several joint meetings toward the end of the process to put the pieces together.

The meetings created unanimity in purpose and direction. Community members and district personnel reached agreement that excellence is not about test scores, but rather about enabling every child to excel in all of his or her abilities, whether that involves learning algebra, playing the trombone, shooting a basketball, or being of service to others. We developed a vision statement that revolves around the whole child:

> The McComb School District is a committed and nurturing community taking responsibility every day for positively impacting the physical, social, and academic well-being of every child and challenging him to become an extraordinary individual empowered to change the world.

A Plan of Action

Once the McComb community made its commitment, district personnel realized that we needed to translate the vision into an unwavering mission. As the first step to creating a school system that would address the needs of the whole child, we looked at the answers to our three questions.

What did community constituents not like about the school district? At the meetings, most participants focused on failures to meet our students' needs. A high proportion of their comments related to students' mental and physical health.

For example, the local hospital administrator complained that the only time doctors saw most of our students was in the emergency room—a practice that resulted in ineffective and costly health care. Most of our students did not receive regular Medicaid screenings because the doctors could not get their parents to bring them to the clinics. Even children with regular private insurance often received inadequate preventive care. School personnel identified cavities and gum disease as a major problem among students.

Businesspeople observed that our students were not ready for work when they graduated. Chamber of commerce personnel pointed out that the schools didn't appear physically inviting. Residents complained that there were too many kids hanging out on the streets as truants or dropouts.

Parents focused on the high number of students lagging behind in reading skills and being placed in special education. Some argued for tighter discipline strategies; others saw the district as too punitive.

Principals and teachers complained about poor attendance that was often the result of such medical conditions as asthma, lice, diabetes, and obesity. Secretaries and administrators worried about having to make medical decisions at school. Teachers said that poor physical facilities inhibited teaching and learning. Food-service directors said that they had a hard time financing the food services because students were skipping the school-provided meals in favor of junk food.

Recreation advocates complained about the lack of formal physical education in the schools, poor facilities, and too little opportunity for students to participate in less-competitive intramural and individual sports after school. Districtwide organized health education for students, they said, was almost nonexistent except as a rainy-day activity. Students had neither the knowledge of health that they needed nor opportunities to put that knowledge into action to make healthy choices.

Mental health advocates cited the prevalence among students of depression, eating disorders, thoughts of suicide, and violent behavior because of families' failure to find and use quality mental health services. Gangs and community violence were creeping into the middle and elementary schools, along with such problems as illegal drugs and alcohol, child abuse, and homelessness. According to the local Youth Court judge, the juvenile violent crime rate for McComb students was escalating. Law enforcement personnel complained about too many suspensions, which left kids roaming the streets unattended. And on and on and on . . .

Thank goodness we finally came to the next question!

What did they want their school district to be like? Community members and district personnel grappled with what the schools should be doing. We approached this question with a consensus that we had to do more for the students than provide traditional academics. At first, however, we disagreed about where the responsibility for our children's well-being should reside.

Community members asserted that schools should play a major part in teaching students how to be healthy and in preventing social and emotional problems that kept them out of school. Teachers and principals countered that with so much emphasis on test scores, they found it hard to spend time on programs that didn't directly connect to academics.

A watershed moment occurred. We all agreed that having the best test scores doesn't make you the best school, especially if the dropout rate is high. We came to an agreement: McComb School District should strive to not only be the best *in* the state and country but also be the best *for* the state and country. If we focused on keeping all of our students in school through graduation instead of on the streets, our test score averages might never be the highest—but we would be serving the needs of our students and our community.

Community members and district personnel agreed not to blame parents, students, or circumstances. Our job was to do for all children what we did for our own—no excuses. We decided to measure our success not just according to the usual criteria of test scores, absenteeism, teacher retention, dropout rates, and graduation rates, but also according to outcomes that were crucial to the community as a whole—recreation opportunities, juvenile Medicaid service rates, juvenile arrest rates, and rates of teenage pregnancy, teen suicide and attempted suicide, drug abuse, and child abuse.

In short, to ensure the future of our society, we joined with parents and community partners in taking responsibility for the whole child. We believed that academic achievement would come for all children only when we addressed their basic needs. This approach would mean truly leaving no child behind!

How did the community want us to get there? Everyone was fired up and excited about the vision—at least until we faced the question, How do we get there? Then the magnitude of our commitment sank in. But the answer was there all along; we just had to rediscover it.

A breakthrough took place when one of our parents, a blue-collar laborer, proposed that we think of our children in school as having the same needs that adults do in their jobs. After all, school is children's job. This analogy led to the question, How do adults accomplish their best work, and what conditions need to be considered in the workplace? Then it was easy to recognize where we needed to look: Maslow's Hierarchy of Needs.

Abraham Maslow asserted that people must satisfy their lower-level needs—physiological well-being, safety, love and belonging, and a sense of competence and recognition—before they can concentrate on the needs involved in meaningful learning, including the cognitive drive to know and explore; the aesthetic drive to appreciate symmetry, order, and beauty; and the self-actualization drive to find self-fulfillment (Maslow & Lowry, 1998). Most educators read Maslow in their college sophomore psychology course. The problem was that we hadn't taken what we learned in that course and applied it to educating our students.

To translate Maslow's concepts into programs our system could implement, we turned to the coordinated school health model developed by the Centers for Disease Control and Prevention (2005). The model provided a framework for school reform based on programs in eight areas: (1) health education, (2) physical education, (3) health services, (4) nutrition services, (5) counseling and psychological services, (6) healthy school environment, (7) health promotion for staff, and (8) family and community involvement. To bring the circle back to teaching and learning, we added a ninth component: academic opportunity.

We had our restructuring plan in place. Our McComb School District vision statement kept us centered on serving the whole child. Maslow's Hierarchy of Needs provided the framework to accomplish that vision by defining what all our students needed. And our McComb nine-component coordinated school health model created the mechanism to meet the needs of all students, regardless of the circumstances.

Implementation of the Plan

During the next five years, every McComb school put into place programs that promoted the nine components of school health. The district mandated that each school tackle at least one component of its choice each year. Some schools worked on two or three components at a time, depending on their needs and available resources. For logistical reasons, the district central office took responsibility for the components of academic opportunity, nutrition services, and family and community involvement. "School Programs to Support the Whole Child" shows a sampling of programs that addressed the nine components.

Aims of Education

> *What then is the education to be? Perhaps we could hardly find a better than that which the experience of the past has already discovered, which consists, I believe, in gymnastic, for the body, and music for the mind.*
>
> —Plato

The funding mechanisms for our districtwide initiative were incremental and evolved over time. First, we made more creative use of our existing funds from local, state, and federal sources. We worked from a zero-based budgeting model, finding funds for the health programs every year before funding anything else. We began to prioritize—for example, by devoting funds to hiring necessary staff before buying "stuff."

Next, we created interagency agreements that gave us access to the services of nurses, therapists, police officers, recreation personnel, and other staff working for the city government, hospitals, service clubs, and other local organizations. This win-win strategy gave the agencies much better access to the children and youth in our community. We also got increased funding by turning all our school clinics into Medicaid-eligible facilities so that we could collect reimbursement dollars for any services provided to Medicaid-eligible students. And, most important for the sustainability of our programs, we began to receive more state funding because our average daily attendance went up and dropout rates went down.

Improved Results

Good feelings from staff and community are positive indicators of success, but in the end, results are what matter. The problems that our community identified in 1997–1998 needed to show improvement in 2004–2005. And they did. The positive results of the coordinated school health approach for our schools and community have shown up in both expected and unexpected ways.

Some results reflect improved student discipline. We hoped that attendance would rise from 93 to 94 percent; in fact, it has stabilized at approximately 96 percent. Out-of-class suspension days have decreased by more than 40 percent. Disciplinary hearings for major infractions have decreased by more than half, from an average of 24 each year to 11.

Academic data are also encouraging. In the two years since the inception of our collaboration with private day-care providers and Head Start facilities, the academic functioning of children entering kindergarten has dramatically improved; the percentage performing below their age level has dropped from 57 percent to 45 percent. Student achievement has risen: For example, a representative sample of students tracked from 3rd through 6th grade showed improved Terra Nova scores in reading (from 32 percent to 46 percent of students exceeding the national norm); language (from 34 percent to 47 percent); and math (from 28 percent to 48 percent). Overall, state accountability levels for our schools have gone from Levels 2 (needs improvement) and 3 (successful) to Levels 3 and 4 (exemplary). Spring 2004 testing found that all but one school in McComb made adequate yearly progress in every category; the school that was the sole exception narrowly missed in special education.

In addition, we are keeping our students in school. Graduation rates rose from 77 percent in 1997 to 92 percent in 2004. Dropout rates in grades 7–12 were below 2 percent in 2004, compared with a national figure of more than 30 percent (Orfield, Losen, Wald, & Swanson, 2004).

The well-being of youth in our community has also improved. For example, the juvenile crime arrest rate in McComb has dropped by 60 percent (from 331 arrests in 1997–1998 to 131 in 2003–2004). The rate of teenagers having second babies—a significant indicator of teen mother dropout rates—has stood at 3 percent in McComb during the last six years, compared with a national average of 21 percent (Mississippi Department of Public Health, 2004).

Perhaps the most telling indicator is that the community is coming back to the public schools. White enrollment has risen to 25 percent, parental complaints to the superintendent's office have decreased by 75 percent (from 110 complaints in 1998 to 28 in 2004), and public funding for school facilities and programs has gained new support.

Overcoming the Odds

McComb School District's success started with the understanding that we had to address the needs of the whole child and then work toward systemwide change for our schools and community. We wanted to enable students to excel in spite of poverty, illiteracy, unhealthy environments, and the violence all around them. Eight years later, it seems to be happening.

Today, we have the same housing projects, the same one-parent households, the same poverty, the same teachers, the same reading program—but we see different results for our students. The common denominators for our success have been a focus on common human needs, a coordinated school health program, and a believing community.

School Programs to Support the Whole Child

Health Education
- Formal nine-week sequential K–8 health education classes for all students every year.
- 1/2 Carnegie Unit health education requirement for high school graduation
- Data collection efforts to identify problem areas and progress of all programs.

Physical Education
- Certified physical education teachers in every elementary and middle school to provide an average of 30 minutes a day of organized P.E. or health for every student.
- Intramural sports leagues.
- Joint city- and school-sponsored summer recreation programs.

Health Services
- One nurse for every 450 students in a school.
- Health and wellness clinics with Medicaid services in each school, open to both students and staff.
- Follow-up referrals and contact with primary-care physicians and dentists.

Nutrition Services
- Redesigned menus that provide more attractive, healthful choices for our students.
- Policies that restrict school fund-raisers to non-food or healthful food items.
- Policy that limits school site vending machines to selling water, 100 percent juice, or milk.

- Policy allowing drinks in the classroom to keep brains hydrated.

Counseling and Psychological Services
- One mental health therapist and one guidance counselor for every 450 students in a school to provide individual, group, and family counseling.
- An interagency health and wellness team in each school, which meets once a week to staff and case-manage troubled students.
- Drug and alcohol counseling services.

Safe and Healthy School Environment
- Annual districtwide safety checks by state department of education staff.
- Modernized and clean school physical plants.
- Security cameras in schools and on buses.
- A toll-free phone number for confidential reporting to law enforcement agencies.

Health Promotion for Staff
- Annual free health check-ups and screenings for all staff.
- School-provided aerobics and fitness classes.
- School nurse case management for staff with chronic illnesses.
- Extended school year beginning August 1, with four nine-week sessions and a nine-day break in between each session for stress relief.

Family and Community Involvement
- Joint community-school health fairs and screenings.

- Parenting classes and conflict resolution classes open to the community.
- Faith-based partnerships for mentoring.

Academic Opportunity

- District family nurturing center and day care for teen mothers and fathers and their babies for prenatal, postnatal, and child care classes and full-time day care while in school.
- Off-site tutoring centers at housing projects and churches in the community.
- Districtwide early childhood coalition (with private day-care providers and Head Start centers) to serve all 3- and 4-year-olds who will enter the McComb School District as kindergartners.

References

Centers for Disease Control and Prevention. (2005). *Healthy youth! Coordinated school health program* [Online]. Available: www.cdc.gov/HealthyYouth/CSHP

Maslow, A., & Lowry, R. (Eds.). (1998). *Toward a psychology of being* (3rd ed.). New York: Wiley & Sons.

Mississippi Department of Public Health. (2004). *Teenage pregnancy in Mississippi: Annual report*. Jackson, MS: Author.

Orfield, G., Losen, D., Wald, J., & Swanson, C. (2004). *Losing our future: How minority youth are being left behind by the graduation rate crisis*. Cambridge, MA: Civil Rights Project at Harvard University.

Pat Cooper is Superintendent of Schools, McComb School District, P.O. Box 868, McComb, MS 39649; 601-684-4661; pcooper@mde.k12.ms.us.

Originally published in the September 2005 issue of *Educational Leadership, 63*(1), pp. 32–36.

Coordinated School Health: Getting It All Together

Joyce V. Fetro, Connie Givens, and Kellie Carroll

Tennessee is implementing coordinated school health statewide—and here's what it looks like.

In 1918, the National Education Association included health as one of seven cardinal principles of education. The authors noted that "'book larnin' may be inhibited by an overworked thyroid or an undernourished body" and "temper tantrums or daydreaming may be induced by hunger" (Oberteuffer, 1918, p. 8). More recently, David Satcher, former U.S. Surgeon General, stated, "Ignoring student health is shortsighted ... because an investment in health is an investment in better academic performance" (Satcher & Bradford, 2003).

Research confirms a strong relationship between student health and school performance (Association of State and Territorial Health Officials & Society of State Directors of Health, Physical Education, and Recreation, 2002; Ehrlich, 2005; Symons, Cinelli, James, & Groff, 1997). So why have U.S. schools and districts minimized or eliminated health and physical education programs; reduced the number of school nurses, counselors, and other health professionals; and focused only on "the basics"? In large part, because of No Child Left Behind (NCLB).

But in these difficult times, one approach can help—coordinated school health. In the short term, this program can provide a safe haven for teaching and learning by addressing the immediate needs of the whole child. In the long term, it can have a significant effect on youth development and academic achievement (Fetro, 2005; Murray, Low, Hollis, Cross, & Davis, 2007).

What Is Coordinated School Health?

Coordinated school health is not another new program to add to schools' already overflowing plates; it's a framework for managing new and existing health-related programs and services in schools and the surrounding community. Such an approach incorporates eight interrelated components that historically have functioned independently: health education; physical education; school health services; counseling, psychological, and social services; nutrition services; staff wellness; a healthy school environment; and family and community involvement. These eight components can help improve students' knowledge, behaviors, attitudes, and skills in health; they can also improve academic and social outcomes (Kolbe, 2002, 2005).

Coordinated school health is an ongoing process. People committed to the health of young people *communicate*; they share what they believe and what they are doing to promote student health. They *cooperate*, functioning independently while supporting one another's programs and services. They *coordinate* by reviewing related program goals and action plans for compatibility and by identifying gaps and duplication. They *collaborate* by working together to develop a common vision and to establish priorities and shared goals. Finally, they *integrate*, developing seamless, blended programs and services with shared responsibility and accountability (Fetro, 2005).

Because every school and district has different programs and services to support students' health-related needs, coordinated school health looks different in every school. Schools need to begin by looking at what they already have in place. Most likely, every school has programs and services that are related, to some degree, to each of the eight components. The ultimate goal, however, is for the eight components to be coordinated.

The Essential Eight

In 2000, recognizing the connection between adolescent health and academic achievement, Tennessee's state legislature funded a five-year pilot program to implement coordinated school health in 10 counties. On the basis of this successful pilot, school health advocates convinced state legislators to expand and fund coordinated school health statewide. Tennessee is now focusing on integrating and coordinating the eight components of the framework.

Health Education

Every day, students are bombarded with new information about health. How can they know what is accurate, what is relevant, and how to use that new health information? The goal of health education is to develop health-literate youth who understand basic health concepts and use personal and social skills—for example, skills related to advocacy, decision making, goal setting, and stress management—to promote and enhance their health (Joint Committee on National Health Education Standards, 2007). Although it rarely occurs, students should receive health education in every grade.

Physical Education

Lack of physical activity among youth is a major concern today. Research has documented the link between physical education and school performance. High-quality physical education programs increase physical competence, fitness, and responsibility, encouraging students to value lifelong physical activity (National Association for Sport and Physical Education, 2005).

In each of its six elementary schools, Tennessee's Loudon County installed a new Beanstalk Fitness Adventure Playground, complete with ropes courses and a tree house. Students scrambled to use the new structures. At one school, an autistic boy came out of his protective shell momentarily and smiled for the first time that year at the sight of the playground.

School Health Services

Despite efforts of parents and guardians, many students arrive at school with health issues that could affect their academic performance. Health services can include first aid, emergency, and diagnostic health care; health assessments and screenings; assistance with medication; and management of acute and chronic health conditions. School health services can work with community health agencies and professionals to provide more comprehensive services.

Students in Tennessee have benefited from routine health screenings. An 8-year-old who didn't pass her school's vision screening was referred to an optometrist who was able to treat the girl for a condition that, if left untreated, might have blinded her. A well-child exam revealed that a kindergartner who was having trouble learning his colors was, in fact, colorblind. A Project Diabetes grant enabled two schools to work closely with 27 students who were at risk for developing type 1 or type 2 diabetes.

Counseling, Psychological, and Social Services

Schools need to provide additional support to students at risk of academic failure as a result of emotional challenges brought about by situations in or out of school. Services in school can include career counseling, peer mentoring and counseling, mental health counseling, peer support groups, and positive alternative programs. In collaboration with community-based programs and services, the school or district can establish a system for early identification, assessment, and referral of students needing assistance.

Nutrition

Many students take advantage of meals offered at school. Food service programs should provide breakfasts and lunches that are not only nutritionally balanced, but also appealing. In addition, the school cafeteria can be a learning laboratory that reinforces what students learn in health classes, encouraging students to make healthier food choices when they are out of school.

With community support, one school in rural Tennessee created an on-site supermarket. The school is developing lesson plans that teach students how to read food labels, what foods are necessary for a healthy diet, and how to prepare food; in addition, students learn about food preservatives, processed foods, hand washing, and food safety. Lessons incorporate math (for example, figuring out percentages of the daily recommended amount of fiber in certain products); language arts (signs in the store are written in both English and Spanish); and social studies.

Staff Wellness

Teachers and other school staff are important role models for students. The more teachers value health, the more their classroom practices support student health. Staff health promotion programs usually are an afterthought, when in reality they are crucial. Programs for teachers and staff include workshops related to healthy dietary patterns; stress management; weight management; cardiovascular fitness; first aid and cardiopulmonary resuscitation (CPR); safety issues; and tobacco, alcohol, and other drug use.

Partnering with the Putnam County Health Department, a Tennessee school system created a weight-loss program for its teachers and administrators, which involved the use of treadmills that the county had purchased. One teacher who lost a substantial amount of weight served as a role model for her students, one of whom asked whether he could come in early and use the treadmill before school started.

A Healthy School Environment

To learn effectively, students and teachers need a healthy school environment, one that is clean, well lit, comfortable, physically safe, and graffiti-free, with minimal noise and other distractions. Equally important, the psychosocial environment should support diversity and promote personal growth, wellness, and healthy relationships. The school should communicate and consistently enforce formal and informal policies and procedures related to student health, safety, and conduct. These policies typically address such issues as the use of tobacco, alcohol, and other drugs; name calling; sexual harassment; violent behaviors; and emergency preparedness.

Family and Community Involvement

Increasing schools' capacity to address students' diverse needs requires family and community involvement. Every school community, no matter how large or small, has untapped resources. Schools should coordinate and integrate activities and initiatives both inside and outside the school. This partnership should be two-way and should include advisory groups and coalitions, advocacy campaigns, family and community outreach programs, and adult mentor programs.

For example, many schools invite in community speakers when discussing health issues in class. As human resources dwindle in schools, parent and community volunteers can assist with coordinated school health activities. Schools can also provide outreach to parents and community members, beginning with awareness sessions and broadening to parenting skills.

Tennessee Takes Action

Tennessee is moving steadily toward full implementation of coordinated school health by the 2012–13 school year. All school districts are striving for compliance with Tennessee school health laws and coordinated school health standards and guidelines. They are hiring full-time coordinators for the program; sending educators to mandatory professional development institutes; and establishing community school health advisory committees, district-level staff coordinating councils, and healthy school teams. Districts are also completing the School Health Index and Youth Risk Behavior Survey—both of which are available from the Centers for Disease Control and Prevention (CDC)—and using the results to develop annual action plans with measurable objectives.

The School Health Index has eight modules, each of which addresses one of the eight components of coordinated school health. The index asks schools such questions as, Do you have 225 minutes of physical education per week? Do you have breakfast and lunch programs? and Do you offer health screening for all staff?

The CDC's Youth Risk Behavior Survey that the schools administered in 2007 had some eye-opening results. Among other findings, it showed that approximately 11 percent of students rarely or never wore a seat belt when riding in a car driven by someone else; that 29 percent of students had recently ridden in a car driven by someone who had been drinking; that 35 percent had been in a physical fight during the 12 months before the survey; that in the previous 30 days, 14.5 percent had seriously considered suicide; and that before the age of 13, 14 percent of students had smoked their first cigarette, 24 percent had tried alcohol, 8 percent had used marijuana, and 7 percent had had sexual intercourse.

A District Success Story

The CDC's Division of Adolescent and School Health selected Gibson County Special School District in western Tennessee as one of six districts across the United States that has an outstanding coordinated school health program. One of the 10 original pilot districts in Tennessee, the school district includes nine schools, with a total enrollment of 3,425 students in grades preK–12.

All Gibson County students explore health concepts and develop health-promoting skills as their schools follow the Michigan Model, a comprehensive school health education program that is currently being implemented in 30 U.S. states as well as in several foreign countries.

Many other programs in Gibson County enhance the health education curriculum. For example, school nurses teach 5th and 6th graders about changes occurring during puberty. Tennessee's National Guard Counterdrug Task Force facilitates a 14-week life skills program to reduce drug use in middle schools. A community partner, Right Choices of West Tennessee, provides a youth development program to help middle school students refrain from engaging in risky behaviors. In collaboration with numerous community partners, each school hosts a health fair.

In addition to providing physical education to all county students, elementary schools participate in the Blue Cross Walking Works for Schools program, which requires students to walk at least 5 minutes every school day for 12 weeks each semester. Five schools incorporate Wii Fit, Wii Yoga, and Wii Sports into their after-school programs. Other elementary schools use PlayStation 2 and Dance Dance Revolution to increase physical activity. Middle school and high school students as well as adults can use the ACES challenge ropes course.

Several activities reinforce positive dietary choices in the cafeteria—for example, Nutri Notes newsletters for students and parents, nutrition bulletin boards, and My Pyramid posters, which remind students ages 6–11 to be physically active and make healthy food choices. A registered dietitian works with healthy school teams to develop individualized nutrition plans for students or staff members needing assistance in this area.

School nurses organize student health screenings for vision, hearing, scoliosis, and body mass index. School staff members receive free health screenings, which address weight, hearing, vision, body mass index, blood pressure, cholesterol levels, blood glucose levels, blood iron levels, and bone density. They also receive professional development about first aid/CPR and blood-borne pathogens, such as hepatitis B and HIV/AIDS. The county is moving toward establishing a school-based health clinic for students, staff, and families.

In addition to day-to-day responsibilities, school counselors provide suicide prevention and intervention training to staff; facilitate a teen parenting program; assist parents and guardians with CoverKids (comprehensive health coverage for uninsured children); and run an anticyberbullying program.

With community partners, Gibson County's Office of Community School Health developed a dramatization of a car crash and presented it to county high schools. Students saw police, medical, and rescue personnel arrive on the scene. They witnessed the police handcuffing the driver and taking him away in a police car, a seriously injured passenger being treated and then airlifted to a hospital, and the reactions of the distraught parents of the injured students.

Outside speakers present at Parent Teacher Organization meetings as requested. A teen action group participates in creating public service announcements to help students make responsible decisions concerning alcohol, tobacco, and other substances. Parent volunteers assist nurses in completing required health screenings. All schools implement a local wellness policy consistent with that of their district.

Gibson County's Office of Coordinated School Health maintains a Web site with helpful links for staff members (see www.gcssd.org/csh/index.htm). All faculty and staff members receive Walk Smart tips, nutrition fact sheets, obesity education information, and a quarterly newsletter on health. Two district schools have staff wellness rooms with fitness equipment and resources. All district employees also receive flu and Hepatitis B shots.

Making It Happen

Currently, the Centers for Disease Control and Prevention provides funding for 22 states to assist schools and school districts in effectively implementing coordinated school health (see www.cdc.gov/healthyyouth). The Massachusetts Department of Education and San Francisco Unified School District also provide professional development and technical support to state and local education agencies in their efforts to effectively implement the program.

But the bottom line is about people. When everyone—from state legislators to county coordinators, to healthy school teams, to community partners, to teachers, to parents—is committed to young people's well-being, coordinated school health can become a reality. It takes time, often years, to put it together. But the Tennessee story is one example of people making it happen.

Joyce V. Fetro is Professor, Distinguished Teacher, and Chair of the Department of Health Education and Recreation at Southern Illinois University, Carbondale; 618-453-2777; jfetro@siu.edu. **Connie Givens** is Director of the Tennessee Office of Coordinated School Health, Tennessee Department of Education, Nashville. **Kellie Carroll** is County Coordinator, Coordinated School Health, Gibson County Special School District, Tennessee.

Originally published in the December 2009/January 2010 issue of *Educational Leadership*, 67(4), pp. 32–37.

Part 7

Rounding Out the Curriculum

Teaching Strategies for Naturalist Intelligence

Thomas Armstrong

Bringing the natural world into classroom learning.

Most of classroom instruction takes place inside of a school building. For children who learn best through nature, this arrangement cuts them off from their most valued source of learning. There are two primary solutions to this dilemma. First, more learning needs to take place for these kids outside in natural settings. Second, more of the natural world needs to be brought into the classroom and other areas of the school building, so that naturalistically inclined students might have greater access to developing their naturalist intelligence while inside of the school building. The strategies that have been selected for inclusion here are all drawn from one or both of these approaches.

Nature Walks

The Nobel Prize–winning physicist Richard Feynman once wrote that he got his start along the path of science by taking walks in nature with his father. It was from the kind of questions that his father would ask him as they walked along (e.g., "What animal do you think made that hole over there?") that his own scientific questioning attitude was formed. In similar fashion, teachers might consider the benefit of "a walk in the woods" (or whatever other natural features are available within walking distance of your school) as a way of reinforcing material being learned inside of the classroom. Virtually any subject lends itself to a nature walk. Science and math, of course, can be examined in the various principles at work in the growth of plants, the weather above, the earth below, and the animals that scurry or fly about. If you're teaching a piece of literature or a history lesson that involves any kind of natural setting (and most do at least somewhere along the way), then you might use a nature walk as an opportunity to reconstruct a scene or two from the story or period of history ("Imagine that this is the meadow where the Pickwick Club had their ridiculous duel in Dickens's *Pickwick Papers*" or "Picture this as the setting of the Battle of Hastings just before the troops arrived on the scene"). Also, nature walks make a superb preparation for getting your class ready to do creative writing, drawing, or other activities.

Windows onto Learning

One of the classic images of an "inattentive" student in the classroom is of a child sitting at a desk looking wistfully out the window while, presumably, fantasizing about what she'd rather be doing! Why do kids want to look out the window? All too often, it's because what they see out there is more interesting than what is going on in the classroom. If this is true, then why not use this "off-task" tendency in students as a positive classroom strategy? In other words, "looking out the window" is a technique that instructors can use to further the curriculum. What can be accomplished, pedagogically speaking, by looking out a window? There are many possibilities, including weather study (have a class weather station to make measurements), bird watching (have binoculars handy), understanding time (study the seasons' effects on the trees, grass, plants, etc.), and creative writing (have students create metaphors based on nature in their writing). In fact, looking out a window can be used as a strategy for just about any subject. As with nature walks, looking out a window can be used to set a scene for literature or history or for scientific observation. Other subjects can take what's beyond the window as a starting point, a place to briefly stop during a lesson, or a final stopping point. Examples include geology or geography ("What nature features do you see in the earth or along the horizon?"), economics ("Investigate the cost of planting the trees just outside the window"), social studies ("How well designed is the area just outside the window for human beings?"), and literature ("As we finish this story, I want you to look out the window and imagine our protagonist walking between the trees there into the distance").

Of course, if you don't have windows in your classroom or your windows look out onto other classrooms or expanses of concrete (a lamentable consequence of using architects who have little of the naturalist in them), then it's not possible to fully realize the possibilities of this strategy. However, even then, you might use the Visualization strategy from spatial intelligence to help your students imagine that they *do* have imaginary windows that they can look out of to gain at least some semblance of connection to the natural world!

Plants as Props

If you can't go out of the classroom on nature walks and don't have windows in your classroom through which to look at nature, then the next viable alternative is to bring nature into your classroom. Many teachers have adorned their windowsills or shelves with house plants simply to create a positive ambiance for learning. However, it is also useful to consider the practical advantage of using plants as learning tools. The fact that the petals of flowers in bloom, for example, often come in multiples is an opportunity to examine the concept of multiplication in a natural setting. Plants can make useful "props" as background scenery for the Classroom Theater and People Sculpture strategies described earlier in this chapter. In teaching about the branches of government, you can use a nearby branching plant as a naturalistic metaphor to illustrate the concept. In science and math, the growth of classroom plants can be measured. In history, their function or usefulness as herbal medicines, foods, or even poisons might be considered. Assigning a particularly difficult child with a naturalistic bent the job of taking care of a plant in the classroom can be a useful way to redirect his or her energies. Finally, I love the idea of using the image of plant growth as a metaphor for the learning that is going on in the classroom—at the beginning of the year, bring in a sprout of a plant, and at the end of the year, point out to the class how much both the plant and the students have grown during the year!

Pet-in-the-Classroom

Many elementary school classrooms already have a "class pet" kept in a gerbil cage, a rabbit hutch, or some other species-appropriate container. This strategy underlines how important this particular addition to the classroom is in terms of sheer instructional value. First of all, having a pet in the classroom automatically creates for many naturalistically inclined students a "safe place" where they can go to have a relationship to the natural world and to feel a sense of caring for nature's beings (some of these kids may be our future veterinarians!). Second, many specific instructional uses can come from having a pet in the classroom. The scientific skill of observation can be developed by having kids keep notes on a pet's behavior. (The naturalist Jane Goodall traces her own love of animals back to an incident at 5 years old where she stayed in a chicken coop for five hours just to see how chickens lay eggs!) Kids can keep math records on their pet's food intake, weight, and other vital statistics. For high school classrooms, teachers can use a class pet as a kind of "alter ego" for the classroom in posing instructional questions (e.g., "How do you think our rabbit Albert would feel about the problem of world hunger?"). Students who relate best to the world through their love of animals might well use Albert's persona in giving voice to their own thinking on the matter. Having a pet in the classroom creates a sort of "reality check" for teachers and students alike, reminding us of our own connection to the animal world and our need sometimes to learn from the wisdom of our pets!

Eco-study

Implied in the concluding statement of the last strategy is the importance of having a sense of respect for the natural world. This is the core idea behind the next strategy: Eco-study. This strategy essentially means that whatever we are teaching, whether it is history, science, math, literature, geography, social studies, art, music, or any other subject, we should keep in mind its relevance to the ecology of the earth. In essence, what I'm suggesting here is that "ecology" shouldn't just be a unit, course, or topic isolated from the rest of the curriculum but that it be integrated into every part of the school day. So, for example, if the topic is fractions or percentages, the teacher can ask students to investigate the fraction of a particular endangered species that exists today as opposed to, say, 50 years ago or the percentage of rain forest left in Brazil compared to what it was in 1900. If the subject is how a bill goes through Congress, students might consider an actual bill having an ecological focus that went through each stage of the process. Or, if a teacher has the option of choosing literature, then a dramatic work like Ibsen's *An Enemy of the People*—an ecological play written before its time—might be assigned or even acted out by the students. For students who are humanity's "earth angels" (those with a particular sensitivity to ecological issues), this sort of strategy can help draw them into the curriculum and at the same time stimulate all students to take a deeper interest in the welfare of our planet's diminishing natural resources.

Thomas Armstrong is the author of five books by ASCD: *Awakening Genius in the Classroom* (1998), *ADD/ADHD Alternatives in the Classroom* (1999), *The Multiple Intelligences of Reading and Writing* (2003), *The Best Schools: How Human Development Research Should Inform Educational Practice* (2006), *Multiple Intelligences in the Classroom*, 3rd Edition (2009); thomas@thomasarmstrong.com.

Originally published in Armstrong, T. (2009). *Multiple intelligences in the classroom* (3rd ed.). (pp. 93–97). Alexandria, VA: ASCD. Reprinted with permission.

Teaching Strategies for Intrapersonal Intelligence

Thomas Armstrong

When students need quiet time and a change of pace.

Most students spend about six hours a day, five days a week in a classroom with 25 to 35 other people. For individuals with strongly developed intrapersonal intelligence and an introverted personality, this intensely social atmosphere can be somewhat claustrophobic. Hence, teachers need to build in frequent opportunities during the day for students to experience themselves as autonomous beings with unique life histories and a sense of deep individuality. Each of the following strategies helps accomplish this aim in a slightly different way.

One-Minute Reflection Periods

During lectures, discussions, project work, or other activities, students should have frequent "time outs" for introspection or focused thinking. One-minute reflection periods offer students time to digest the information presented or to connect it to happenings in their own lives. They also provide a refreshing change of pace that helps students stay alert and ready for the next activity.

A one-minute reflection period can occur anytime during the school day, but it may be particularly useful after the presentation of information that is especially challenging or central to the curriculum. During this one-minute period (which can be extended or shortened to accommodate differing attention spans), there is to be no talking and students are to simply think about what has been presented in any way they'd like. Silence is usually the best environment for reflection, but you occasionally might try using background "thinking" music as an option. Also, students should not feel compelled to "share" what they thought about, but this activity can be combined with Peer Sharing to make it both an intra- and interpersonal activity.

Personal Connections

The big question that accompanies strongly intrapersonal students through their school career is: "What does all this have to do with *my* life?" Most students have probably asked this question in one way or another during their time in school. It's up to teachers to help answer this question by continually making connections between what is being taught and the personal lives of their students. This strategy, then, asks you to weave students' personal associations, feelings, and experiences into your instruction. You may do so through questions ("How many of you have ever. . . ?"), statements ("You may wonder what this has to do with your lives. Well, if you ever plan on … "), or requests ("I'd like you to think back in your life to a time when … "). For instance, to introduce a lesson on the skeletal system, you might ask, "How many people here have ever broken a bone?" Students then share stories and experiences before going on to the anatomy lesson itself. Or, for a lesson on world geography, you might ask, "Has anybody ever been to another country? What country?" Students then identify the countries they've visited and locate them on the map.

Choice Time

Giving students choices is as much a fundamental principle of good teaching as it is a specific intrapersonal teaching strategy. Essentially, choice time consists of building in opportunities for students to make decisions about their learning experiences. Making choices is like lifting weights. The more frequently students choose from a group of options, the thicker their "responsibility muscles" become. The choices may be small and limited ("You can choose to work on the problems on page 12 or 14"), or they may be significant and open-ended ("Select the kind of project you'd like to do this semester"). Choices may be related to content ("Decide which topic you'd like to explore") or to process ("Choose from this list a method of presenting your final project"). Choices may be informal and spur of the moment ("Okay, would you rather stop now or continue talking about this?"), or they may be carefully developed and highly structured (as in the use of a learning contract for each student). How do you currently provide for choice in your classroom? Think of ways to expand the choice-making experiences your students have in school.

Feeling-Toned Moments

One of the sadder findings of John Goodlad's "A Study of Schooling" (2004) was that most of the 1,000 classrooms observed had few experiences of true feeling—that is, expressions of excitement, amazement, anger, joy, or caring. All too often, teachers present information to students in an emotionally neutral way. Yet we know that human beings possess an "emotional brain" consisting of several subcortical structures (see Goleman, 2006). To feed that emotional brain, educators need to teach with feeling. This strategy suggests that educators are responsible for creating moments in teaching where students laugh, feel angry, express strong opinions, get excited about a topic, or feel a wide range of other emotions. You can help create feeling-toned moments in a number of ways: first, by modeling those emotions yourself as you teach; second, by making it safe for students to have feelings in the classroom (giving permission, discouraging criticism, and acknowledging feelings when they occur); and finally, by providing experiences (such as movies, books, and controversial ideas) that evoke feeling-toned reactions.

Goal-Setting Sessions

One of the characteristics of highly developed intrapersonal learners is their capacity to set realistic goals for themselves. This ability certainly has to be among the most important skills necessary for leading a successful life. Consequently, educators help students immeasurably in their preparation for life when they provide opportunities for setting goals. These goals may be short-term ("I want everybody to list three things they'd like to learn today") or long-term ("Tell me what you see yourself doing 25 years from now"). The goal-setting sessions may last only a few minutes, or they may involve in-depth planning over several months' time. The goals themselves can relate to academic outcomes ("What grades are you setting for yourself this term?"), wider learning outcomes ("What do you want to know how to do by the time you graduate?"), or life goals ("What kind of occupation do you see yourself involved with after you leave school?"). Try to allow time *every day* for students to set goals for themselves. You may also want to show students different ways of representing those goals (through words, pictures, etc.) and methods for charting their progress along the way (through graphs, charts, journals, and time lines).

Thomas Armstrong is the author of five books by ASCD: *Awakening Genius in the Classroom* (1998), *ADD/ADHD Alternatives in the Classroom* (1999), *The Multiple Intelligences of Reading and Writing* (2003), *The Best Schools: How Human Development Research Should Inform Educational Practice* (2006), *Multiple Intelligences in the Classroom, 3rd Edition* (2009); thomas@thomasarmstrong.com.

Originally published in Armstrong, T. (2009). *Multiple intelligences in the classroom* (3rd ed.). (pp. 91–93). Alexandria, VA: ASCD. Reprinted with permission.

Teaching Strategies for Bodily-Kinesthetic Intelligence

Thomas Armstrong

How to make physical learning a part of everyday learning.

Students may leave their textbooks and folders behind when they leave school, but they take their bodies with them wherever they go. Consequently, finding ways to help students integrate learning at a "gut" level can be very important to increasing their retention, understanding, and interest. Traditionally, physical learning has been considered the province of physical education and vocational education. The following strategies, however, show how easy it is to integrate hands-on and kinesthetic learning activities into traditional academic subjects like reading, math, and science.

Body Answers

Ask students to respond to instruction by using their bodies as a medium of expression. The simplest and most overused example of this strategy is asking students to raise their hands to indicate understanding. This strategy can be varied in any number of ways, however. Instead of raising hands, students could smile, blink one eye, hold up fingers (one finger to indicate just a little understanding, five fingers to show complete understanding), make flying motions with their arms, and so forth. Students can provide "body answers" during a lecture ("If you understand what I've just said, put your finger on your temple; if you don't understand, scratch your head"), while going through a textbook ("Anytime you come to something in the text that seems outdated, I want you to frown"), or in answering questions that have a limited number of answers ("If you think this sentence has parallel construction, I want you to raise your two hands high like a referee indicating a touchdown; if you think it's not parallel, put your hands together over your head like the peak of a house").

Classroom Theater

To bring out the actor in each of your students, ask them to enact the texts, problems, or other material to be learned by dramatizing or role-playing the content. For example, students might dramatize a math problem involving three-step problem solving by putting on a three-act play. Classroom Theater can be as informal as a one-minute improvisation of a reading passage during class or as formal as a one-hour play at the end of the semester that sums up students' understanding of a broad learning theme. It can be done without any materials, or it may involve substantial use of props. Students may themselves act in plays and skits, or they may produce puppet shows or dramatizations in miniature (e.g., showing how a battle was fought by putting miniature soldiers on a plywood battlefield and moving them around to show troop movements). To help older students who may initially feel reluctant to engage in dramatic activities, try some warm-up exercises (see Spolin, 1986).

Kinesthetic Concepts

The game of charades has long been a favorite of partygoers because of the way it challenges participants to express knowledge in unconventional ways. The Kinesthetic Concepts strategy involves introducing students to concepts through physical illustrations or asking students to pantomime specific concepts or terms from the lesson. This strategy requires students to translate information from linguistic or logical symbol systems into purely bodily-kinesthetic expression. The range of subjects is endless. Here are just a few examples of concepts that might be expressed through physical gestures or movements: soil erosion, cell mitosis, political revolution, supply and demand, subtraction (of numbers), the epiphany (of a novel), and biodiversity in an ecosystem. Simple pantomimes can also be extended into more elaborate creative movement experiences or dances (such as dancing the periodic table of the elements).

Hands-On Thinking

Students who are highly developed in the fine-motor aspect of bodily-kinesthetic intelligence should have opportunities to learn by manipulating objects or by making things with their hands. Many educators have already provided such opportunities by incorporating manipulatives (e.g., Cuisenaire rods) into math instruction and involving students in experiments or lab work in science. In thematic projects, too, students can use hands-on thinking—for instance, in constructing adobe huts for a unit on Native American traditions or in building dioramas of the rain forest for an ecology theme. You can extend this general strategy into many other curricular areas as well. At a rote level, students can study spelling words or new vocabulary words by forming them in clay or with pipe cleaners. At a higher cognitive level, students can express complex concepts by creating clay or wood sculptures, collages, or other assemblages. For example, students could convey an understanding of the term "deficit" (in its economic sense) using only clay (or some other available material) and then share their productions during a class discussion.

Body Maps

The human body provides a convenient pedagogical tool when transformed into a reference point or "map" for specific knowledge domains.

One of the most common examples of this approach is the use of fingers in counting and calculating (elaborate finger-counting systems such as Chisanbop have been adapted for classroom use). We can map out many other domains onto the body. In geography, for example, the body might represent the United States (if the head represents the northern United States, where is Florida located?). The body can also be used to map out a problem-solving strategy in math. For example, in multiplying a two-digit number by a one-digit number, the feet could be the two-digit number, and the right knee could be the one-digit number. Students could then perform the following actions in "solving" the problem: tap the right knee and the right foot to get the first product (indicated by tapping the thighs); tap the right knee and the left foot to get the second product (indicated by tapping the stomach); tap the thighs and the stomach (to indicate adding the two products), and tap the head (to indicate the final product). By repeating physical movements that represent a specific process or idea, students can gradually internalize the process or idea.

Thomas Armstrong is the author of five books by ASCD: *Awakening Genius in the Classroom* (1998), *ADD/ADHD Alternatives in the Classroom* (1999), *The Multiple Intelligences of Reading and Writing* (2003), *The Best Schools: How Human Development Research Should Inform Educational Practice* (2006), *Multiple Intelligences in the Classroom, 3rd Edition* (2009); thomas@thomasarmstrong.com.

Originally published in Armstrong, T. (2009). *Multiple intelligences in the classroom* (3rd ed.). (pp. 82–85). Alexandria, VA: ASCD. Reprinted with permission.

Appendix

Keeping the Whole Child
Healthy and Safe

Learning, Teaching, and Leading in ASCD's Healthy School Communities

Principal leadership matters. In fact, the recent evaluation of the Healthy School Communities (HSC) pilot project showed that the role of the principal was the most critical piece of the puzzle in implementing meaningful school change and school improvement. Other elements were crucial—such as an understanding that health improvement supports school improvement, authentic community collaboration, and the ability to make systemic rather than merely programmatic change—but these pieces more often than not arose through the influence and role the principal took in the implementation of Healthy School Communities.

What Are Healthy School Communities?

Healthy School Communities is a worldwide effort to promote the integration of health and learning and the benefits of school-community collaboration. It is part of a large, multiyear plan to shift public dialogue about education from a narrow focus centered on curriculum and accountability systems to a whole child approach that encompasses all factors required for successful student outcomes.

Healthy school communities are school settings in which students, staff, and community members work collaboratively to ensure that each student is emotionally and physically healthy, safe, engaged, supported, and challenged. Every school has students who are absent for physical health-related issues, such as asthma and upper respiratory infections, or students who struggle to concentrate because of pain from cavities or other injuries. In other cases, students may be preoccupied with conflict at home or may feel unsafe or, for a variety of reasons, unsupported at school. And in all too many cases, students are disengaged by lesson content and left unchallenged by rote memorization of facts for an invalid assessment. Each and every one of these situations and conditions impede students' ability to perform to their best and, indeed, teachers' ability to teach most effectively. Until the school is a healthy, safe, engaging, supportive, and challenging place to be, many of the best school improvement initiatives will fall short.

In the spring of 2006, ASCD launched Healthy School Communities and commenced a pilot study of school-community partnerships in the United States and Canada that focused on effective school improvement efforts. ASCD engaged an evaluator from the initiation of the project to follow school-community teams as they used the Healthy School Report Card (HSRC); gauge fidelity of HSC implementation; and gather feedback from sites on the full range of technical support provided. At its core, the evaluation sought to find out, *What levers of change in a school community allow for the initiation and implementation of best practice and policy for improving school health?* The results from the evaluation provide guidance on how sites can best implement change, as well as overarching findings to improve school improvement effectiveness and ultimately increase student success.

HEALTHY SCHOOL COMMUNITIES
ARE BUILT ON

- **Belief in the Whole Child.** They demonstrate the belief that successful learners are emotionally and physically healthy, knowledgeable, motivated, and engaged.
- **Best Practice Leadership.** They demonstrate best practices in leadership and instruction across the school.

- **Strong Collaborations.** They create and sustain strong collaborations between the school and community stakeholders and institutions.
- **A Systems Approach.** They use evidence-based systems and policies to support the physical and emotional well-being of students and staff.
- **A Healthy Environment.** They provide an environment in which students can practice what they learn about making healthy decisions and staff can practice and model healthy behaviors.
- **Data.** They use appropriate data to continuously improve.
- **Networking.** They network with other school communities to share best practices.

Key Findings

The evaluation identified nine levers that catalyzed significant change in the culture of the participating school communities. The most effective sites demonstrated all of these levers to a great extent, with these levers working in concert to support sustainability of the change.

The Nine Levers of School Change

1. Principal as leader.
2. The creation or modification in school policy related to Healthy School Communities.
3. Authentic and mutually beneficial community collaborations.
4. Integration with the school improvement process.

5. Effective use of the Healthy Schools Report Card and planning process for continuous improvement.
6. Effective and distributive team leadership.
7. Active and engaged leadership.
8. Ongoing and embedded professional development.
9. Stakeholder support of the local Healthy School Communities effort.

Several findings, however, stood out as pivotal to ensure change. Without these elements, schools found implementation more difficult and sustainability in jeopardy.

Principal as Leader

Effective leadership was imperative. However, what was most interesting was the impact the principal had in driving both implementation of Healthy School Communities and improvements through using the Healthy Schools Report Card with the school community. The influence of the principal was paramount. It was clear that at sites where the principal was not only onboard but also actively engaged in leading the process, the Healthy School Communities initiative was more quickly and fully embedded in the school improvement process. Successful Healthy School Communities teams had a principal who was not merely supportive of the initiative but rather key in organizing and leading the team through the process. Principal leadership in these sites not only provided an automatic "educational acceptance" of the initiative to the wider school body, but also used the interpersonal and managerial skill of the principal in aligning stakeholders.

Principal-led teams were found to develop more diverse committees, involve more stakeholders, and initiate more systemic change to school policy and process. Further study into the specific skills and assets that principals bring to the table is warranted, but principal leadership of the process takes what may have been seen as merely a "health issue"— which might be considered beneficial but somewhat separate from education—and positions it directly under the responsibility of the principal and the school improvement process.

The findings indicate that it is not sufficient for a principal to merely give permission for this work, and a school community cannot expect a high level of success if the principal delegates the lead role to another individual, such as a school health coordinator. The principal must lead or co-lead this effort for it to be systemic and sustainable. Current school health practices that designate a staff coordinator to lead the team and rely only on administrator buy-in will continue to leave health on the periphery, rather than allowing it to move into the central position it must play within school improvement.

What also became clear during the evaluation was how these elements are interrelated. Principal-led Healthy School Communities teams were able to engage the community; provide educational acceptance to the initiative; promote systemic change; and address the foundational criteria that influence all aspects of school effectiveness. In short, principal leadership became the pivot from which other elements of success could grow.

Systemic Rather Than Programmatic Approach

For change to be meaningful and sustainable, it needs to address school improvement at the systemic level, rather than just the programmatic level. Programmatic changes are more likely to be tried and rolled back or become "siloed" as the property of a particular staff member or department. Systemic change allows for improvement across the school and subsequently will affect programs and policies. Systemic changes become embedded into the everyday running of the school and are not necessarily affected when key staff transfer, change roles, or retire. Authority to make systemic changes often resides with the principal, the administration, and the school board.

The evaluation found that when the Healthy School Communities team leadership did not include these parties, the teams were both less likely to have a diverse stakeholder representation on the team—including key community stakeholders— and more likely to focus on a programmatic rather than systemic approach.

Authentic Community Collaboration
The most effective Healthy School Communities teams engaged community organizations and members in the early stages of the work. These collaborations involved joint assessment and engagement in solving problems and identifying and sharing resources. Although the Healthy Schools Report Card does not prescribe predetermined steps, it does strongly recommend the engagement of community members on the Healthy School Communities committee as it discusses and formulates the Healthy School and School Improvement Plans. Community members who are part of the Healthy School Communities committee become engaged and empowered as they are granted the same opportunities for input and ownership as other school-based stakeholders. Their involvement significantly contributes to plan development that is relevant and achievable within each unique setting and often supports evaluation of plan efforts.

Health Improvement Supports School Improvement
A healthy school environment provides the foundation for other programs, projects, and initiatives. It is this foundational environment that allows a positive school climate to develop, a healthy school culture to grow, and effective programs and curriculum to be successfully introduced to enhance teaching and learning and, ultimately, ensure the success of students.

But what is meant by the term health? When health is discussed in the context of Healthy School Communities, it is not referring only to the physical, and it is not referring only to the health of the students. It is a broad understanding or view of health. It encapsulates the physical, mental, social, and emotional well-being of participants in the school community and an environment that supports the ability to be healthy.

The evaluation team found that sites that used the Healthy Schools Report Card within the context of the school improvement process were more likely to engage in meaningful and integrated planning than sites that did not.

Conclusion

If principals wish to effectively implement systemic school improvement through using tools such as the Healthy Schools Report Card, then they need to lead the team and the process. Principal leadership dispels any notion that an initiative is extraneous to the school or the educational process and allows community stakeholders into the workings of the school. Principal leadership, however, does not necessarily mean principal-run. The creation of an effective and distributive team leadership was also one of the nine levers of change cited in the findings. Schools that engage and use stakeholders, both inside and outside the school walls, are able to access a wide array of skills, knowledge, and resources; spread ownership; empower and unite teams; and, ultimately, increase the effectiveness of the school and improve the educational process.

In turn, schools that focus efforts on the foundational aspects of their school and their school improvement process are able to provide a setting in which effective teaching and learning can excel. By directing resources onto the health—in its broadest definition—of the school environment, staff, and students, schools are dramatically affecting all actions, programs, and processes that take place in the school setting.

The health of the school and its participants cannot be underestimated as a precursor to effective teaching and learning. Students must feel safe or connected to their schools; staff must feel supported and secure; parents must feel welcome; and individuals must not feel physically restricted, for any number of reasons, from being able to perform at school. Otherwise, their ability to teach and learn effectively will be affected. Schools must address these foundational issues to effectively implement meaningful school change through using the school improvement process—a process that is best initiated through principal leadership that starts with a core understanding of the benefits of a healthy environment and a positive school culture that empowers and authentically involves community and that targets systemic rather than programmatic improvement.

> **KEY RECOMMENDATIONS**
>
> **ASCD recommends the following key elements for school sites wishing to initiate and sustain meaningful school change and school improvement:**
>
> 1. Planning teams should be principal-led.
> 2. Plans should address systemic issues at the school.
> 3. Collaboration should commence from the start of the planning process.
> 4. HSC planning should align with and be the basis of the overall school improvement process.
> 5. Planning should focus on those aspects revealed by assessment to have the most need.
> 6. Team leadership should aim to build a team to facilitate the process.
> 7. Team leadership should ensure all stakeholders understand the value of their involvement.
> 8. Ongoing purposeful professional development should be integrated to support the process.
> 9. School administration should actively seek out and access community resources.

Study Guide

Keeping the Whole Child
Healthy and Safe

Study Guide for Keeping the Whole Child Healthy and Safe

PART 1. Back to Whole

What Does It Mean to Educate the Whole Child?, *Educational Leadership*, September 2005
Healthy and Ready to Learn, *Educational Leadership*, September 2005

In "What Does It Mean to Educate the Whole Child?" Nel Noddings looks at the seven aims of education identified by the National Education Association in 1918: command of academic fundamentals, health, vocation, citizenship, worthy family membership, worthy use of leisure, and ethical character.

- Do you agree that these are important aims of education? Do you believe that schools today concentrate on academic fundamentals? What does your school do to integrate the other aims?
- Ask teachers to brainstorm activities or lessons they might introduce in upcoming months that would, as Noddings says, "stretch their subjects" by incorporating health, citizenship, and the other elements Noddings mentions into their teaching. Have teachers share ideas and see if they've identified any common activities or concepts. How could these ideas be worked into cotaught lessons or units?

Consider Noddings's comment that "Most of us want to be treated as persons, not as the 'sinus case in treatment room 3' or the 'refund request on line 4.'" She adds, "But we live under the legacy of bureaucratic thought." Discuss what might make students and families victims of bureaucracy and compartmentalization at school. How could educators change some of these practices to create a healthy, more caring environment?

PART 2. Promoting a Healthy Life

Finding Our Way Back to Healthy Eating: A Conversation with David A. Kessler, *Educational Leadership*, December 2009/January 2010
A Supersize Problem, *Education Update*, January 2007
Sleep: The E-zzz Intervention, *Educational Leadership*, December 2009/January 2010
A Place for Healthy Risk-Taking, *Educational Leadership*, December 2009/January 2010
Keeping Teachers Healthy, *Curriculum Update*, Winter 2004

Christi Bergin and David Bergin ("Sleep: The E-zzz Intervention") discuss sleep deprivation. Probe how big a problem this is for your students: For two weeks, notice how many students in one of your classes put their heads down or close their eyes during the period. How many students do you see exhibiting grogginess throughout the class? Compare notes with other teachers.

For high school and middle school teachers:
Set aside a time to talk openly with students about the fact that as students grow older, their need for sleep diminishes. However, when they reach puberty, adolescents typically need more sleep—9 to 10 hours each night. Ask how many of your students knew that their sleep needs increased once they hit puberty and find out if any of them have made adjustments. You might even survey several classes of students about

their typical amount of sleep each night. Ask them to make a graph to use as they discuss the issue. Have students brainstorm what things in their environment–including habits they have some control over—act as "sleep stealers" that interrupt their night's slumber.

Some schools have established staff wellness programs to help teachers improve their own health, such as the Washoe County School District effort described in "Keeping Teachers Healthy" by Rick Allen (www.ascd.org/publications/curriculum_update/winter2004/Keeping_Teachers_Healthy.aspx).

- What does your school system do to promote staff wellness? How much do you feel the system's efforts affect your behavior?
- What is one step you could take to improve your own health? What support would you need to take that step?

PART 3. Protecting Students, Rehabilitating Bullies

Bullying—Not Just a Kid Thing, *Educational Leadership*, March 2003
Civility Speaks Up, *Educational Leadership*, September 2008
Words Can Hurt Forever, *Educational Leadership*, March 2003
Fights Like a Girl, *Education Update*, April 2006
How We Treat One Another in School, *Educational Leadership*, May 2007
R U Safe? *Educational Leadership*, March 2009

Do your students feel safe at school? Do they know that their safety concerns are taken seriously by adults? In their article "Bullying—Not Just a Kid Thing," Doug Cooper and Jennie Snell propose a list of misconceptions about bullying, including "boys will be boys," "only a small number of children are affected," and "adults are already doing all they need to do."

- Besides these misconceptions, what are some other reasons that adults ignore bullying?
- Which of the methods mentioned in this article, including adult involvement and effective supervision, writing an anti-bullying policy, staff training, and developing routines for transitions, has your school tried and what were the effects?
- If your school doesn't have an effective plan, develop one with colleagues.

Keeping school bully-free must go beyond rule-setting, according to Donna San Antonio and Elizabeth A. Salzfass's article "How We Treat One Another in School." After interviewing 211 middle schoolers, these authors concluded that efforts to curb antisocial behavior among students must have a school climate shift at the core:

> Schools should not frame the issue of how students and educators treat one another as an issue of behavior. Instead, they should opt for a more comprehensive set of goals that address social and moral development, school and classroom climate, teacher training, school policies, and community values, along with student behavior.

- Discuss how to create a positive school climate. Beyond setting classroom rules that curb bullying or inconsiderate behavior, what kinds of actions could you take to create a classroom climate in which kind acts, small and large, are both encouraged and openly affirmed?
- How might you help students understand that they should treat one another well because of common beliefs or values about respect, rather than just to avoid getting into trouble?

PART 4. Helping Students Cope with Life Challenges

Success With Less Stress, *Educational Leadership*, December 2009/January 2010

Helping Self-Harming Students, *Educational Leadership*, December 2009/January 2010

Reaching the Fragile Student, *Educational Leadership*, September 2008

Peers Helping Peers, *Educational Leadership*, February 2007

Silence Is Golden, *Educational Leadership*, December 2009/January 2010

When a Student Dies, *Educational Leadership*, November 2007

True wellness does not begin and end with physical health. Mental health is also crucial. To achieve and maintain mental health, students need to learn to cope with stress in healthy ways.

In "Success with Less Stress," Jerusha Conner, Denise Pope, and Mollie Galloway describe a study in which they discovered that many high-achieving students feel overwhelmed by stress. They indicate that "the stress these students feel not only compromises their learning experience, but also takes a toll on their health and well-being." Discuss in your group:

- What stressors do you see interfering with students' mental health? How do your students cope with stress? What, if any, changes have you noticed in the nature of student stress in recent years?
- At what point does academic pressure become too great?
- What can teachers do to reduce academic stress without reducing rigor? Consider the strategies the authors suggest. How well do you think these strategies would work with your students? What other ideas do you have?

In "Helping Self-Harming Students," Matthew D. Selekman discusses cutting and other coping mechanisms that preteens and adolescents use to alleviate anxiety.

- Have you encountered students who engage in self-harming behavior? How did you respond? What did you learn from the experience? What, if anything, might you do differently today? (Keep student confidentiality in mind when sharing your answers.)
- What mental health services does your school have in place? How well are these services meeting students' needs?

PART 5. Teaching Values, Building Character

Democracy at Risk, *Educational Leadership*, May 2009
"Hobo" Is Not a Respectful Word, *Educational Leadership*, May 2009
No More Haves and Have Nots, *Educational Leadership*, May 2007
Waging Peace, *Educational Leadership*, September 2008

What better guarantee that schools are a safe environment could we have than assurance that students within our schools respect others' rights, value social justice, and practice self-control? As Deborah Meier notes in "Democracy at Risk," schools are the ideal laboratory for students to practice skills they need to live in a democracy.

In "No More Haves and Have-Nots," Joyce Huguelet, principal of a school with wide diversity in students' family circumstances, writes: "To provide an emotionally safe learning environment, we needed to level the playing field so students could focus on interacting and learning." How level is the playing field at your school? Are there ways your school's setup might unwittingly give an advantage to students whose families have more money, education, or social capital?

- Set up a group to take a "walk-through" of your school for an afternoon, observing classes, sports practices, lunch, the computer lab, and so on with an eye to rules, resources, and even cherished school traditions that might lead to enhanced opportunities for wealthier students. Debrief together. Is the playing field at your school truly level? What changes could you make, or advocate, to usher in greater equality?

Social justice doesn't have to be an add-on. According to Sarah Hershey ("'Hobo' Is Not a Respectful Word"), service projects can be integrated into the curriculum in such a way that they enable students to learn academic content as they work to make a difference. Hershey points readers to the Learn and Serve Clearinghouse's definition of service learning. According to Learn and Serve, service learning not only "enhances the community through the service provided, but it also has powerful learning consequences for the students or others participating in providing a service."

- Take a look at the curriculum for your classes and consider how you might connect some of your academic objectives with opportunities to serve the wider world. How might you introduce such opportunities to students?
- What kinds of school-based service projects have you been involved in, either as a participant or a planner? What did students learn from the experience? Would you characterize the project as an add-on or as true service learning? If it was an add-on, what might be done to improve the project?

PART 6. Creating Healthy and Safe Schools

Centers of Hope, *Educational Leadership*, April 2008

A Full-Service School, *Educational Leadership*, April 2008

A Coordinated School Health Plan, *Educational Leadership*, September 2005

Coordinated School Health: Getting It All Together, *Educational Leadership*, December 2009/January 2010

In their article "Coordinated School Health: Getting It All Together," Joyce C. Fetro, Connie Givens, and Kellie Carroll list eight components essential to promoting health in schools:

- Health education
- Physical education
- School health services
- Counseling, psychological, and social services
- Nutrition
- Staff wellness
- A healthy school environment
- Family and community involvement

Consider each of these components. In which areas is your school doing well, and in which areas is improvement needed? Choose one of these components to research further. Look for stories of how schools have promoted this aspect of health, and develop a strategy for what your school can do.

Ellen Santiago, JoAnne Ferrara, and Marty Blank ("A Full-Service School Fulfills Its Promise") list actions that educators who want to connect their school more closely to their community and its needs should focus on. Topping the list: "Take a broad view of developmental growth and learning, beyond a narrow focus on test scores."

- With this recommendation in mind, think about the students in one of your classes. How can you ascertain whether students are growing in the qualities they will most need to thrive in your community? For example, should you know more about their families' social support systems? Students' academic English skills? Each student's awareness of postsecondary schools in the area, and how he or she might prepare to be eligible to attend those schools?

PART 7. Rounding Out the Curriculum

Teaching Strategies for Naturalist Intelligence
Teaching Strategies for Intrapersonal Intelligence
Teaching Strategies for Bodily-Kinesthetic Intelligence
(From *Multiple Intelligences in the Classroom, 3rd edition*, by Thomas Armstrong)

- Select two strategies from these excerpts that intrigue you and that you haven't already used in your classroom. Do background reading or consult with colleagues as needed, and develop lesson plans that describe exactly how you will apply the strategies. Try out these lessons and evaluate the results. How would you modify each strategy in the future to make it more successful?
- Develop a broad learning experience for your students that incorporates at least one of the strategies for naturalist, intrapersonal, and bodily-kinesthetic intelligences. For example, develop a unit that involves nature walks, reflection, and movements. Work alone or as part of an interdisciplinary team.

Naomi Thiers is Associate Editor, *Educational Leadership*, nthiers@ascd.org.
Teresa Preston is Associate Editor, *Educational Leadership*, tpreston@ascd.org.

DON'T MISS A SINGLE ISSUE OF ASCD'S AWARD-WINNING MAGAZINE,

EDUCATIONAL LEADERSHIP

If you belong to a Professional Learning Community, you may be looking for a way to get your fellow educators' minds around a complex topic. Why not delve into a relevant theme issue of *Educational Leadership*, the journal written by educators for educators.

Subscribe now, or buy back issues of ASCD's flagship publication at **www.ascd.org/ELbackissues.**

Single issues cost $7 (for issues dated September 2006–May 2013) or $8.95 (for issues dated September 2013 and later). Buy 10 or more of the same issue, and you'll save 10 percent. Buy 50 or more of the same issue, and you'll save 15 percent. For discounts on purchases of 200 or more copies, contact **programteam@ascd.org**; 1-800-933-2723, ext. 5773.

To see more details about these and other popular issues of *Educational Leadership*, visit **www.ascd.org/ELarchive.**

LEARN. TEACH. LEAD.

1703 North Beauregard Street
Alexandria, VA 22311-1714 USA

www.ascd.org/el

www.ingramcontent.com/pod-product-compliance
Lightning Source LLC
Chambersburg PA
CBHW071857290426
44110CB00013B/1189